*To Don -*
*baseball fan!*

# TURNING
# TWO

## BASEBALL'S CLASSIC
## KEYSTONE COMBINATIONS

*My very best wishes!*
*John Valerino 10/25/08*

BY JOHN VALERINO

FOREWORD BY BOBBY RICHARDSON

INTRODUCTION BY ALAN TRAMMELL

ADDITIONAL RESEARCH
& EDITED BY MICHAEL F. VALERINO

*Baseball Hall of Fame Library*
*Yogi Berra Museum Library*
*- 2008 -*

Printed in the United States of America.

ISBN: 978-1-59571-210-3

Library of Congress Control Number: 2007934473

Word Association Publishers
205 Fifth Avenue
Tarentum, Pennsylvania 15084
www.wordassociation.com
1-800-827-7903

Book Design: Gina Datres, Word Association Publishers

# DEDICATION

THIS BOOK IS DEDICATED TO MY ALL-TIME FAVORITE

KEYSTONE COMBINATION: MY WIFE, LORRAINE, AND MY LATE

FATHER, MICHAEL (1919-2006). THEIR INSPIRATION AND CONSTANT

ENCOURAGEMENT MADE THIS BOOK POSSIBLE.

A DOUBLE PLAY

IS THE ACT OF

MAKING TWO OUTS

DURING THE SAME

CONTINUOUS

PLAYING ACTION.

## IN MEMORY

TO MY MOTHER, BETTY WRIGHT VALERINO (1920-1998),

WHOSE FAVORITE PLAYERS WERE HER TWO SONS

AND JOE DIMAGGIO.

# TABLE OF CONTENTS

Acknowledgments 8

Foreword 14

Introduction 17

Chapter 1   The Many Variations of the Double Play: A Review   21

Chapter 2   Johnny Evers and Joe Tinker, Chicago Cubs   29

Chapter 3   Charlie Gehringer and Billy Rogell, Detroit Tigers   47

Chapter 4   Joe Gordon and Phil Rizzuto, New York Yankees   67

Chapter 5   Bobby Doerr and Johnny Pesky, Boston Red Sox   89

Chapter 6   Jackie Robinson and Pee Wee Reese, Brooklyn Dodgers   110

Chapter 7   Nellie Fox and Luis Aparicio, Chicago White Sox   133

Chapter 8   Bobby Richardson and Tony Kubek, New York Yankees   155

Chapter 9   Bill Mazeroski and Gene Alley, Pittsburgh Pirates   177

Chapter 10   Glenn Beckert and Don Kessinger, Chicago Cubs   199

Chapter 11   Joe Morgan and Dave Concepcion, Cincinnati Reds   219

Chapter 12   Tom Herr and Ozzie Smith, St. Louis Cardinals   243

Chapter 13   Bill Ripken and Cal Ripken Jr., Baltimore Orioles   266

Chapter 14   Lou Whitaker and Alan Trammell, Detroit Tigers   289

Chapter 15   The Best of the Rest   313

Chapter 16   The Keystoners' First Basemen and Top 25 all-time   323

Chapter 17   Baseball's Top Second Basemen & Shortstops by the Numbers   337

## THE PLAYERS & MANAGERS

THE AUTHOR WOULD LIKE TO THANK THE FOLLOWING MAJOR

LEAGUE BASEBALL PLAYERS, MANAGERS, HISTORIANS,

TEAMS AND FRIENDS FOR THEIR INTERVIEWS, COOPERATION

AND INTEREST IN THE PUBLICATION OF THIS BOOK:

*HF denotes Hall of Famer*

## ACKNOWLEDGMENTS

**Gene Alley,** shortstop, Pirates, 1963-73.

**Sparky Anderson (HF),** manager, Reds, 1970-78; Tigers, 1979-95.

**Elden Auker,** pitcher, Tigers, 1933-38; Red Sox, 1939; Browns, 1940-42.

**Ernie Banks (HF),** shortstop, first baseman, Cubs, 1953-71.

**Glenn Beckert,** second base, Cubs,1965-73; Padres, 1974-75.

**Yogi Berra (HF),** catcher, outfielder, Yankees, 1946-65.

**Jack Billingham,** pitcher, Dodgers, 1968; Astros, 1969-71; Reds, 1972-77; Tigers, 1978-79.

**Dom DiMaggio,** outfielder, Red Sox, 1940-53.

**Bobby Doerr (HF),** second base, Red Sox, 1937-51.

**Carl Erskine,** pitcher, Dodgers, 1948-59.

**Bob Feller (HF),** pitcher, Indians, 1936-41; 1945-56.

**Bob Friend,** pitcher, Pirates, 1951-65; Yankees, 1966; Mets, 1966.

**Ron Hansen,** shortstop, Orioles, 1958-62; White Sox, 1963-67; Senators, 1968; White Sox, 1968-69; Yankees, 1970-71; Royals, 1972.

**Whitey Herzog,** manager, Rangers, 1973; Angels, 1974; Royals, 1975-79; Cardinals, 1980-90; first base, outfielder, Senators, 1956-58; Athletics, 1958-60; Orioles, 1961-62; Tigers, 1963.

**Ralph Houk,** manager, Yankees, 1961-63; 1966-73; Tigers, 1974-78; Red Sox, 1981-84; catcher, Yankees, 1947-54.

**Tom Herr,** second base, Cardinals, 1979-88; Twins, 1988; Phillies, 1989-90; Mets, 1991.

**Don Kessinger,** shortstop, Cubs, 1964-75; Cardinals, 1976-77; White Sox, 1977-79.

**Clyde King,** pitcher, Dodgers, 1944-45; 1947-48; 1951-52; Reds, 1953; manager, Giants, 1969-70; Braves, 1974-75; Yankees, 1982.

**Tony Kubek,** shortstop, outfielder, Yankees, 1957-65.

**Jim Landis,** outfielder, White Sox, 1957-64; Athletics, 1965; Indians, 1966; Astros, Tigers and Red Sox, 1967.

**Jim Leyland,** manager, Pirates, 1986-1996; Marlins, 1997-98; Rockies, 1999; Tigers, 2006-07.

**Al Lopez (HF),** manager, Indians, 1951-56; White Sox, 1957-65; 1968-69; catcher, Dodgers, 1928, 1930-35; Braves, 1936-40; Pirates, 1940-46; Indians, 1947.

**Joe Morgan (HF),** second base, Astros, 1963-71; Reds, 1972-79; Astros, 1980; Giants, 1981-82; Phillies, 1983; Athletics, 1984.

**Johnny Pesky,** shortstop, third base, Red Sox, 1942-52; Tigers, 1952-54; Senators, 1954.

**Billy Pierce,** pitcher, Tigers, 1945, 1948; White Sox, 1949-61; Giants, 1962-64.

**Bobby Richardson,** second base, Yankees, 1955-66.

**Bill Ripken,** second base, Orioles, 1987-92, 1996; Rangers, 1993-94, 1997; Indians, 1995; Tigers, 1998.

**Cal Ripken, Jr. (HF),** shortstop, third base, Orioles, 1981-2001.

**Eddie Robinson,** first base, Indians, 1942, 1946-48, 1957; Senators, 1949-50; White Sox, 1950-52; Phillies, 1953; Yankees, 1954-56; Athletics, 1956; Tigers and Orioles, 1957.

**Bob Shaw,** pitcher, Tigers, 1957-58; White Sox, 1958-61; Athletics, 1961; Braves, 1962-63; Giants, 1964-66; Mets, 1966-67; Cubs, 1967.

**Ozzie Smith (HF),** shortstop, Padres, 1978-81; Cardinals, 1982-96.

**Alan Trammell,** shortstop, Tigers, 1977-96; manager, Tigers, 2003-05.

**Bill Virdon,** outfielder, Cardinals, 1955-56; Pirates, 1956-68; manager, Pirates, 1972-73; Yankees, 1974-75; Astros, 1975-82; Expos, 1983-84.

**Lou Whitaker,** second base, Tigers, 1977-95.

**Jimmy Wynn,** outfielder, Astros, 1963-73; Dodgers, 1974-75; Braves, 1976; Yankees and Brewers, 1977.

**Don Zimmer,** infielder, Dodgers, 1954-59, 1963; Cubs, 1960-61; Mets and Reds, 1962; Senators, 1963-65; manager, Padres, 1972-73; Red Sox, 1976-80; Rangers, 1981-82; Cubs, 1988-91.

HISTORIANS

**David W. Anderson,** author of "More Than Merkle" *(University of Nebraska Press).*

**Dick Bresciana,** Boston Red Sox, vice president/publications and archives.

**Ernie Harwell,** Hall of Fame television and radio broadcaster.

**Jerome Holtzman,** Major League Baseball's official historian.

**Lew Matlin,** baseball historian.

GENERAL SOURCES

Baseball-Almanac.com

*Baseball Autograph Collector's Handbook* by Jack Smalling

*Baseball's Book of Firsts* by Lloyd Johnson *(Courage Books)*

*Baseball Digest*

BaseballLibrary.com

Baseball-Reference.com

MajorLeagueBaseball.com

*The New York Evening Mail*

*The New York Times*

*The Washington Post*

*Wikipedia Encyclopedia*

## TEAM SOURCES

| | |
|---|---|
| Baltimore Orioles | www.orioles.com |
| Boston Red Sox | www.redsox.com |
| Chicago Cubs | www.chicagocubs.com |
| Chicago White Sox | www.whitesox.com |
| Cincinnati Reds | www.cincinnatireds.com |
| Detroit Tigers | www.detroittigers.com |
| Los Angeles Dodgers | www.ladodgers.com |
| New York Yankees | www.newyorkyankees.com |
| Pittsburgh Pirates | www.pittsburghpirates.com |
| St. Louis Cardinals | www.stlouiscardinals.com |

## NATIONAL BASEBALL HALL OF FAME RESEARCH DEPARTMENT

A special tip of the cap to Gabriel Schechter, research associate, for his critical eye, counsel and insight.

**John Horne,** photo coordinator.

## SPECIAL THANKS

**Mike Cobb,** Detroit Tigers beat writer, *The (Lakeland, Fla.) Ledger*

**Debra L. Dennler,** Dennler Financial Management, PC, St. Louis.

**Robert Dvorchak,** *Pittsburgh Post-Gazette,* sports writer

**Dan Ewald,** former Detroit Tigers public relations director

**Leanne Bloeth Green,** graphic artist, Auburndale, Fla.

**Bob Grim,** Chicago White Sox, senior director, broadcasting & business development

**Dan Hart,** Pittsburgh Pirates, manager of media services

**Dave Kaplan,** director, Yogi Berra Museum & Learning Center

**John Maroon,** vice-president of communications, Ripken Baseball.

**Carmen Molina,** public relations coordinator, Tampa Bay Devil Rays
**Keith Niebuhr,** *St. Petersburg (Fla.) Times,* sports writer
**Ambreen Qureshi,** *Associated Press* photo images
**Patrick Zier,** former Detroit Tigers beat writer, *The (Lakeland, Fla.) Ledger*

THE SUPPORTERS
Thank you to the following: Dr. Robin Wooten, Dr. Stuart Tullis, Charles
Carlton, Ted Hoffman, Rick Korber, Father Matt Mello and the Resurrection
School and Church Community in Lakeland, Fla.; Victor Troiano, Jim Lee,
Ed Diaz, Dan McGowan, Terry and Debbie Miggins, Dick Scanlon, Dr.
Matthew Smith, Denise Vaughn, Rob Word, Carol Ponton; my brother, Jim
Valerino, and my cousins, Denny Caruso and Brian Valerino.

Special thanks to my two daughters, Mackenzie and Quinn, who patiently
waited for me to get off the computer, as well as our English Springer
Spaniels, Max and Tobie, who patiently waited for me at the base of our
staircase each day.

WORD ASSOCIATION PUBLISHING
Thank you to publishers Tom and Francine Costello, book designer
Gina Datres, and the rest of the staff for their promptness and patience
answering all of the author's questions and helping make a goal
become a reality.

"BASEBALL FOR DUMMIES" BY JOE MORGAN
Thank you to Joe Morgan and Wiley Publishing, Inc., of Hoboken, N.J.,
for allowing the author to use passages from Morgan's book, *"Baseball for
Dummies,"* 3rd edition, in Chapter 11.

PHOTO CREDITS
**National Baseball Hall of Fame, Cooperstown, N.Y.:** Tinker-Evers (page 29);
Gehringer (47); Rogell (48); Gordon (67); Rizzuto (68); Fox (133); Aparicio
(134); Fox-Aparicio (135); Richardson (155); Kubek (156); Alley (178);
Mazeroski (181) Beckert (199); Kessinger (200); Morgan (219); Concepcion
(220); Herr (243); Smith (244); the Ripkens (266); Whitaker (289); Trammell
(290).

**Associated Press Photo Images:** Doerr-Pesky (page 89); Robinson-Reese
and other Dodgers (110).

**Courtesy of the Pittsburgh Pirates:** Mazeroski (page 177).

# FOREWORD

I receive quite a bit of mail each week. Most letters are from autograph seekers, others are invitations to speak at various sports and religious functions around the country.

In August 2005, I received an unusual letter from John Valerino of Lakeland, Fla., who was trying to track down and talk to former Major League Baseball second basemen and shortstops who played together. His goal was to compile a list of the game's most-talented and most-unforgettable "classic keystone" —or double-play—combinations.

It's no secret that for a team to be successful, it must be strong defensively up the middle: the catcher, second baseman, shortstop and center fielder. The keystone of that group is the second baseman and shortstop, who anticipate each other's moves and turn rally-ending double plays.

I think Hall of Fame shortstop Ozzie Smith, formerly of the St. Louis Cardinals, sums it up best in Chapter 12 when he says: "The middle of the (baseball) diamond is where you have the people you can rely on. It's one of the reasons why you put your strongest people up the middle. The team wants to have confidence in its second baseman and shortstop, as well as your center fielder."

Of course, it takes hours of practice to form a successful keystone combination. Shortstop Don Kessinger of the Chicago Cubs, whose keystone mate was Glenn Beckert for nine years (1965-73), probably explains it best in Chapter 10 when he says: "Glenn and I would spend hours fielding balls and tossing the ball to each other in the exact same spot on every play. Your double-play partner needs to know where the ball is coming. Throwing the ball in a general area isn't good enough. It has to be in the same spot every time. Glenn and I knew exactly where we wanted the ball. All that practice paid off."

I thought for a few moments and recalled how fortunate I was to have played second base with the New York Yankees alongside a talented and dedicated shortstop named Tony Kubek for nine seasons (1957-65). We spent hours playing catch, fielding groundballs and honing our skills around the second base bag.

We also had a pretty-good player, Hall of Famer Mickey Mantle, backing us up in center field and two talented catchers, Hall of Famer Yogi Berra and later Elston Howard.

John's project started out as a means of daily therapy for an illness, major clinical depression, which he's been fighting since 1993. The illness forced the award-winning journalist to leave the newspaper business after 31 years (1973-2003). Thirty of those years were spent with the same company. Talk about loyalty! That is hard to find today, both in professional sports and in the business world. In baseball, the "classic keystone combination" requires team loyalty, but today it's a lost art because players move from one team to another far too often. As you'll read in Chapter 8, three years following my retirement, the Atlanta Braves approached me about making a comeback. A loyal Yankee even to this day, my reply was, "Once a Yankee, always a Yankee."

So, what started out as a means of therapy at the urging of his doctor, Robin Wooten of Lakeland, snowballed into this interesting baseball book devoted exclusively to the play of major league second basemen and shortstops, the first of its kind, according to the National Baseball Hall of Fame.

John's criteria for inclusion among the "classic combos" was that a tandem had to play together for the same team for a minimum of five years. There are two exceptions, however: the Yankees' Joe Gordon and Phil Rizzuto, and the Red Sox's Bobby Doerr and Johnny Pesky. Their years of playing together were interrupted two to three years each because of military service during World War II. They should not, John says, be penalized for serving their country.

After spending nearly a month of playing telephone tag, John and I finally hooked up and enjoyed a lengthy conversation about my New York Yankees of the late 1950s and early-to-mid 1960s, my double-play relationship with Tony, the championships, the fun times and my teammates. This project also reunited me with one of my former Yankee managers, Ralph Houk.

John's therapeutic project led to interviews with Hall of Famers like Bob Feller, Ernie Banks, Bobby Doerr, Al Lopez, Ozzie Smith and Sparky Anderson, to name a few. Take a careful look at the "Acknowledgments" and you'll find an impressive list of former players, managers and historians who contributed to this book.

Tony and I are pleased to be included in this unique book, which showcases 13 "classic keystone combinations" as well as 13 "best of the rest." From Tinker-to-Evers in the early 1900s to Whitaker-to-Trammell from 1977-1995, John's research and interviews have produced an easy-to-read historical look at some of the game's greatest—and funniest—characters in baseball. So, sit back and read about the very best second basemen and shortstops who have executed the most-overlooked, yet most-exciting play in baseball—the double play.

BOBBY RICHARDSON

*New York Yankees, 1955-66*
*Seven-time American League All-Star*
*Five-time Gold Glove Award winner*
*Three-time World Champion*
*1960 World Series Most Valuable Player*

## INTRODUCTION

Ask any baseball pitcher, regardless of the level of play, and he'll tell you that a double play is his "best friend."

Research tells us that 70 percent of all double plays start with either the second baseman or shortstop. The most-common double play takes place with a runner on first and a ball is hit to the shortstop, who tosses the ball to the second baseman for the forceout (first out). The second baseman then throws the ball to first to get the batter running down the first-base line (second out).

The second most-common double play occurs when a batted ball is hit to the second baseman, who tosses the ball to the shortstop covering the second base bag. The shortstop then throws to first to complete the double play.

There are many other ways to "turn two." For example, with a runner on first, a third baseman can field a grounder and throw to the second baseman for the forceout. Since this particular double play, called "around the horn," takes more time to complete, the second baseman must use his quick release and arm strength to get the ball to the first baseman for the second out.

Also, a shortstop can catch a line drive (first out), then throw to first to force out the base runner who wandered too far off the base. The same play can take place between the second and first basemen. It's plays like these that cause a difference in the number of double plays turned by a second baseman and shortstop during a season.

Many pitchers, especially sinkerballers, have been saved by what is considered the game's most-exciting play. That's why baseball organizations spend a great deal of time grooming individuals to play the game's two most-demanding positions. When a manager talks about being "strong up the middle defensively," he's referring to his catcher, second baseman, shortstop and centerfielder.

In baseball, the term "keystone" refers to "strength and stability" at the second base and shortstop positions, thus the term "keystone combination."

There are many special qualities that go into a successful keystone combination. Both players should be strong defensively with good range and good arms. The two most-important qualities are timing and longevity. The more a second baseman and shortstop play together, the more comfortable they become with one another. They learn each other's habits. They know exactly where to make the toss to each other at second base. They think alike. They become comrades.

I was fortunate to play a record 19 major league seasons with one of the game's finest second basemen, Lou Whitaker. After a couple of years together, "turning two" became natural for us. There were no secrets. Lou knew where I'd be and I knew where Lou would be. From 1977 through 1995, all with the Detroit Tigers, Lou was involved in a team-record 1,527 double plays. I managed 1,292. Along the way, we won the 1984 World Series and the 1987 American League East title.

Let me take you back to 1976, when our "keystone combination" began. Lou was drafted by the Detroit Tigers in 1974. I followed in 1975. Lou spent the 1976 season playing third base for the Lakeland (Fla.) Tigers of the Florida State League (Class A). His manager was a guy named Jim Leyland, who in 2006 guided the Detroit Tigers to the World Series before falling to the St. Louis Cardinals in five games. After his stay in the minors, Leyland worked his way up to coach with the Chicago White Sox during the early 1980s under Tony LaRussa, the manager of the 2006 world champion Cardinals. Leyland then became manager of Pittsburgh (1986-96), where he won three National League East titles. In 1997, Jim led the young Florida Marlins to the World Series crown over Cleveland.

While Lou was winning Most Valuable Player honors and an FSL championship in 1976 in Lakeland, I was in Bristol, Va., of the Appalachian Rookie League. Later that season, I was promoted to Class AA ball in Montgomery, Ala. Our seasons ended at about the same time, so Lou and I reported to the Tigers' Instructional League team in St. Petersburg, Fla. That's where our relationship as a "keystone combination" began.

On Sept. 18, the first day of instructional ball, Tiger executives moved Lou to second base and the two of us started working together from that day forward.

We worked under the guidance of former major league shortstop Eddie Brinkman for two months, then played for Eddie in 1977 with the Montgomery Rebels and won the Southern League (Class AA) championship.

Eddie spent 15 seasons in the majors (1961-75), including four with the Tigers (1971-74). He was not a threat at the plate (.224 lifetime), but he was a wizard defensively and knew baseball. He was an All-Star and won a Gold Glove. He did a lot of little things to help his teams win. Twice he ranked among the top 10 in singles, triples and sacrifices. He also turned more than a thousand career double plays.

For Lou and myself, it all happened so fast: two months in instructional ball, one full season in the Southern League, then a call-up to Detroit in September of 1977. From that time through September of 1995, Lou and I formed the longest double-play combination in the history of baseball.

During that time, Lou and I had the privilege of playing 17 seasons for who we believed was the best manager in the game, Sparky Anderson. Sparky really taught us how to play the game and, more importantly, how to be a true professional on and off the field.

Many baseball fans believe our "career highlights" are the statistics and the individual accomplishments. That was never the case for Lou and myself. Our most-important accomplishments were to play the game right and that the team always came first. To be included in award-winning journalist John Valerino's book as one of "baseball's classic keystone combinations" is quite an honor. Over the years, there have been some great ones. Being a history buff of the game, I enjoyed reading John's accounts of the various "keystone combos" that played during the 1900s. I think you'll learn a great deal about these men and, at the same time, enjoy a few laughs.

Here's hoping that another "classic keystone combination" comes along during the next several years and challenges the 19 seasons Lou and I played together. And let's hope they have the same goal Lou and I had —the team always comes first.

**And, by the way, remember to keep those pitchers happy.**

ALAN TRAMMELL
*Detroit Tigers, 1977-1996*
*Six-time American League All-Star*
*Four-time Gold Glove Award winner*
*1984 World Series Champion and Most Valuable Player*

## CHAPTER ONE

# THE MANY VARIATIONS OF THE DOUBLE PLAY

A double play is the act of making two outs during the same continuous playing action.

There are many ways to "**turn two**." As Alan Trammell explained in his Introduction, the most-common "DP" occurs when there is a base runner on first, a batted ball is fielded by the shortstop, who flips to the second baseman, who then throws to first. The second most-common double play goes to the second baseman, through the shortstop covering second, then to first.

It's important to remember that although a large majority of double plays involve the second baseman and shortstop as a unit playing together, many do not. This is one of the reasons why a shortstop or second baseman may have more career double plays than his keystone mate.

For example, in Chapter 2 on the Chicago Cubs' keystone combination of second baseman Johnny Evers and shortstop Joe Tinker, the record books tell us that Tinker was involved in 584 double plays during the 11 seasons (1902-12) he played with Evers, who recorded 455. The 129 difference in DPs is due to many factors, including the number of games played by each player, late-inning substitutions, injuries, a position change and the number of double plays Tinker participated in that did not involve Evers.

Chapter 8 tells us that New York Yankee second baseman Bobby Richardson had 869 double plays during the nine seasons (1957-65) he played alongside his keystone mate, shortstop Tony Kubek, who had 583. The 286 difference is due to the same factors mentioned for Evers-Tinker and then some. During his "keystone" days with Richardson, Kubek also played 145 games in the outfield and 55 at third base. Kubek also appeared in just 45 games in 1962 due to his National Guard commitment.

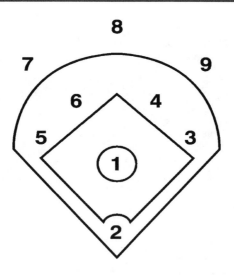

**TO SIMPLIFY THINGS IT'S BEST FOR THE FAN TO UNDERSTAND THAT EACH DEFENSIVE POSITION ON THE BASEBALL FIELD IS ASSIGNED A NUMBER. THEY ARE:**

**1** PITCHER
**2** CATCHER
**3** FIRST BASEMAN
**4** SECOND BASEMAN
**5** THIRD BASEMAN
**6** SHORTSTOP
**7** LEFT FIELDER
**8** CENTER FIELDER
**9** RIGHT FIELDER

There are many forms of double plays that involve the shortstop, but not the second baseman.

*Examples:*

> **THE SITUATION:** RUNNER ON FIRST BASE.

DP #1: The batter hits a line drive to the shortstop (first out), then throws to first to get the base runner who strayed too far from the bag (second out). **Score it 6-3, shortstop to first.**

DP #2: The batter hits a ground ball to the pitcher, who turns and throws to the shortstop covering second (first out). The shortstop then throws to first (second out). **Score it 1-6-3.**

DP #3: A groundball is hit to the first baseman, who throws to the shortstop covering second base (first out). The shortstop then throws back to first for the second out. **Score it 3-6-3.**

DP #4: The same play as DP #3, but the pitcher covers first base and takes the throw from the shortstop. **Score it 3-6-1.**

DP #5: A batter bunts the ball in front of home plate. The catcher retrieves the ball, then throws it to the shortstop covering second base (first out). The shortstop then throws to first (second out). **Score it 2-6-3.**

DP #6: The batter strikes out. The catcher then throws to the shortstop, who is covering second base to catch a would-be base stealer. **Score it 2-6.**

> **THE SITUATION:** RUNNER ON SECOND BASE.

**DP #7:** The batter hits a line drive to the first baseman (first out), then throws to the shortstop covering second base to force out the base runner who strayed too far from the bag. **Score it 3-6.**

**DP #8:** The batter hits a line drive to the shortstop, who then steps on second base to get the runner who strayed too far from the bag. **Score it 6, an unassisted double play.**

> **THE SITUATION:** BASES LOADED.

**DP #9:** In a close game, the infielders play several steps closer to home plate. The batter hits a ground ball to the shortstop, who throws home for the forceout (first out), then the catcher throws to first for the second out. **Score it 6-2-3.**

**The classic 6-4-3:** If the defensive team has a healthy lead, the fielders play their normal depth. A batted ball is hit to the shortstop, who flips the ball to the second baseman, who throws to first.

These examples are just a few of the DP possibilities for the shortstop. As one can see, the shortstop stays quite active during the course of a game and has more opportunities to turn two than the second baseman.

In Chapter 13, former Baltimore Oriole Cal Ripken Jr., whose 1,565 career double plays ranked third all-time for major league shortstops through the 2007 season, had this to say about the position he mastered for 16 of his 21 seasons:

"I always enjoyed playing shortstop because I believe it is a position that, when handled properly, can take charge of a game and serve as an anchor for the defense. Intelligence, positioning and having an understanding of all of the possible scenarios that could happen when the ball is hit is vital to the success of a shortstop."

Now let's not underestimate the importance of the other half of the keystone combination, the second baseman. There are several forms of double plays that involve the second baseman, but not the shortstop.

*Examples:*

> **THE SITUATION:** RUNNER ON FIRST BASE.

DP #1: The batter hits a line drive to the second baseman (first out), then throws to first to get the base runner who strayed too far from the bag (second out). **Score it 4-3.**

DP #2: The batter hits a ground ball to the pitcher, who turns and throws to the second baseman (first out). The second baseman then throws to first (second out). **Score it 1-4-3.**

DP #3: A groundball is hit to the first baseman, who throws to the second baseman (first out). The second baseman then throws back to first for the second out. **Score it 3-4-3.**

DP #4: The same play as DP #3, but the pitcher covers first base and takes the throw from the second baseman. **Score it 3-4-1.**

DP #5: A batter bunts the ball in front of home plate. The catcher retrieves the ball, then throws it to the second baseman (first out). The second baseman then throws to first (second out). **Score it 2-4-3.**

NOTE: In DPs #2 through #5, it's more common for the shortstop to take the throw at second base because his momentum takes him in the direction of first base, thus making for an easier throw, but there are occasions when the second baseman is in a better position to handle the play.

DP #6: A ball is hit to the second baseman, who tags the base runner going to second (first out), then throws to first for the second out. **Score it 4-3.**

**> THE SITUATION:** RUNNER ON SECOND BASE.

DP #7: The batter hits a line drive to the second baseman, who then steps on second base to get the runner who strayed too far from the bag. **Score it 4, an unassisted double play.**

**> THE SITUATION:** BASES LOADED.

DP #8: The batter hits a ground ball to the second baseman, who throws home for the forceout (first out), then the catcher throws to first for the second out. **Score it 4-2-3.**

DP #9: A ball is hit to the third baseman, who turns and throws to the second baseman (first out), who throws the ball to first (second out). **"Around the horn, 5-4-3."**

**The classic 4-6-3:** A batted ball is hit to the second baseman, who flips the ball to the shortstop, who throws to first.

THE OUTFIELDERS
Outfielders with strong and accurate arms can also be involved in double plays. The most-common DP takes place when a runner is on third base and the batter hits a fly ball to one of the outfielders (first out). Once the ball is caught, the base runner can leave third base—called "tagging up"—and race for home. The outfielder then attempts to throw that runner out at home plate for the double play. Left fielders and right fielders have more success doubling up a runner than a center fielder, who often has a further distance to throw the ball. As a result, **score it 7-2 or 8-2 or 9-2.**

Another common double play involves the right fielder and third baseman. A runner on second base may attempt to "tag up" and advance to third after the right fielder has caught a deep fly ball. Right fielders with strong, accurate arms many times throw the runner out at third base. **Score it 9-5.**

The all-time record for double plays by an outfielder is held by Tris Speaker with 139. Speaker, who spent 22 seasons (1907-28) in the majors with the Red Sox, Indians, Senators and Athletics, led the American League in that category five times.

Max Carey, who played 20 seasons (1910-29), holds the National League mark with 86. Seventeen of those 20 seasons were with the Pirates, the other three with the Dodgers.

Willie Mays, a center fielder for the Giants for 21 seasons, led the National League four times and totaled 60 double plays in his career. He spent his final season (1973) with the Mets.

Another player who will always be remembered for his "rifle arm" is former Pirate right fielder Roberto Clemente, who was involved in 42 double plays during his 18-year career (1955-72).

Many times four players can take part in a DP. For example, with a runner on first, the batter hits the ball back to the mound, where it hits the pitcher's glove. The shortstop retrieves the ball, tosses it to his second baseman (first out), who then throws to first for the double play. This DP would be scored **1-6-4-3.**

There are a countless number of ways to complete a double play. Many times it involves an odd event or a base-running mistake.

Whatever the situation, the Yankees' Kubek probably sums it up best in Chapter 13: "Our (Yankee) coach, Frank Crosetti, told us that you make the double play and you make it as quickly as possible. He didn't believe in the 'Let's-get-at-least-one-out' theory. Double plays prevent rallies and win games."

Joe Tinker (left) and
Johnny Evers (right)
played side-by-side for
11 seasons, yet they
didn't talk to each other
for 34 years.

CHAPTER TWO

# 2B JOHNNY EVERS & SS JOE TINKER
# CHICAGO CUBS, 1902-12

**NAME: John Joseph Evers**
**Nickname:** The Crab
**Born:** July 21, 1881, Troy, N.Y.
**Died:** March 28, 1947, Albany, N.Y.
**Batted/threw:** Left/right
**Height/weight:** 5-feet-9, 115 pounds
**Major league seasons:** 18 (Chicago Cubs, 1902-13; Boston Braves, 1914-17, 1929; Philadelphia, 1917; Chicago White Sox, 1922)
**Major league debut:** Sept. 1, 1902 (**Cubs 5,** Phillies 1)
**Final major league game:** Oct. 6, 1929 (Giants 9, **Braves 4**)
**Position:** Second base
**Career games:** 1,784
**Career double plays:** 692
**DPs with Cubs at second base (1902-12):** 455
**Career errors:** 447
**Career assists:** 5,215
**Career putouts:** 3,806
**Career fielding percentage:** .953
**Gold Gloves:** The Rawlings Gold Glove Award began in 1957
**All-Star:** All-Star selections began in 1933
**World Series:** 3-1
**Career batting average:** .270
**Turning two:** After being traded from the Cubs to Boston in 1914, Evers won the Most Valuable Player Award, helped the Braves win 68 of their last 87 games, the National League pennant and the World Series over the Philadelphia A's.
**Hall of Fame:** Class of 1946.

**NAME: Joseph Bert Tinker.**

**Nickname:** Joe

**Born:** July 27, 1880, Muscotah, Kan.

**Died:** July 27, 1948, Orlando, Fla.

**Batted/threw:** Right/right

**Height/weight:** 5-feet-9, 175 pounds

**Major league seasons:** 15 (Chicago Cubs, 1902-12, 1916; Cincinnati, 1913; Chicago of the Federal League, 1914-15)

**Major league debut:** April 17, 1902 (**Cubs 6,** Reds 1)

**Final major league game:** Sept. 22, 1916 (Giants 6, **Cubs 0**)

**Position:** Shortstop

**Career games:** 1,804

**Career double plays:** 671

**DPs with Cubs at shortstop (1902-12):** 584

**Career errors:** 648

**Career assists:** 5,943

**Career putouts:** 3,816

**Career fielding percentage:** .938

**Gold Gloves:** The Rawlings Gold Glove Award began in 1957

**All-Star:** All-Star selections began in 1933

**World Series:** 2-2

**Career batting average:** .262

**Turning two:** Tinker was among the National League leaders in home runs in 1908 and 1909 with 6 and 4, respectively. First baseman Tim Jordan of Brooklyn led the league in 1908 with 12 homers, while Red Murray of the Giants was the 1909 leader with 7.

**Hall of Fame:** Class of 1946

On Sept. 15, 1902, second baseman Johnny Evers, shortstop Joe Tinker and first baseman Frank Chance turned their first double play for the Chicago Cubs in a 6-3 victory over the Cincinnati Reds.

It wasn't your typical double play, though. A sharply hit groundball to the left of Tinker bounced off his shoe and ricocheted to Evers at second, who touched the bag and threw to Chance at first to complete the twin killer.

Baseball's first dynamic double-play combination had been born. They're credited with perfecting the modern double play thanks to their smart, hard-nosed and scrappy style of play, which led the Cubs to four National League pennants and two World Series crowns between 1906 and 1910.

In the 1907 World Series, which opened with a 12-inning, 3-3 tie, the Cubs ran wild, beating the Detroit Tigers in five games, thanks to 16 stolen bases and the bats of third baseman Harry Steinfeldt (.471) and Evers (.350). The Cubs' pitching staff, which allowed just six runs, held the Tigers scoreless in 43 of the 48 innings played and stymied 20-year-old batting champion Ty Cobb (.350) to an anemic .200 mark in the Series.

It was more of the same in 1908 against Detroit as Evers, Tinker and Chance led the Cubs to a four-game World Series win, becoming the first team in Major League Baseball history to win back-to-back championships. The Tigers couldn't touch Cubs righty Mordecai Brown, who won two games and did not allow a run in his two Series starts. Chance batted .421, while outfielder Frank Schulte hit .389.

The Cubs also won National League pennants in 1906 and 1910, but lost to their cross-town rivals, the White Sox in six, and Philadelphia in five, respectively, in the World Series.

The Cubs' success started with Tinker-to-Evers-to-Chance. Their acrobatic fielding, despite poor playing conditions and small gloves that resembled garden gloves with no laces or padding, were immortalized in a poem titled *"Baseball's Sad Lexicon"* by sports writer Franklin Adams of *The New York Evening Mail*:

*"These are the saddest of possible words,*
*"Tinker to Evers to Chance.*
*"Trio of bear cubs and fleeter than birds,*
*"Tinkers to Evers to Chance.*
*"Thoughtlessly pricking our gonfalon bubble,*
*"Making a Giant hit into a double.*
*"Words that are weighty with nothing but trouble,*
*"Tinkers to Evers to Chance."*

Adams later admitted he penned the eight-line poem when his editor informed him that one of his game stories between the Cubs and Giants was eight lines too short.

Although they weren't major threats at the plate—Tinker had a career average of .262, Evers .270—and their fielding percentages are embarrassing by today's standards, many baseball historians believe Adams' poem immortalized the three players and secured their spots in the National Baseball Hall of Fame in 1946 in Cooperstown, N.Y.

Not so, according to David W. Anderson, who spent five years researching and writing about the threesome for the book *"More Than Merkle"* (University of Nebraska Press, 2000), which focuses on the Cubs' 1908 season, the last year they won a World Series.

"They're in the Hall of Fame because together they won," Anderson said. "These three guys were winners. They won by anyway they could. Their (offensive) numbers were down, but whose numbers weren't down during that dead-ball era?"

The threesome patrolled the Cubs' infield together for 10 seasons (1902-11). The keystone combo of Evers and Tinker played together for 11 seasons (1902-12) and totaled 1,039 double plays—584 by Tinker and 455 by Evers.

"They probably didn't make the most double plays back then," Anderson said, "simply because they had such a great pitching staff back then."

True. The Pittsburgh Pirates, who beat Detroit in the 1909 World Series, had a solid DP combination in second baseman Dots Miller and shortstop Honus Wagner, who totaled 335 double plays from 1909 to 1911.

Wagner had a Hall of Fame (1936) career. He played for the old Louisville Colonels from 1897-1899, then was traded to the Pirates in 1900 in a deal that involved 16 players and $25,000 in cash. The Pirates easily got the best of the trade, as Wagner spent 18 seasons in Pittsburgh, won eight batting titles, batted a career .327 with 1,732 runs-batted-in. He didn't hit for power (101 career homers), but he had 722 stolen bases and 252 triples. Mainly a shortstop, he was involved in 963 double plays. Known as "The Flying Dutchman," his T206 tobacco baseball card has been purchased for as high as $2.3 million. About 60 of the "Mona Lisa of baseball cards" exist.

The Giants were also strong in the middle infield with second baseman Larry Doyle and shortstop Al Bridwell, who totaled 357 double plays in 3.5 seasons (1909-1912).

The Cubs' pitching staff during the century's first decade was deep and stingy. It featured several 20-game winners, including Brown, Jock Menefee, Orval Overall, Jack Pfiester, Ed Reulbach, Jack Taylor, Jack Weimer and Bob Wicker.

Their best season defensively came in 1912 when Tinker had 73 DPs and Evers 71. Both players were prone to errors, though. Four times between 1902 and 1912, Tinker had more errors than double plays, including 72 miscues in 1902. He did, however, lead National League shortstops in fielding percentage four times. Evers had more errors than DPs twice.

More importantly, according to Anderson, Tinker and Evers did bring more attention to the defensive side of the game, "coming up with new ways to defend against the hit-and-run, bunts and stolen bases, which were the strategies teams used during the dead-ball era," he said.

Tinker, whose parents wanted him to be a wallpaper hanger, was a player of several "firsts:"

1) He was the first Cub to hit a home run in a World Series game, that coming on Oct. 11, 1908, in a 6-1 victory over Detroit;

2) He was baseball's first holdout, demanding a $1,000 raise prior to the 1909 season. Two weeks into the season, he accepted a $200 increase.

3) He was the first player to steal home plate twice in one game, that coming on June 28, 1910 in an 11-1 win over Cincinnati. He finished with 18 home steals in his career, far behind all-time career leader Ty Cobb's 50.

4) Tinker was the first major league player from the American League and National League to jump ship and sign with the rival Federal League, which was formed in 1914 by James A. Gilmore. The league offered big contracts, some as high as $25,000, four times the amount the AL and NL teams were paying. Tinker couldn't resist, joining the Chicago Whales as player and manager. He was successful, leading the Whales to a second-place finish in 1914 and the league pennant in 1915. The league folded, so Tinker returned to Chicago in 1916 when he skippered the Cubs to a fifth-place finish. Later on, he kicked around the minors as president and manager of several teams, including the old Orlando Gulls of the Class A Florida State League. A stadium in Orlando, Fla., bears his name.

The scrappy Evers was generally regarded the best player of the Chicago infield, picking up the nickname "The Crab" for his ability to cover the right side of the infield.

Anderson chuckled, saying the nickname was really a result of Evers' disposition.

"Evers was 'The Crab' more for his personality," Anderson said. "He was very gruff, a real tough guy. If you look at pictures of the players of that era you'll see they were all very tough-looking characters."

Evers, who devoured candy in an attempt to keep his weight above 100 pounds, was the original "Mr. October" in the 1907 and 1908 World Series wins over Detroit, batting .350 each year for the champion Cubs. Later in his career, he helped lead the Boston Braves from last place in July to the National League pennant and a four-game sweep of the Philadelphia Athletics in the 1914 World Series to become the first player in baseball history to win three Series rings. Named the National League's Most Valuable Player that season, Evers batted .438 in the Series.

Chance, nicknamed "Husk" for "husky" because of his size (6-feet, 190 pounds) and strength, was the leader of the Cubs. As player-manager from 1905 to 1912, the first baseman led the Cubs to the four NL pennants, including the 1906 squad that won a then-record 116 games. That 1906 squad won 60-of-75 games on the road.

Chance was named the Cubs' player-manager in 1905 when Frank Selee developed tuberculosis. Selee was one of the most-successful skippers in the early days of the game. He managed the Boston Braves for 12 seasons (1890-1901), won 1,004 games, five National League pennants and the 1892 "World Championship" over the Cleveland Spiders. In 1902, he joined the Cubs and enjoyed three successful seasons before he was forced to step down due to his illness 65 games into the 1905 campaign, which is when Chance took charge.

Selee, who died at the age of 49 in 1909, but was selected to the Hall of Fame 90 years later by the Veterans Committee, concluded his managerial career with 1,284 wins and 862 losses, a winning percentage of .598.

As player-manager, Chance had no equals. "The Peerless Leader," as he was called by his players, was a tough character with a temper, several times needing police escorts from the field of play after flinging bats at taunting fans. He holds the distinction of being the first player to be ejected from a World Series game, that coming in Game 3 of the Cubs' five-game Series loss to Philadelphia in 1910.

"Chance didn't get along with anybody," Anderson said. "Not even his own teammates. His basic concept was, do it my way or hit the highway."

Chance, a career .290 hitter and good defensive first baseman (.987 fielding percentage), had strong opinions about everything and never backed away from a debate. He was especially hard on Evers and Tinker, who didn't care for his militant-like approach to managing. As a result, the keystone combo had little to do with their skipper-first baseman off the field and socially.

"Because a man is placed in charge of a club does not make it necessary for him to be a taskmaster or a tyrant," Tinker said, according to the National Baseball Hall of Fame.

Those who played and were forced to put up with Chance's antics included outfielders Jimmy "Shorty" Slagle (5-feet-6), Jimmy Sheckard and Schulte, catcher Pat Moran and utility player Heinie Zimmerman, who actually got into a fist fight with the Cubs' skipper, according to Anderson.

The pitching staff was led by Overall, who threw a Game 5 shutout to seal the Cubs' last World Series championship in 1908; two-time 20-game winner Weimer; Carl Lundgren, who posted a career earned-run-average of 2.42 in eight seasons; and Reulbach, who won seven World Series games for the Cubs.

Chance, whose last full season as a player was 1909, also managed the New York Yankees in 1913 and 1914, then the Boston Red Sox in 1923 before retiring with a career mark of 946 victories and 648 losses, a winning percentage of .593. He posted an impressive 768-389 record with the Cubs. His Chicago teams won more than 100 games four times in eight seasons.

As his career came down to its final year, *The New York Times* wrote: "Chance was a born fighter, a determined, able and magnetic leader of men who could always inspire his men with extraordinary enthusiasm. He combined all the qualities of an ideal baseball general."

Evers, who often said, "My favorite umpire is a dead one," understood the rules of baseball, more so than the umpires. He spent hours studying the rulebook. Thanks to the tiny, 115-pound second baseman, one play in 1908 turned the National League pennant race in the Cubs' favor with the infamous "Fred Merkle Play," which is covered in detail in Anderson's book.

The date was Sept. 23, 1908. With first place at stake in the National League standings, Chance's Cubs were in New York's Polo Grounds to play John McGraw's Giants.

Christy Mathewson, who spent 17 years with New York and won 373 games, was on the mound for the Giants, while the Cubs countered with Jack Pfiester, who had a record of 12-10.

The two pitchers were masterful, holding their opponents to one run through eight innings.

THEN CAME THE NINTH

With the bases loaded, two outs and the score tied at 1 in the bottom half of the inning, the Giants' Merkle was on first. Teammate Moose McCormick stood on third with the potential winning run. The Giants' Al Bridwell hit a sharp liner to right center to score McCormick with what was believed to be the winning run. However, Cubs center fielder Solly Hoffman threw the ball towards Evers at second base. Merkle, meanwhile, did not advance to second. Instead, he ran off the field.

Evers pointed out to umpires Hank O'Day and Bob Emslie that Merkle didn't run out the play and, as a result, was forced at second for the third out, thus negating the winning run. After giving the play some thought and realizing it would be too difficult to clear the field of 25,000 celebrating Giants fans, O'Day waited several hours before ruling in favor of the Cubs and declaring the game a 1-1 tie. The next day, *The New York Times* called Merkle's base running "considerable stupidity."

"In his defense, Merkle ran to the clubhouse, not wanting to get caught up in the middle of a celebration," Anderson said. "At that time, players were actually afraid to be on the field with the fans. It got rough out there at times."

Some accounts question if the ball Evers had in his glove to force Merkle at second base was actually the official game ball, that center fielder Hoffman's throw into the infield got away from the Chicago fielders and Giants third base coach Joe McGinnity picked it up and threw the ball into the stands.

Kid Kroh of the Cubs eventually got the ball—or a ball—flipped it to third baseman Steinfeldt, who tossed it to Tinker, who threw it to Evers standing on second.

Some Giants players, realizing their teammate never touched second, frantically yelled at Merkle to get back on the field and run to second base. Some accounts say a couple of Chicago Cubs grabbed Merkle so he couldn't reach second base until Evers had the ball for the official forceout.

Merkle was somewhat philosophical about the play, saying years later, "I suppose when I die, they'll put on my tombstone, 'Here Lies Bonehead Merkle.'"

Merkle was just 19 years old when "the play" took place and he was used sparingly during the regular season. He considered quitting after his running error, but McGraw talked him out of it. Despite hitting .187 the following season, McGraw stuck with the first baseman.

In the meantime, NL President Harry Pulliam was criticized for nearly a year by the media for not rescheduling a makeup game between the two teams the day after the 1-1 "Merkle game" on Sept. 23. The constant harassment eventually led to his suicide on July 28, 1909, a gunshot to the head.

Chance, meanwhile, took matters into his own hands and figured that the 1-1 tie would be replayed on Sept. 24 before the regularly scheduled game against the Giants, so he instructed his team to report to the Polo Grounds several hours early. When the Giants didn't show, Chance tried to gain the win by forfeit, but the league didn't go along with him. The Giants won the scheduled game, 5-4. At the end of play on Sept. 24, the Cubs stood 90-54, the Giants 88-50.

The Cubs, who won their last four and 12-of-14, concluded the regular season with a 98-55 record. Pitcher Reulbach played a major role in the Cubs' late-season drive, becoming the only pitcher in baseball history to pitch back-to-back, complete game shutouts on the same day. His two masterpieces came on Sept. 26 against Brooklyn, 5-0 and 3-0.

With the Cubs' season completed, the Giants, whose record was 95-55, still had three games to play. On Oct. 5-6-7 at the Polo Grounds, the weary Giants swept a three-game series from Boston to tie the Cubs for first with 98-55 records, then were forced to play the one-game playoff the next day.

The Oct. 8 playoff between the two teams was played at New York's Polo Grounds. The Cubs prevailed against future Hall-of-Famer Mathewson and the Giants, 4-2, thanks to Tinker's two-run double. The Cubs then went on to defeat Cobb's Detroit Tigers in the World Series.

Lost in the shuffle that 1908 season was the fact the Pittsburgh Pirates, like the Giants, finished one game behind the Cubs in the final NL standings. On Oct. 4, the final day of the regular season for both clubs, the Pirates, led by Wagner's .354 average and 109 runs-batted-in, lost to the Cubs, 5-2. Had the Pirates won that game, they would have won the pennant outright.

**Final 1908 NL Standings**

| Team | W | L | Pct. | GB |
| --- | --- | --- | --- | --- |
| Chicago | 99 | 55 | .643 | — |
| Pittsburgh | 98 | 56 | .636 | 1.0 |
| N.Y. Giants | 98 | 56 | .636 | 1.0 |
| Philadelphia | 83 | 71 | .539 | 16.0 |
| Cincinnati | 73 | 81 | .474 | 26.0 |
| Boston Braves | 63 | 91 | .409 | 36.0 |
| Brooklyn | 53 | 101 | .344 | 46.0 |
| St. Louis | 49 | 105 | .318 | 50.0 |

Evers eventually took over for Chance as the Cubs' manager in 1913 and again in 1921, finishing third and seventh, respectively. He managed the cross-town White Sox in 1924 to a sixth-place finish. He's the only man in baseball history to manage both the Cubs and the White Sox.

As successful as they were, Tinker and Evers had a terrible relationship during and after their playing days following a Sept. 14, 1905 fist fight in Washington, Ind. The ugly on-field incident took place prior to an exhibition game. Evers left for the ballpark in a taxi, leaving his keystone partner in the hotel lobby.

"That was Evers for you," Anderson said.

That didn't sit well with Tinker and he let Evers know it at the park. The two did not speak to one another for 34 years.

"Tinker and myself hated each other, but we loved the Cubs," Evers said years later, according to Baseball-Almanac.com. "We wouldn't fight for each other, but we'd come close to killing people for our team. That was one of the answers to the Cubs' success."

The silence ended in 1938 when the two retired players were secretly invited to help with the radio broadcast of the Cubs' four-game World Series loss to the New York Yankees. The two former teammates spent most of the first game emotionally reminiscing about their playing days together.

The fact the two teammates didn't talk to one another while they were still playing side-by-side surprised longtime baseball player, coach and manager Don Zimmer.

"A second baseman and shortstop have to be like twin brothers," said the 76-year-old Zimmer, a second baseman, shortstop and third baseman who played 12 seasons (1954-65) for the Dodgers, Cubs, Mets, Reds and Senators. "They should play catch with one another before every game, but I guess if you don't like a guy, you don't want to play catch with him."

After his playing days, Zimmer spent 13 seasons managing the Padres, Red Sox, Rangers and Cubs. He's also been a bench coach for the Yankees and Devil Rays. He has a handful of World Series rings earned as a player and coach.

And whatever happened to Fred Merkle? He played 16 seasons in the majors for the Giants, Dodgers, Cubs and Yankees, and had a career batting average of .273. He ranked among the top 10 in homers four times, runs-batted-in five times and finished seventh in the 1911 Most Valuable Player voting. A first baseman, he sported a solid .985 fielding percentage. Merkle appeared in five World Series, batting .239 in 27 games, but was never a member of a championship team.

Unfortunately, Merkle was involved in another not-so-memorable play in the eighth game of the 1912 World Series against the Boston Red Sox. With the Red Sox trailing the Giants by a run in the bottom of the 10th inning, Tris Speaker hit a foul ball between catcher Chief Meyers and Merkle at first. The two players let the ball drop between them, giving Speaker new life. Speaker followed with a game-tying single. Larry Gardner then ended the contest with a sacrifice fly that scored Josh Devore for a 3-2 win and a Red Sox World Series title.

Merkle refused to grant interviews the rest of his life, not wanting to relive his controversial plays. He died at the age of 67 in Daytona Beach, Fla. In the obituary that appeared in the Saturday, May 3, 1956 edition of *The New York Times*, the subhead read, "Giant 1st Baseman's 'Boner' in Failing to Touch 2nd Led to Loss of '08 Pennant."

Anderson shared a story about Merkle that Keith Olbermann, formerly of ESPN and now a popular TV news host on MSNBC, wrote in the Foreword of his book.

"About 25 years after 'the bonehead' play, a minister paid a visit to a church in Florida and opened by admitting he was from 'Fred Bonehead Merkle's hometown' (of Toledo, Ohio)," Anderson said. "One of Merkle's daughters shared the story with Olbermann."

"Following the minister's announcement," Anderson said, "Fred Merkle, in attendance at the church, stood up and led his family out the door."

Through the 2007 season, Chicago fans remained frustrated over the fact that their beloved "Cubbies" hadn't won a World Series since 1908 or appeared in a Series since 1945, when they lost to Detroit in seven games. Since the 1908 championship, the Cubs were 0-7 in World Series play. They advanced to postseason play five other times.

# DEFENSE BY THE NUMBERS

A look at the individual fielding statistics of Johnny Evers and Joe Tinker during the time period they played for the Chicago Cubs at their primary positions, second base and shortstop (PO – putouts; AST – assists; E – errors; DP – double plays; PCT. – fielding percentage):

| YEAR | JOHNNY EVERS, 2B PO | AST | E | DP | PCT. | JOE TINKER, SS PO | AST | E | DP | PCT. |
|---|---|---|---|---|---|---|---|---|---|---|
| 1902 | 38 | 58 | 1 | 5 | .990 | 243 | 453 | 72 | 46 | .906 |
| 1903 | 245 | 306 | 37 | 39 | .937 | 229 | 362 | 61 | 37 | .906 |
| 1904 | 381 | 518 | 54 | 53 | .943 | 327 | 465 | 64 | 54 | .925 |
| 1905 | 249 | 290 | 36 | 38 | .937 | 345 | 527 | 56 | 67 | .940 |
| 1906 | 344 | 441 | 44 | 51 | .947 | 288 | 472 | 45 | 55 | .944 |
| 1907 | 346 | 500 | 32 | 58 | .964 | 215 | 390 | 39 | 45 | .939 |
| 1908 | 237 | 361 | 25 | 39 | .960 | 314 | 570 | 39 | 48 | .958 |
| 1909 | 262 | 354 | 38 | 29 | .942 | 320 | 470 | 50 | 49 | .940 |
| 1910 | 282 | 347 | 33 | 55 | .950 | 277 | 411 | 42 | 54 | .942 |
| 1911 | 66 | 90 | 4 | 17 | .975 | 333 | 486 | 55 | 56 | .937 |
| 1912 | 319 | 439 | 32 | 71 | .959 | 354 | 470 | 50 | 73 | .931 |
| Totals | 2,769 | 3,704 | 336 | 455 | .955 | 3,245 | 5,076 | 573 | 584 | .933 |

NOTE: *Although a large majority of the seasonal and career double plays listed above involved the two keystone partners as a unit playing together at the same time during the noted time period, some were obviously not. The difference is due to many factors, including the number of games played, late-inning substitutions, injuries, a position change, DPs converted independent of each other and, in some cases, games missed due to military service.*

The mild-mannered Charlie Gehringer, shown making the tag at second, missed his Hall of Fame induction ceremony because it was on the same day as his wedding.

CHAPTER THREE

# 2B CHARLIE GEHRINGER & SS BILLY ROGELL DETROIT TIGERS, 1932-38

**NAME: Charles Leonard Gehringer**
Nickname: The Mechanical Man
Born: May 11, 1903, Fowlerville, Mich.
Died: Jan. 21, 1993, Bloomfield Hills, Mich.
Batted/threw: Left/right
Height/weight: 5-feet-11, 180 pounds
Major league seasons: 19 (Detroit, 1924-42)
Major league debut: Sept. 22, 1924 (**Tigers 9,** Red Sox 1)
Final major league game: Sept. 27, 1942 (Indians 8, **Tigers 0**)
Position: Second base
Career games: 2,323
Career double plays: 1,447
DPs with Tigers at second base (1932-38): 753
Career errors: 310
Career assists: 7,091
Career putouts: 5,446
Career fielding percentage: .976
Gold Gloves: The Rawlings Gold Glove Award began in 1957
All-Star: 6 times
World Series: 1-2
Career batting average: .320
Turning two: Gehringer signed his autograph "Chas." Gehringer, saying, "Why use seven letters when four will do?"
Hall of Fame: Class of 1949

Chatter-box Billy Rogell
knocked out St. Louis Cardinals pitcher Dizzy Dean with
a thrown ball in the 1934
World Series.

**NAME: William George Rogell**
Nickname: Billy
Born: Nov. 24, 1904, Springfield, Ill.
Died: Aug. 9, 2003, Sterling Heights, Mich.
Batted/threw: Both/right
Height/weight: 5-feet-11, 163 pounds
Major league seasons: 14 (Boston Red Sox, 1925, 1927-28; Detroit, 1930-39; Chicago Cubs, 1940)
Major league debut: April 14, 1925 (Athletics 9, **Red Sox 8**)
Final major league game: Aug. 25, 1940 (Giants 12, **Cubs 8**)
Position: Shortstop (also third base: 104 games; second base: 78)
Career games: 1,482
Career double plays: 862
DPs with Tigers at shortstop (1932-38): 709
Career errors: 324
Career assists: 4,315
Career putouts: 2,611
Career fielding percentage: .955
Gold Gloves: The Rawlings Gold Glove Award began in 1957
All-Star: 0 times
World Series: 1-1
Career batting average: .267
Turning two: Rogell holds the Detroit team record for most doubles in a season by a switch-hitter with 42 (1933).
Hall of Fame: No

He was called "The Mechanical Man," a nickname New York Yankee pitcher and Hall of Famer Lefty Gomez gave him in the 1930s.

"Gomez said, 'You can wind him up in the spring and he'll hit .320 to .350 with 40 doubles and 100 RBIs,'" explained 85-year-old Detroit Tiger historian Lew Matlin. "And you know something, it was true."

"His teammates also joked that on opening day, Charlie would say 'hello,' then on the final day of the season he'd say 'goodbye,'" Matlin continued. "Between those two days, he'd say nothing."

That wasn't quite true, according to Baseball Hall of Fame broadcaster Ernie Harwell, who announced major league games on television and radio for 55 years, including 42 with the Tigers.

"Charlie Gehringer was a very modest, almost shy person, but he wasn't as much of a non-talker as he's been made out to be," Harwell said. "If he knew you, he'd talk quite a bit."

The bottom line was, Gehringer could play second base with the best of them, especially in the 1930s when he led the Detroit Tigers to three American League pennants (1934, 1935, 1940) and their first World Series title in 1935. That's when he picked up the nickname "Mechanical Man." Everything he did at the plate and in the field was "mechanical," picture perfect.

Off the field, Gehringer was a devoted son and husband.

"He was always the perfect gentleman," Matlin said. "He always dressed neatly, was very charming and well liked by everyone."

Gehringer remained a bachelor during his playing days because he felt an obligation to take care of his mother, who was diabetic. Only after her death did he marry.

When he did get married, he missed his own Hall of Fame induction ceremony in Cooperstown, N.Y.

"Charlie had agreed to marry Josephine Stillen on a particular date in California," Harwell recalled with a chuckle. "Well, wouldn't you know it, it was the same day in 1949 as the Hall of Fame induction ceremonies. Charlie wisely attended his own wedding instead."

At shortstop, the Tigers had a feisty rebel named Billy Rogell. When you wound him up, he talked and talked and talked. Actually, Matlin said, Rogell didn't need winding up. It just came natural for him to gab non-stop.

Rogell talked so much that he used to get on the nerves of Hall of Famer and former Cleveland Indians pitcher Bob Feller.

"He was a know-it-all. He talked way too much. I didn't care for him," said Feller, who won 266 career games, including six seasons of 20-or-more, for the Indians.

Feller was the author of three no-hitters and 12 one-hitters, so it took a lot to get on his nerves. He would have easily won more than 300 games had it not been for the four years he served his country in the Navy in World War II.

Despite their opposite personalities, the "odd couple" of Gehringer and

Rogell set the standard for keystone combinations during the 1930s. Between 1932 and 1938, they totaled 1,462 double plays—753 by Gehringer, 709 by Rogell.

"Billy was definitely a talker," Tiger pitcher Elden Auker said several months before his death at the age of 96 in August 2006.

A submarine pitcher who won 77 games for the Tigers in six seasons (1933-38), Auker was the last living member of the Tigers' 1935 World Series championship team and the last living pitcher to face Babe Ruth. An All-Big Six selection in football, basketball and baseball at Kansas State University, Auker nearly turned to football as a profession, but Tiger owner Frank Navin talked him into becoming a pitcher.

"I guess Billy bothered a lot of people. Others just ignored him," Auker said. "On the other hand, Charlie was pretty quiet and just went about his business."

"Gehringer was real smooth," Feller said. "He moved smoothly in the infield. He wasn't a colorful person, but he was a great person."

"A lot of players around the league loved Charlie, but they didn't like Rogell," Matlin recalled. "I remember Billy and Rick Ferrell got into an awful fist fight. Rogell came in hard (at home) and they fought."

Ferrell, a catcher for the Browns, Red Sox and Senators during an 18-year Hall of Fame career, "was a real tough guy," Matlin said. "He was a fighter, but Rogell stood his ground."

Ironically, nearly 30 years later, Ferrell, who was originally signed by Detroit in 1926 but opted for the Browns as a free agent in 1928, became an executive with the Tigers and earned a World Series ring from the club's 1968 victory over the St. Louis Cardinals.

"Billy was a great defensive player, a great little shortstop." Auker said. "I'd put him in the same category as Phil (Rizzuto of the Yankees) and Pee Wee (Reese of the Dodgers). Billy really belongs in the Hall of Fame with Pee Wee (1984) and Rizzuto (1994)."

One can draw their own conclusion when comparing the three shortstops' statistics:

### Rogell vs. Reese & Rizzuto

|  | Reese | Rizzuto | Rogell |
|---|---|---|---|
| Major league seasons | 16 | 13 | 14 |
| Games played per season | 135.4 | 127.8 | 105.9 |
| Career batting average | .269 | .273 | .267 |
| Hits per season | 135.6 | 122.2 | 98.2 |
| Home runs per season | 7.9 | 2.9 | 3.0 |
| Runs-batted-in per season | 55.3 | 43.3 | 43.5 |
| Double plays per season | 78.4 | 93.6 | 61.6 |
| Errors per season | 25.4 | 20.2 | 23.1 |
| Assists per season | 383.2 | 359.0 | 308.2 |
| Putouts per season | 257.8 | 247.7 | 186.5 |
| Career fielding percentage | .962 | .968 | .955 |
| World Series record | 1-6 | 7-2 | 1-1 |

Although the numbers strongly favor Reese and Rizzuto, it should be noted that Rogell did not play in at least 100 games in six different seasons due to various injuries, accounting for 349 contests.

The right-handed Auker, who developed his underhanded style of pitching after suffering a shoulder injury while playing football at Kansas State, did admit that compared to today's players and statistics, Reese, Rizzuto and Rogell "probably wouldn't stand a chance of making the Hall."

"A lot of the people who vote today don't take into account defense, bunting a runner over, stealing a base or the leadership qualities these players from the past possessed," Auker said. "Now, it's how many homers you hit and how high your average is."

"I think they've been overlooked and the double play has been taken for granted," Auker added. "That's a shame."

Despite their different personalities and styles, Auker said Gehringer and Rogell "really complemented each other. As a double-play combination, they were Hall of Famers."

"As a pitcher, I always felt comfortable with those two backing me up," Auker said.

"Charlie was the best I ever saw," Auker said. "Fielding, hitting….he did everything perfect. And he did it so gracefully and quietly."

Auker recalled an incident when Rogell roamed over from his shortstop position to the right side of the infield to catch a pop fly intended for Gehringer. In the process of catching the ball, Rogell stepped on and spiked Gehringer's foot.

"Charlie calmly said, 'I can catch balls, too,' and he went back to his second base position like nothing had happened," Auker said.

For 16 full seasons (1926-41) and 2,323 games, Gehringer patrolled second base for the Tigers, turning 1,447 double plays, second only to another second baseman, Lou Whitaker (1977-95) with 1,527, in club history. Gehringer led the American League in fielding average nine times and in assists seven.

At the plate, Gehringer was a line-drive hitter. For his career, he hit .320, topping the .300 mark 14 times, including 1937 when he batted an American League-high .371 and won the league's Most Valuable Player Award. He was among the top 10 in the American League's MVP voting eight times. Gehringer also had 184 career homers and 574 doubles, including an astounding 60 in 1936, and 146 triples.

Gehringer was also a tough out, striking out just 372 times in 8,860 career at-bats. He was also an "iron man," having played in 98 percent of the Tigers' games during his career.

As an All-Star, Gehringer played every inning of the first six All-Star Games (1933-38) and batted a then-record .500. Seven-time (1998-2002, 2004, 2006) All-Star Derek Jeter of the New York Yankees has since broken that mark, going 7-for-13 for a .538 average.

"Gehringer was my hero growing up," said Hall of Famer Bobby Doerr, who played second base for the Boston Red Sox from 1937-1951. "I had read about him in the papers. I never saw him because we had no TV, but when I did get to see him play when I joined the Red Sox, it was a big thrill."

"He goes down as one of the greatest fielders and hitters to play the game," Doerr said.

Gehringer was so well thought of as a player, he was featured on boxes of "Wheaties" cereal in 1938.

As a youngster, Gehringer grew up on a farm, where one of his daily chores was slopping pigs. He loved baseball, so he and his brother carved out a baseball diamond and played ball everyday.

He attended the University of Michigan for one year, then decided to sign with Detroit in 1924 based on the recommendation of Bobby Veach, a former Tiger outfielder. Veach spent 12 seasons with the Tigers (1912-1923) and had a career batting average of .310 before becoming a Detroit scout.

Gehringer's first manager, Ty Cobb, publicly said he didn't believe the youngster would amount to anything in the major leagues. Cobb, probably the game's fiercest competitor, served as the Tigers' player-manager from 1921 to 1926 before being traded to Philadelphia. He skippered the Tigers to five winning seasons in his six years, the best mark coming in 1924 when the club finished 86-68.

Gehringer was eager to impress his manager, who retired in 1928 with a career-record batting average of .367, 12 batting titles and 90 records during his 24 years as a player.

Publicly, Cobb was quite gruff with Gehringer, but in reality, he liked the young second baseman and took him under his wings. Cobb was so anxious to sign the youngster that he rushed to the front office after a game in his uniform instead of waiting until he showered and changed into his street clothes.

After appearing in just 13 games in 1924 and 1925, Gehringer batted

.277 in 1926. He followed that in 1927 with a .317 mark, starting a streak of .300-plus batting averages in 14 of the next 15 seasons.

As Gehringer's career progressed, Cobb called him, aside from Eddie Collins of the Athletics and White Sox, "the greatest second baseman (he) ever saw."

His double-play partner at second in 1926-27-28 was Jackie "The Rabbit" Tavener, a fair hitter, but a weak fielder. In 1929, the Tigers tried Heinie Schuble (.233 and 46 errors in 86 games) and Yats Wuestling (.200 and 13 errors in 52 games).

Rogell joined Detroit in 1930 after spending three seasons with the Red Sox. He struggled when he first arrived in Detroit, so much that the Tigers acquired Mark Koenig from the New York Yankees. Koenig was a member of the Yankees' famed "Murderers' Row" lineup of Gehrig, Ruth, Lazzeri, Meusel and Combs.

It wasn't until the end of the 1931 season when Rogell blossomed into the player he became and the perfect sidekick to Gehringer. As a result, the Tigers released Koenig and Rogell was the club's starting shortstop on opening day in 1932.

Koenig, whose career covered 12 years, played five more productive seasons (1932-36) with the Cubs, Reds and Giants. He retired with a career batting average of .279 and two World Series rings, which he earned with the 1927 and 1928 Yankees.

Rogell's .955 career fielding percentage was an eye sore, but he made up for that with his hustle and desire to win. He did lead American League shortstops in fielding percentage three straight seasons (1935-37) and in assists twice (1934-35).

He was especially proud to be a Tiger and part of the club's "tough gang" image. At 5-feet-10, 155 pounds, he never backed down from anyone. He often said the only way the Tigers could lose on the road was if their opponents and fans ganged up and ran the team out of town.

Even though his last named started with an "R," he liked being associated with the Tigers' feared "G-Men Attack" of Gehringer, first baseman Hank Greenberg and outfielder Goose Goslin during the mid-1930s.

The three "G-Men," all members of the Hall of Fame, terrorized American League pitching in 1934 when they combined for 366 runs-batted-in en route to the American League flag with a then team-best 101 victories, seven more than the second-place Yankees. For good measure, Rogell contributed another 100 RBIs.

Manager-catcher Mickey Cochrane's Tigers did not win the 1934 World Series, though, losing to the St. Louis Cardinals' "Gas House Gang" in seven games. Brothers Dizzy and Paul Dean, who won 30 and 19 games, respectively, during the regular season, pitched and won all four Series games for the victorious Cards, who featured some real characters in the clubhouse. Leading the "gang" was Pepper Martin, who had more fun playing the banjo and washboard than he did baseball.

A third baseman and outfielder, Martin was a .298 career hitter in 13 seasons with the Cards. In two World Series (1931 and 1934), both Cardinal victories, he batted .418.

Game 4 of the 1934 Series featured one of the most unusual plays and, of course, it involved Rogell. Auker, who was the Tiger pitcher, was cruising along with a 10-4 lead that would even the Series at two games apiece. "I remember as if it happened yesterday," Auker said of what should have been an inning-ending Gehringer-to-Rogell-to-Greenberg double play. "I can still see it in my mind vividly."

"We were ahead, 10-4, late in the game and Cardinal manager Frankie Frisch puts his ace pitcher, Dizzy Dean, into the game as a pinch runner. Now how stupid was that? You're down 10-4 and you put Dizzy in. My gosh, he could have broken his leg or something."

The Cardinals' Pat Crawford hit a grounder to Gehringer, who flipped the ball to Rogell at second. Rogell then made his throw to first base in an attempt to complete the double play.

"Rogell's throw hit Dean in the head," Auker said. "Dean went down like he had been shot. The only thing that saved his life was the bill of his cap. Rogell's throw hit Dizzy's bill."

"They rushed Dizzy to the hospital and he was OK. Of course, the headline the next day in the *St. Louis Dispatch* read, 'X-rays Show Nothing in Dizzy's Head.' We all got a kick out of that."

Dean will always be remembered as one of baseball's all-time great "characters." He quit school in the second grade, picked cotton until he was 16 and joined the Army. His sergeant gave him the name "Dizzy" because of his goof-ball antics. He did learn how to pitch during his stint in the Army and played for a semi-pro team in San Antonio, Texas, where he caught the eye of a St. Louis scout.

Dean made his major league pitching debut on the last day of the 1930 season. He held the Pittsburgh Pirates to three hits in a 3-1 complete-game victory. The big, 6-feet-2 righty went on to win 150 games during his 12-year career.

With Dean recovered from his beaning, he started Game 5 the next day, lasting eight innings in a 3-1 loss to the Tigers. Dizzy did start and win the decisive seventh game, 11-0. Auker was the starting pitcher and loser for the Tigers.

"It's obvious I didn't have it that day," Auker sheepishly said. "Boy, I'd like to get that game back and start over again."

That final game was almost called after six innings because of a near riot. With the Tigers trailing, 9-0, Joe Medwick of the Cards tripled and barreled into Tiger third baseman Marv Owen. The two players got involved in a shoving match, but order was restored...for the time being.

When Medwick went to his left field position in the bottom of the sixth, he was greeted by a variety of flying objects, including tomatoes and apples from the Tiger faithful. Commissioner Kenesaw Mountain Landis considered suspending play, but instead ordered Medwick to leave the game.

Cochrane's Tigers finally won their first World Series in 1935 after failed attempts in 1907-08-09 and 1934, dispatching the Cubs in six games. Cochrane went on to manage the Tigers through 1938, compiling a 348-250 record.

His playing career covered 13 seasons with the Athletics (1925-33) and Tigers (1934-37). A .320 career hitter and a member of the Hall of Fame, Cochrane was a rugged catcher who was known for his defense and blocking the plate for runners trying to score. He played on the Athletics' 1929 and 1930 World Series championship teams, and was named the American League's Most Valuable Player in 1928 and 1934. Ironically, in the 1934 voting, he nudged out teammate Gehringer by two votes. The outcome of the voting raised a few eyebrows, as these 1934 statistics show:

## MVP: Cochrane or Gehringer?

| | Cochrane | Gehringer |
|---|---|---|
| Games | 129 | 154 |
| At-bats | 437 | 601 |
| Runs | 74 | 134 |
| Hits | 140 | 214 |
| Doubles | 32 | 50 |
| Triples | 1 | 7 |
| Home runs | 2 | 11 |
| Runs-batted-in | 76 | 127 |
| Batting average | .320 | .356 |
| On-base percentage | .428 | .450 |
| Slugging percentage | .412 | .517 |

Overlooked in the 1934 MVP voting was the Yankees' Lou Gehrig, who won the Triple Crown (.363 average, 49 homers, 165 runs-batted-in), yet finished fifth in the voting.

Cochrane's 1935 Tiger squad was again led by the "G-Men" as Gehringer, Greenberg and Goslin combined for 387 runs-batted-in. Gehringer led the hit parade with a .330 mark, followed by Greenberg at .325 and Goslin at .292.

In the field, Gehringer was involved in 99 DPs, Rogell 104 as the Tigers posted a 93-58 record, three games ahead of the second-place Yankees.

The Cubs, managed by Charlie Grimm, came out of no where to win the National League flag, winning 21 consecutive games in September to post a 100-54 mark.

The 1935 World Series got off to a rough start for the Tigers. They lost the opener, 3-0, behind the Cubs' Lee Wanrneke's four-hit, complete game.

In Game 2, the Tigers appeared doomed. They lost Greenberg for the Series when he broke his wrist trying to score from first base. Before the injury, though, the big first baseman hit a two-run homer to ignite a four-run first. Gehringer had two hits and three runs-batted-in, while Rogell chipped in a pair of singles to back the six-hit pitching of Tommy Bridges in an 8-3 Tiger win.

"We missed Hank greatly," Auker said. "But we all told ourselves we had a job to do. The other guys picked it up and we made it."

One player who especially picked it up was right fielder Pete Fox. A consistent .290-.300 hitter for the Tigers (1933-40), Fox led all hitters in the Series, going 10-for-26 for a .385 mark.

"Pete really got us going," Auker said. "He was a good player, a good out-fielder with a great throwing arm."

In Game 3, Gehringer, Goslin, Rogell and Fox combined for 10 hits and four runs-batted-in as the Tigers nipped the Cubs, 6-5, in 11 innings. Jo-Jo White knocked home the game-winner in the top of the 11th and pitcher Schoolboy Rowe got the victory with four strong innings of relief. The Tigers took a 3-1 Series lead with Gehringer driving in a run and pitcher Alvin Crowder going the distance in a 2-1 victory. The Tigers received a little help from the Cubs' defense as left fielder Augie Galan and shortstop Billy Jurges committed costly errors that led to the eventual game-winning run in the sixth inning.

The Tigers wrapped up their first championship in Game 6 when Goslin doubled home Cochrane in the bottom of the ninth for a 4-3 victory, much to the delight of the crowd of 48,420 at Navin Field in Detroit. Bridges was again strong on the mound, scattering 12 hits in the complete-game performance.

Gehringer had a remarkable Series with nine hits and a .375 average. In the three World Series he appeared in (20 games), he posted a .321 average.

After four mediocre seasons, the Tigers were back in the World Series again in 1940 against Cincinnati, but minus Rogell, who had been traded to the Cubs; Goslin, who retired, and Cochrane.

Cochrane's career had ended abruptly 27 games into the 1937 season when he was hit in the head by a Bump Hadley fastball. Hadley's high, inside pitch had so much velocity that when the ball hit Cochrane, it bounced back to the Yankee pitcher. Cochrane was unconscious for several days with a fractured skull. He never played again.

Gehringer, Greenberg and Rudy York powered the 1940 Tiger offense, while Bobo Newsom and Schoolboy Rowe led the pitching staff.

Newsom pitched three complete games in the Series, but the third one was a heartbreaking 2-1 loss in Game 7 to the Reds' Paul Derringer.

The championship was especially gratifying for Cincinnati, which had not won a World Series since the tainted victory over the 1919 Chicago "Black Sox." The Reds had played the Yankees in the 1939 Series, but got swept four straight.

Rogell's final season in Detroit was in 1939, when he appeared in just 74 games due to a variety of injuries. He was traded to the Chicago Cubs for shortstop Dick Bartell in a transaction the baseball writers called "a swap of sore shoulders." With the Tigers, Rogell turned 709 double plays at short, including a career-high 116 in 1933. He punched out a .267 career batting average.

He appeared in 33 games for Chicago in 1940, then, ironically, was released so the Cubs could make room for a pitcher by the name of Dizzy Dean.

Bartell was no slouch, having played 18 seasons (1927-43 and 1946) with the Pirates, Giants, Phillies, Cubs and Tigers. A career .284 hitter, he was handy with the bat, twice leading the American League in sacrifice bunts in 1932 with 35 and 1933 with 37. He ranked among the top five in that category eight times and totaled 269 for his career. In his one full season with the Tigers (1940), though, he hit just .233. He signed with the Giants in 1941 after being released by the Tigers. Defensively, Bartell turned 1,072 double plays from the shortstop position.

Following his playing days, Rogell kicked around the minors for several years as a manager, then served as a Detroit city council member for 38 years. And just like he was on the field, he was a mover and a shaker in Detroit city government.

He was honored by the Tigers on Sept. 27, 1999 by throwing out the ceremonial first pitch before the final game in the history of Tiger Stadium, which opened in 1912. He died four years later of pneumonia at the age of 98.

Gehringer, meanwhile, batted .313 in 1940, then slumped to .220 the following year. In 1942, his last season, he was hitting .267 in 45 games before joining the Navy for three years. He considered a comeback in 1945 in an effort to reach 3,000 career hits, but decided against it. As a result, he came up 161 hits shy of 3,000. He spent the 1950s working in the Tigers' front office, including that of general manager, before retiring for good in 1960.

When all was said and done, Gehringer ranked among the top 10 in batting six times, runs scored 12, hits nine, doubles and triples six times, and total bases eight.

Like Rogell, Gehringer lived long enough to see his beloved Tigers win World Series crowns in 1968 over the St. Louis Cardinals and in 1984 over the San Diego Padres.

Today, a statue of Gehringer is located in the left-field walkway at Comerica Park in Detroit.

# DEFENSE BY THE NUMBERS

A look at the individual fielding statistics of Charlie Gehringer and Billy Rogell during the time period they played for the Detroit Tigers at their primary positions, second base and shortstop (PO – putouts; AST – assists; E – errors; DP – double plays; PCT. – fielding percentage):

| | CHARLIE GEHRINGER, 2B | | | | | BILLY ROGELL, SS | | | | |
|---|---|---|---|---|---|---|---|---|---|---|
| YEAR | PO | AST | E | DP | PCT | PO | AST | E | DP | PCT. |
| 1932 | 396 | 495 | 30 | 110 | .967 | 275 | 433 | 42 | 88 | .944 |
| 1933 | 358 | 542 | 17 | 111 | .981 | 326 | 526 | 51 | 116 | .944 |
| 1934 | 355 | 516 | 17 | 100 | .981 | 259 | 518 | 31 | 99 | .962 |
| 1935 | 349 | 489 | 13 | 99 | .985 | 280 | 512 | 24 | 104 | .971 |
| 1936 | 397 | 524 | 25 | 116 | .974 | 286 | 462 | 27 | 98 | .965 |
| 1937 | 331 | 485 | 12 | 102 | .986 | 323 | 451 | 26 | 103 | .968 |
| 1938 | 393 | 455 | 21 | 115 | .976 | 291 | 431 | 31 | 101 | .959 |
| Totals | 2,579 | 3,506 | 135 | 753 | .979 | 2,040 | 3,333 | 232 | 709 | .959 |

NOTE: *Although a large majority of the seasonal and career double plays listed involved the two keystone partners as a unit playing together at the same time during the noted time period, some were obviously not. The difference is due to many factors, including the number of games played, late-inning substitutions, injuries, a position change, DPs converted independent of each other and, in some cases, games missed due to military service.*

### CHAPTER FOUR

# 2B JOE GORDON & SS PHIL RIZZUTO
## N.Y. YANKEES, 1941-42, 1946

**NAME: Joseph Lowell Gordon**
Nickname: Flash
Born: Feb. 18, 1915, Los Angeles, Calif.
Died: April 14, 1978, Sacramento, Calif.
Batted/threw: Right/right
Height/weight: 5-feet-10, 180 pounds
Major league seasons: 11 (N.Y. Yankees, 1938-43, 1946; Cleveland, 1947-50)
Major league debut: April 18, 1938 (Red Sox 8, Yankees 4)
Final major league game: Sept. 30, 1950 (Tigers 3, Indians 1)
Position: Second base
Career games: 1,566
Career double plays: 1,196
DPs with Yankees at second base (1941-42, 1946): 317
Career errors: 264
Career assists: 4,726
Career putouts: 3,826
Career fielding percentage: .970
Gold Gloves: The Rawlings Gold Glove Award began in 1957
All-Star: 9 times
World Series: 5-1
Career batting average: .268
Turning two: The second baseman hit 20 or more homers in seven of the 11 seasons he played, with a high of 32 in 1948.
Hall of Fame: No

**NAME: Philip Francis Rizzuto**
**Nickname:** Scooter
**Born:** Sept. 25, 1917, Brooklyn, N.Y.
**Died:** August 14, 2007
**Batted/threw:** Right/right
**Height/weight:** 5-feet-6, 160 pounds
**Major league seasons:** 13 (N.Y. Yankees, 1941-42, 1946-56)
**Major league debut:** April 14, 1941 (**Yankees 3,** Senators 0)
**Final major league game:** Aug. 16, 1956 (Red Sox 2, **Yankees 1**)
**Position:** Shortstop
**Career games:** 1,661
**Career double plays:** 1,217
**DPs with Yankees at shortstop (1941-42, 1946):** 320
**Career errors:** 263
**Career assists:** 4,666
**Career putouts:** 3,220
**Career fielding percentage:** .968
**Gold Gloves:** The Rawlings Gold Glove Award began in 1957
**All-Star:** 5 times
**World Series:** 7-2
**Career batting average:** .273
**Turning two:** Rizzuto was the first mystery guest on the television show
"What's My Line?" in 1950.
**Hall of Fame:** Class of 1994

There were a lot of shenanigans going on in Major League Baseball during the 1940s and early 1950s. Two of the many culprits—and victims—were New York Yankee second baseman Joe Gordon and shortstop Phil Rizzuto.

Rizzuto was the funny man who loved pranks, as long as they weren't played on him. A durable and happy-go-lucky shortstop, he spent 13 seasons with the Yankees, won nine pennants, seven World Series and the Most Valuable Player Award in 1950 when he hit .324.

Gordon combined acrobatic defensive skills at second and was a clutch hitter who had power. He was low-key and pretty much went about his business, but he was known to throw in a zinger now and then. Gordon played for the Yankees for seven seasons, won four-of-five World Series and was named the Most Valuable Player in 1942 when he hit .322

"I guess you could characterize them as a comedy team," former Yankee player, manager and executive Ralph Houk said with a chuckle.

"Phil always liked to kid with people. Joe was pretty reserved. I don't want to start any rumors, though, but Joe had some tricks of his own."

When Rizzuto and Gordon formed one of baseball's classic keystone combos (1941-42, 1946) that was, unfortunately, interrupted by World War II, fielders routinely left their gloves on the playing field at the end of an inning. This, baseball officials believed, would speed up the game 10-20 minutes, cutting down on the amount of time players spent looking for their gloves in the dugout at the end of an inning.

Critics like Joe Cronin, Hank Greenberg and Houk insisted that leaving the gloves on the field could cause injuries to the players on the field.

And on more than one occasion, batted balls hitting the unused gloves interfered with play on the field. The 1905 American League pennant race between Philadelphia and Chicago, for example, was decided when a batted ball hit an unused glove on the field, thus allowing the Athletics to score the winning run and win the AL flag.

In 1954, baseball declared that all defensive fielders would carry their gloves back to the dugout at the conclusion of an inning. If a player was stranded on second base, one of his defensive teammates could bring him his glove.

Prior to 1954, though, baseball was full of comedians who loved to leave a little surprise in their opponents' gloves, surprises like limburger cheese, mice and, in one case, the deadly queen of spades.

According to former Yankee catcher and Hall of Famer Yogi Berra, "Phil was pretty squeamish about those things. He didn't like finding things in his glove."

That didn't stop his opponents, though.

Former Boston Red Sox shortstop Johnny Pesky remembers that Rizzuto was a favorite target.

"Phil would put on his glove, feel something in it and jump 20 feet," recalled Pesky, who played several years during the Rizzuto era. "He'd find a dead mouse or worm or a little chewing tobacco or something in his glove. It was all in fun."

"I actually saw frogs hop out of gloves when Phil or someone tried to put their gloves on," said Eddie Robinson, who spent 13 seasons (1942, 1946-57) playing first base for the Indians, Senators, White Sox, Tigers, Yankees and Athletics. "Everyone knew Phil didn't like those things. That's why players picked on him."

Gordon used to annoy opposing pitchers, especially Bobo Newsom, by cutting up pieces of white paper and dropping the debris in front of the pitcher's mound as he ran to the dugout from second base. Newsom, who pitched for nine teams and won 211 games during a 20-year career, would not pitch until the ground crew picked up every scrap of paper.

When Eddie "The Brat" Stanky was with the St. Louis Cardinals, he once hid New York Giant Bill Rigney's glove *under* second base. "Players were trying to get more creative with their little tricks," Pesky said.

"I loved to play the card game 'Hearts,'" Pesky said. "One day I found the queen of spades in my glove. That shook me up pretty good."

Longtime baseball guru Don Zimmer, who's been in the game for more than 50 years, laughs when he recalls some of the pranks he saw.

"I saw guys put little garden snakes in a player's glove," said Zimmer, who spent 12 seasons playing second, short and third (1954-65) for the Dodgers, Cubs, Mets, Reds and Senators before becoming a manager and coach. "I saw shaving cream. A player would put the glove on and his fingers would be covered with shaving cream. Some of the players back then were real comedians."

The comedy and fun aside, Gordon and Rizzuto formed as close to a perfect keystone combination as there's been, according to their peers.

During their three seasons playing the keystone positions, they totaled 637 double plays—317 by Gordon, 320 by Rizzuto.

It's unfortunate that World War II cost the two All-Stars a combined five years of playing time together. Rizzuto served in the Navy for three years (1943-45) and Gordon was in the Army for two (1944-45).

"Both Phil and Joe were superb fielders," Houk said. "They had great range. Phil had the quick release, probably the quickest I've seen. He could do it all. He played the hitters well. And Joe had the great arm."

"Rizzuto was very quick," Pesky said. "He didn't play a deep shortstop, but he had the quickness and great range. He was like a mosquito. He was everywhere."

"Gordon was as good as anyone at second," Pesky continued. "He was the perfect player. I'd put him in the same class as (Boston's) Bobby Doerr and (Detroit's) Charlie Gehringer."

"They were as good of a double-play combination as I have ever seen," added Pesky, who's been around the majors since 1942.

"Gordon was a real acrobat and a good money player," said Hall of Fame pitcher Bob Feller, who won 266 games for Cleveland. "Rizzuto had the fastest hands I've seen, and that includes (Pittsburgh's Bill) Mazeroski and (New York's Bobby) Richardson."

"Had they not missed those seasons due to the war, there's no telling what they could have accomplished," said 10-year pitching veteran Elden Auker, who won 130 games for the Tigers, Red Sox and Browns from 1933-42.

"Rizzuto could do it all at short and at the plate, probably a little better than our shortstop back in Detroit, Billy Rogell," Auker said. "Joe was a classy guy, just like our second baseman (in Detroit), Charlie Gehringer. They were about equal making the plays in the field. At the plate, Charlie hit for a higher average (.320 to Gordon's .268), but Joe had more power (23 homers per season compared to Gehringer's 9.5) and probably drove in more runs (90 to 75 per season).

"I've followed the game closely since I retired," said Auker, who passed away in August 2006 at the age of 96. "I don't think I've seen better double-play combinations than Rizzuto-Gordon and Rogell-Gehringer."

Gordon quickly picked up the nickname "Flash" for his quick feet around second base and in reference to the popular comic book hero of the 1930s, "Flash Gordon."

Gordon signed with the Yankees in 1936 as a free agent after attending the University of Oregon, where he starred in baseball, football, gymnastics, soccer, the long jump and even the violin.

In his first professional season in 1937 with the Newark (N.J.) Bears, Gordon played a steady second base and hit .280. The Bears had a powerful team, going 109-43 during the regular International League season, then 8-0 in the playoffs.

In the Junior World Series against Columbus (Ohio), the American Association champion, Newark, fell behind 3 games to 0, but rallied to win four straight for the title.

In Gordon's first season with the Yankees in 1938, he teamed with shortstop Frank Crosetti, who was in his seventh season with the club. The two formed a fine tandem during the next three seasons (1938-40), helping the Yankees to a pair of World Series championships in 1938 over the Cubs and 1939 over the Reds, both four-game sweeps.

Gordon replaced one of the most-popular Yankees of that era, Tony Lazzeri, who won five World Series playing with the likes of Babe Ruth, Lou Gehrig and Joe DiMaggio. Lazzeri, a Hall of Famer, played 12 seasons with the Yanks, then was traded to the Chicago Cubs prior to the 1938 season to make room for the young Gordon.

The 23-year-old Gordon had some big shoes to fill at second as Lazzeri had a career batting average of .292, drove in more than 100 runs seven times and turned 785 double plays with New York.

Gordon was quick to contribute, not only during the regular season when he hit .255 with 25 homers and 97 runs-batted-in, but in the postseason as well. In the four-game sweep of the Chicago Cubs in the 1938 World Series, Gordon batted .400 and drove home six runs.

Gordon had the distinction of playing next to Hall of Famer and first baseman Lou Gehrig in 1938 and a short period of time in 1939, when "The Iron Horse" developed Amyotrophic Lateral Sclerosis, a rare neurological disorder that to this day is incurable. Today, the disease is called "Lou Gehrig's Disease." The date was May 2, 1939 when a sick Gehrig took himself out of the starting lineup against Detroit, snapping a streak of 2,130 consecutive games played. He died on June 2, 1941 at the age of 37. Ironically, his death came 16 years to the day that his playing streak began.

Gordon's first three seasons were solid with batting averages of .255, .284, .281, a total of 83 home runs and 311 runs-batted-in. Crosetti, however, stumbled badly with a .194 average in 1940, one of the reasons why the Yankees finished two games behind Detroit for the American League pennant.

Waiting in the wings was the 23-year-old Rizzuto, who had signed with the Yanks prior to the 1937 season.

When then-Brooklyn manager Casey Stengel first saw the 5-feet-6 Rizzuto at a Dodger tryout camp, he told the shortstop that he was too small and that he should consider shining shoes for a career. Little did Stengel know that Rizzuto would play a big role in his success as manager of the Yankees in the 1950s.

The Dodgers passed on Rizzuto, as did the New York Giants. Bill Terry, the Giants' skipper, wouldn't even let Rizzuto on the field because of his size.

The Yankees and manager Joe McCarthy, though, saw a lot of energy in Rizzuto. They were impressed with the shortstop's ability in the field and at the plate as a bunter.

As a minor league player, Rizzuto was nicknamed "the absorber" for his excellent fielding range. It wasn't until spring training 1941 when Rizzuto picked up the nickname "Scooter."

"Billy Hitchcock was on the team with me. You know my legs are short and when he saw me run, he said, 'Man, you're not running, you're scootin.' And from that, I got 'Scooter.' I've been called a lot worse names than that," Rizzuto explained in an interview with the National Baseball Hall of Fame in 2000.

Hitchcock never played a game for the Yankees. A utility infielder, he spent nine seasons with five clubs. He then managed the Orioles for two seasons (1962-63) and Atlanta for 1.5 years (1966-67). He compiled a career managerial record of 274-261.

Rizzuto made an immediate impact as the Yankees won the 1941 American League pennant by 17 games with a 101-53 record. He batted .307 and played a solid shortstop with 109 double plays. His keystone mate, Gordon, added a .276 mark, 24 homers, 87 runs-batted-in and 109 more double plays.

Gordon and Rizzuto had a little help winning the 1941 American League crown. Manager McCarthy's everyday lineup included outfielders DiMaggio (.357), Charlie Keller (.298) and Tommy Henrich (.277), all of whom crashed more than 30 homers. The pitching staff featured 15-game winners Red Ruffing and Lefty Gomez, and Marius Russo, who added 14 victories. Managing the pitching staff was catcher Bill Dickey.

In the 1941 Series, the Yankees took cross-town rival Brooklyn in five games. Gordon again was a force at the plate, hitting .500 and posting a slugging percentage of .929.

It was more of the same in 1942, as McCarthy's Yankees won 103 games to win the American League title by nine games over Boston before losing to the Cardinals in five in the World Series. Gordon was named the league's Most Valuable Player. Finishing second in the MVP voting was Boston's Ted Williams, who had won the Triple Crown. A comparison of the two players' stats in 1942:

## MVP: Gordon or Williams?

|  | Gordon | Williams |
|---|---|---|
| Games played | 147 | 150 |
| At-bats | 538 | 522 |
| Runs | 88 | 141 |
| Hits | 173 | 186 |
| Doubles | 29 | 34 |
| Triples | 4 | 5 |
| Homers | 18 | 36 |
| Runs-batted-in | 103 | 137 |
| Stolen bases | 12 | 3 |
| Base-on-balls | 79 | 145 |
| Average | .322 | .356 |
| On-base percentage | .409 | 499 |
| Slugging percentage. | 491 | .648 |

There were three reasons why Gordon won the Most Valuable Player Award: He led the Yankees to a 103-51 record and the American League pennant. Williams' Red Sox were second, nine games behind. Gordon's numbers were easily impressive enough to win the award. Even at the age of 23, Williams had already rubbed sports writers the wrong way. He created enemies among the media, which swung votes Gordon's way.

The MVP balloting was close, though, as Gordon collected 12 first-place votes, Williams nine. Gordon had 270 voting points, Williams 249. Williams won another Triple Crown in 1947, but lost the MVP honor by one vote to DiMaggio. The difference in the voting? One sports writer left Williams completely off his ballot.

Rizzuto did his part in his second full season in 1942, hitting .284 and enjoying another solid season at short with 114 double plays. Gordon added 121.

Rizzuto became an excellent bunter, four times leading the league in sacrifices. He also became a threat to steal bases, eight times ranking among the top six in the league in that category.

Tiny Bonham led the 1942 pitching staff with 21 wins, followed by Spud Chandler's 16, Hank Borowy's 15 and Ruffing's 14.

The next three years (1943-45) saw the Yankees use a merry-go-round of second basemen and shortstops due to the war with Rizzuto and Gordon overseas. Also gone for three seasons (1943-45) was DiMaggio, who served in the Army.

YANKEES' MAKESHIFT INFIELD
The Yankees' infield looked like this from 1943 to 1945:

| Year | First | Second | Short | Third |
|------|-------|--------|-------|-------|
| 1943 | Nick Etten | Gordon | Crosetti Snuffy Stirnweiss | Billy Johnson |
| 1944 | Etten | Stirnweiss | Milosevich | Oscar Grimes |
| 1945 | Etten | Stirnweiss | Milosevich | Grimes |

The 1943 team—minus DiMaggio and Rizzuto—surprisingly ran away with the American League pennant by 13 games over Washington, then took care of St. Louis in five games in the World Series.

The 1944 and 1945 teams, however, stumbled, finishing third and fourth, respectively.

In 1946, the Yankee stars were back. DiMaggio returned to center, and

Gordon and Rizzuto were back at second and short. Yankee fans anticipated a return to the top of the American League standings, but there was just too much rust after the war years.

For the first time in his career, DiMaggio failed to hit .300 and drive in at least 100 runs. Gordon had a rough season at the plate, batting .210 with just 47 runs-batted-in. Rizzuto managed a .257 mark. His assists and putouts were down, and his errors were up. Rizzuto was involved in 97 double plays, Gordon 87.

There were also two changes at the top. Manager McCarthy was replaced by Bill Dickey who was replaced by Johnny Neun. At the end of the 1946 season, the Yankees finished third, 17 games behind league champion Boston.

Things got so bad that Rizzuto, who was very superstitious, started putting a piece of chewing gum on his hat for good luck.

"The only time I would take it (the gum) off is when we lost a game," Rizzuto said in his interview with the Hall of Fame. "There was a time, though, where we had set the record for winning consecutive games and nobody would sit next to me on the bench. Oh, it smelled awful, but I couldn't take it off. They (teammates) tried to hide it and throw the hat away, but that was just one of the things. You could never step on the white line going to your position."

One Yankee cap still containing a Rizzuto wad of chewed gum was sold at auction for $8,190 by Geppi's Memorabilia Road Show in September 2006.

"Ball players are very superstitious," Rizzuto said. "It seems silly, but some guys were worse than me. They would wear a (unwashed) sweatshirt for a long time and that's bad if you're in a winning streak."

Following the disappointing third-place 1946 season, the Yankees and new manager Bucky Harris shipped Gordon to Cleveland for pitcher Allie Reynolds, breaking up one of the game's finest double-play tandems.

"Like a lot of us, Gordon lost two good years to the military, then when he came back for one season, the Yankees traded him," Pesky said. "I was really surprised the Yankees traded Joe because he was one of the best."

Oddly enough, Gordon played in 1,000 games for the Yankees and collected 1,000 base hits.

The trade benefited both the Yankees and the Indians. Reynolds posted a 131-60 record in eight seasons in New York, including a pair of no-hitters in 1951, and was 7-2 in six World Series, all Yankee victories.

Gordon enjoyed four productive seasons in Cleveland, playing alongside Hall of Fame shortstop-manager Lou Boudreau. The two formed an excellent keystone combo, exceeding the 200 mark in 1947, 1948 and 1949. They began to fade in 1950, missing a combined 130 games due to injuries and the team's need to break-in younger players.

Gordon did win a fifth career World Series in six tries, this one coming in 1948 with the Tribe in six games over the Boston Braves. During the season, Gordon batted .280, smacked 32 homers and drove home 124 runs, powerful statistics for a second baseman during that era.

The Indians took the 1948 AL crown after beating Boston, 8-3, in a one-game playoff at Fenway Park on Oct. 4. Both teams finished the season 96-58, setting the stage for the playoff and a World Series date against the Braves.

"We could have won the pennant outright, but we lost to the Tigers (7-1) in Cleveland on the final day of the season," recalled the Indians' Eddie Robinson. "So we had to ride the train to Boston all night, check into the hotel and right away report to the ballpark."

"We figured the Red Sox pitcher would be Mel Parnell, but we were surprised to see it was Denny Galehouse," Robinson said.

Parnell, a hard-throwing, 26-year-old southpaw, had gone 15-8 in 1948 with an earned-run-average of 3.14. At age 36, Galehouse was 8-8. The Sox couldn't use their other aces—Joe Dobson (16-10), Ellis Kinder (10-7), Jack Kramer (18-5) and Parnell—because they had used them up during a four-game winning streak at the end of the season to pull even in the AL standings with the Indians.

Cleveland pitcher Gene Beardon shut the Sox down to pick up his 20th win of the season against seven defeats. The Tribe's staff also included 20-game winner Bob Lemon and 19-game winner Bob Feller. Catcher Jim Hegan managed the staff.

The Cleveland infield featured Robinson at first, Gordon at second, Boudreau at short and Kenny Keltner at third. In the outfield, Boudreau had Larry Doby, Dale Mitchell and Thurman Tucker.

"Without Joe, we wouldn't have won the pennant," Robinson said. "Joe was a real team leader. He kept the team loose and was an excellent clutch performer."

"He was my roommate and he was a great roommate," added Robinson, who had 16 homers, 83 runs-batted-in and a .254 batting average in the Tribe's 1948 pennant run. "After all, who wouldn't want to room with an ex-Yankee like Joe Gordon?"

Defensively, Robinson, who committed just seven errors in 1948, was the beneficiary of 123 double plays at first, thanks to the tandem of Gordon and Boudreau.

The 1948 season would be Gordon's last hurrah. In 1949, his average dipped to .251, but he still played a solid second base, turning a career-high 123 double plays while committing just 15 errors in 145 games.

He was released by the Tribe in 1950 with a career average of .268. He also averaged 23 home runs and 90 runs-batted-in during his 11-season career and turned 1,196 double plays. He led American League second basemen in double plays three times and in assists four.

Gordon, the first second baseman in major league history to hit 20 or more home runs in a season (25 in 1938), is often called "the lost Yankee" or "the greatest Yankee no one talks about," which is probably why he never made the Hall of Fame.

"Joe belongs in the Hall," said former Red Sox second baseman Bobby Doerr, a Hall of Famer himself. "It's always been a mystery to me as to why he isn't."

The Veterans Committee first considered Gordon for the Hall in March of 1988, along with Rizzuto, Leo Durocher and Gil Hodges, but did not elect anyone for the first time in 33 years. Gordon had appeared on the writers' ballot 11 times, but never came close to earning the necessary 75 percent of the votes. Durocher and Rizzuto eventually made the Hall, but Hodges, who spent 16 seasons with the Dodgers and produced impressive credentials like Gordon, didn't.

After managing in the Pacific Coast League and serving as a scout for the Detroit Tigers, Gordon skippered four different teams, starting in Cleveland (1958-60), where he posted a 184-151 mark. At one point during the 1959 season, Cleveland general manager Frank Lane fired Gordon, then rehired him the next day due to adverse fan reaction.

Then, during the 1960 season, Gordon was actually traded to Detroit for manager Jimmy Dykes. The bizarre trade still stands as the only swap of managers.

The trade was the brainstorm of Detroit general manager Bill DeWitt and Lane, who had several run-ins with Gordon.

The trade took place more than halfway through the 1960 season, with Gordon managing the Tigers to a 26-31 mark. Dykes led the Indians to a 26-32 mark. Neither team challenged for the pennant, as the Indians finished 76-78 and the Tigers 71-83.

"Lane and DeWitt liked to do kooky things like that," explained Hall of Fame TV and radio broadcaster Ernie Harwell, who joined the Tigers in 1960 after stints with the Brooklyn Dodgers (1948-49), New York Giants (1950-53) and Baltimore Orioles (1954-59).

"The trade didn't make a whole lot of difference to the players," he continued. "Everyone in Detroit loved Jimmy Dykes. He was easy going, and so was Joe (Gordon). They weren't taskmasters or anything like that. Lane and DeWitt just wanted to shake things up."

"I didn't know anything about it (in advance)," said Harwell, who spent 42 years calling Detroit games. "I don't think anyone did. But it didn't bother me. I liked both Jimmy and Joe."

Dykes had a long career as a manager, first spending 13 seasons (1934-46) with the White Sox. He spent three seasons with the Athletics (1951-53), then one in Baltimore (1954). He replaced Birdie Tebbetts in Cincinnati late in the 1958 campaign before moving on to Detroit in 1959. His career record: 1,406 wins, 1,541 losses.

As a player, Dykes spent 22 seasons in the big leagues with the Philadelphia Athletics (1918-32) and White Sox (1933-39). He played every infield position, except catcher, had a career batting average of .280 and won a pair of World Series with Philly in 1929 and 1930.

In 1961, Gordon became manager of the Kansas City Athletics. He was surprisingly fired by Charles Finley after a 26-33 start and replaced by former Yankee Hank Bauer, who went 35-67. In 1969, Gordon returned to the majors and managed the Kansas City Royals to a 69-93 record. As a result, he was the only person to manage both the Athletics and the Royals in Kansas City. His career mark as a manager was 305-308.

Rizzuto remained the Yankees' primary shortstop through the 1953 season. He was as steady as ever for manager Stengel, both at the plate and in the field. With Gordon gone, he played next to several different second basemen, including Snuffy Stirnweiss, Jerry Coleman, Billy Martin and Gil McDougald.

Because of his ability to lay down sacrifice bunts—or in this case, a suicide squeeze—Rizzuto was involved in a game that clinched the pennant for the Yankees, but left the Cleveland Indians annoyed. The date was Sept. 17, 1951 at Yankee Stadium. The score was tied at 1 in the bottom half of the Yankee ninth. Rizzuto recalled the play in his interview with the Hall of Fame:

"Joe DiMaggio was on third base and I was at bat. The score was tied and we had the squeeze play on. I was allowed to give the squeeze play sign to whoever was on third base, and I would do it by holding the bat horizontally at chest level. I would always take one pitch, hoping that it would be a strike and I would turn around and argue with the umpire. I would hold the bat like that, trying to decoy them. Well, DiMaggio got a running start and was just about seven or eight feet away from the plate."

"Bob Lemon was the pitcher and he threw it right at my head and I had to jump up to bunt it or it would have hit me right in the face. Well the beauty of the whole thing was that some photographer had gotten a picture of it and in the on-deck circle (rookie) Mickey Mantle was jumping up and down like a little kid. DiMaggio crossed home plate and Lemon took his glove and threw it up on the screen in back of home plate and Al Rosen, who was the first baseman, picked the ball up, threw it up there and I snuck around and got to first base. I got a base hit on it!"

In 1954, Rizzuto began to stumble, hitting a paltry .190 in 127 games. He saw limited action in 1955 and 1956, then was released by the Yankees, who were in the process of a major facelift under the guidance of Stengel, who was interested in playing "his players." Unfortunately, as great as DiMaggio and the heart-broken Rizzuto were, Stengel felt like he had "inherited them."

Berra had settled in as the Yankees' all-star catcher, as did Mantle in center field. The infield featured Bill Skowron at first, Martin at second, McDougald at short and Andy Carey at third. Bauer and Elston Howard joined Mantle in the outfield.

By 1958 and 1959, names like second baseman Bobby Richardson, shortstop Tony Kubek and third baseman Clete Boyer appeared in the New York starting lineup. In 1960, Roger Maris had taken over the right field position.

Rizzuto, meanwhile, was inducted into the Baseball Hall of Fame in 1994 by the Veterans Committee with impressive credentials: seven World Series championships, two fielding titles for a shortstop and the top shortstop in terms of double plays three times. His good friend, DiMaggio, lobbied hard for Rizzuto's induction. His longtime rival and friend, Ted Williams, was also a Rizzuto supporter, many times saying the difference between his Red Sox and the Yankees was the little, scrappy shortstop from Brooklyn.

According to Baseball-Almanac.com, prior to his election, Rizzuto jokingly said, "I'll take anyway to get into the Hall of Fame. If they want a batboy, I'll go in as a batboy."

Rizzuto took his induction seriously. He wasn't sure if he deserved to be selected, but his old buddy from the National League, the Dodgers' Pee Wee Reese, gained entry into the Hall in 1984. Statistically, Rizzuto outhit Reese, career-wise, .273 to .269, both were equal in the field and the Yankee played a major role in seven World Series titles to Reese's one.

Following his playing days, Rizzuto spent four decades in the Yankees'

TV and radio broadcast booth where his trademark phrase was "Holy cow!" He is probably best remembered for his call of Roger Maris' 61st home run on the final day of the 1961 season to break Babe Ruth's single-season mark of 60.

"When he hit the 61st home run, I screamed so loud I had a headache for about a week," Rizzuto said.

In addition to his popular "Holy cow" phrase, Rizzuto also came up with the term "huckleberry" for umpires, both as a player and as a broadcaster. His thinking was he couldn't be thrown out of a game if he called an umpire a "huckleberry." Sure enough, he never got tossed.

Some of Rizzuto's broadcasting sidekicks included many of the game's finest, including Mel Allen, Red Barber, Joe Garagiola, Jerry Coleman and Frank Messer.

Rizzuto's broadcasting career, which began in 1957, came to a temporary halt on Aug. 18, 1995, when the television station airing Yankee baseball refused to allow him to miss a game so he could attend Mantle's funeral. Rizzuto, upset and full of emotion during the broadcast on the eve of Mantle's funeral, left the broadcast booth halfway through the game and attended the funeral anyway. The station eventually asked him to return to the broadcast booth. His last season in the booth was 1996.

Prior to his death, Rizzuto was involved with several charitable organizations, especially the St. Joseph's School for the Blind in Jersey City, N.J. During the same auction that netted $8,190 for his "bubble gum Yankee cap," his 1950 Most Valuable Player Award netted $175,000. Three of his World Series rings garnered $84,825. A majority of the funds went to the school for the blind.

DEFENSE BY THE NUMBERS

A look at the individual fielding statistics of Joe Gordon and Phil Rizzuto during the time period they played for the New York Yankees at their primary positions, second base and shortstop (PO – putouts; AST – assists; E – errors; DP – double plays; PCT. – fielding percentage):

| YEAR | JOE GORDON, 2B | | | | | PHIL RIZZUTO, SS | | | | |
|---|---|---|---|---|---|---|---|---|---|---|
| | PO | AST | E | DP | PCT. | PO | AST | E | DP | PCT. |
| 1941 | 332 | 397 | 32 | 109 | .958 | 252 | 399 | 29 | 109 | .957 |
| 1942 | 354 | 442 | 28 | 121 | .966 | 324 | 445 | 30 | 114 | .949 |
| 1946 | 281 | 346 | 17 | 87 | .974 | 267 | 378 | 26 | 97 | .961 |
| Totals | 967 | 1,185 | 77 | 317 | .966 | 843 | 1,222 | 85 | 320 | .957 |

NOTE: *Although a large majority of the seasonal and career double plays listed above involved the two keystone partners as a unit playing together at the same time during the noted time period, some were obviously not. The difference is due to many factors, including the number of games played, late-inning substitutions, injuries, a position change, DPs converted independent of each other and, in some cases, games missed due to military service.*

Former pitcher Elden Auker said "Doerr (left) and Pesky (right) were slick—almost magical—they could turn the double play as well as anyone."

## CHAPTER FIVE

# 2B BOBBY DOERR & SS JOHNNY PESKY BOSTON RED SOX, 1942, 1946-47, 1951

**NAME: Robert Pershing Doerr**

Nickname: Bobby

Born: April 7, 1918, Los Angeles, Calif.

Died: Still throwing as of October 1, 2007

Batted/threw: Right/right

Height/weight: 5-feet-11, 175 pounds

Major league seasons: 14 (Boston, 1937-44; 1946-51)

Major league debut: April 20, 1937 (**Red Sox 11,** Athletics 5)

Final major league game: Sept. 7, 1951 (**Red Sox 8,** Athletics 5)

Position: Second base

Career games: 1,865

Career double plays: 1,507

DPs with Red Sox at second base (**1942; 1946-47; 1951**): 451

Career errors: 214

Career assists: 5,710

Career putouts: 4,928

Career fielding percentage: .980

Gold Gloves: The Rawlings Gold Glove Award began in 1957

All-Star: 9 times

World Series: 0-1

Career batting average: .288

Turning two: Doerr drove home more than 100 runs six times, including 1950 when he knocked in 120

Hall of Fame: Class of 1986

**NAME: John Michael Pesky**
Nickname: Needle nose
Born: Sept. 27, 1919, Portland, Ore.
Died: Still throwing as of October 1, 2007
Batted/threw: Left/right
Height/weight: 5-feet-9, 168 pounds
Major league seasons: 10 (Boston, 1942; 1946-52; Detroit, 1952-54; Washington, 1954)
Major league debut: April 14, 1942 (**Red Sox 8,** Athletics 3)
Final major league game: Sept. 24, 1954 (**Senators 1,** Red Sox 0)
Position: Shortstop (also third base: 460 games; second base: 137)
Career games: 1,270
Career double plays: 594
DPs with Red Sox at shortstop (1942; 1946-47; 1951): 354
Career errors: 178
Career assists: 3,114
Career putouts: 1,987
Career fielding percentage: .966
Gold Gloves: The Rawlings Gold Glove Award began in 1957
All-Star: 1 time
World Series: 0-1
Career batting average: .307
Turning two: Pesky averaged 207 hits in 1942, 1946 and 1947 to lead the American League
Hall of Fame: No

Although they played side-by-side for only four seasons due to World War II and a strange position shift by Boston manager Joe McCarthy, second baseman Bobby Doerr and shortstop Johnny Pesky formed one of the game's finest keystone combinations in the 1940s, one that was constantly being compared to the Yankees' talented duo of Joe Gordon and Phil Rizzuto.

Unfortunately, as slick as he was in the field and as productive as he was at the plate, Pesky's 10-year career is still clouded by "the play" some Boston fans say he didn't make against the St. Louis Cardinals in the seventh game of the 1946 World Series. Teammates Dom DiMaggio and Doerr are still quick to come to his defense, but around New England, they still occasionally talk about the time "Pesky held the ball."

The Red Sox rolled to the 1946 American League pennant with a 104-50 record, a whopping 12 games ahead of Detroit and 17 ahead of New York. It was their first American League flag since 1918, when they beat the Chicago Cubs in six World Series games.

That 1946 Boston team was led by first baseman Rudy York (.276 and 119 runs-batted-in), Doerr (.271, 116 RBIs), Pesky (.335), left fielder and American League Most Valuable Player Ted Williams (.342, 38 homers, 123 RBIs) and center fielder DiMaggio (.316).

Dave Ferriss led the pitching staff with a 25-6 record, while Tex Hughson added a 20-11 mark.

The Cardinals, 98-58, outlasted the Brooklyn Dodgers in a wild National League pennant race that was determined by a best-two-out-of-three playoff at the end of the season. Both teams finished 96-58, but the Cardinals made quick work of the Dodgers in the playoff series, winning the first two games by counts of 4-2 and 8-4.

The Cards' standouts that season were first baseman and Most Valuable Player Stan Musial (.365, 16 homers, 103 RBIs), third baseman Whitey Kurowski (.301, 14, 89) and a spunky outfielder named Enos Slaughter (.300, 18, 130).

Doerr said he was concerned about the Series because the Red Sox had the American League pennant wrapped up in mid-September, while the Cardinals had to maintain their edge and momentum to win the National League flag in a playoff.

"Maybe we weren't as pumped up as the Cardinals," Doerr admitted.

After the two teams split the first four games, pitcher Joe Dobson gave the Red Sox a 3-2 World Series lead with a four-hit, 6-3 victory at Fenway Park. Two days later at Sportsman's Park in St. Louis, pitcher Harry Breechen turned back the Bostonians, 4-1, in Game 6 to set up a dramatic and memorable Game 7.

"The play"—or "The Mad Dash," as it's commonly called in St. Louis—took place the following day on Oct. 15. The hometown Cardinals led, 3-1, in the eighth, but the Sox tied it at 3 on DiMaggio's two-run double. While rounding first, however, DiMaggio pulled a leg muscle and was forced to leave the game. Replacing the defensive-minded DiMaggio in center was the less-experienced Leon Culberson, who appeared in 370 games during his six-year career (1943-48), five with the Red Sox and one with Washington. Career-wise, he was a .266 hitter and was actually considered a solid outfielder, committing just 21 errors.

The Cardinals reclaimed the lead in the bottom of the eighth with what is still one of baseball's most-dramatic plays.

With Bob Klinger on the mound for the Red Sox and two outs, the left-handed hitting Slaughter singled. Up to the plate came Harry Walker, who blooped a hit into left-center field. Slaughter was running on the pitch and he never stopped, making a mad dash around third for home despite a frantic "stop" sign by Cardinals third base coach Mike Gonzalez.

Culberson fielded the ball, then threw to Pesky, the cutoff man who had his back to the plate. When Pesky turned, he was startled that Slaughter was making a dash for home. Pesky threw home to catcher Roy Partee, but it was too late. Slaughter scored, giving the Cardinals a 4-3 lead.

The Cardinals' Brecheen entered the game in the ninth and got into trouble as the Red Sox put two men on base with no outs, but the righty worked his way out of the jam with the help of a clutch play by second baseman Red Schoendienst with the tying run at third to give St. Louis the World Series crown.

Schoendienst, a second baseman by trade during his 19-year playing career, would later manage the Cardinals for 12 seasons (1965-76), winning more than 1,000 games, two National League pennants and a World Series crown in 1967 against—who else?—the Red Sox.

Following the game, Pesky simply said, "I'm the goat."

"I didn't like taking the heat," Pesky recalled of Slaughter's mad dash. "But I took it all in stride. I accepted the responsibility. If they wanted to blame me, that's fine."

Film clips of the play do show a *very slight* hesitation on Pesky's part, but even without it, Slaughter would have scored.

"If I had been in center field, I would have had a chance to get Slaughter at third base," DiMaggio still claims to this day. "Culberson was a good player, but with Slaughter at first, Harry Walker came up. Now Harry loved to hit the ball to left center. We kept waving Culberson to move more toward left center, but he took only a few steps."

"Had I been out there," DiMaggio said, "I would have played Walker differently and taken a different angle on the ball and thrown the ball to third to get Slaughter. Instead, Culberson threw the ball to Pesky, the cutoff man."

Several years after the play, Slaughter himself said he believed Pesky got a bum rap, stating that with his back to the infield for the cutoff throw, the shortstop needed verbal help from his Red Sox teammates.

"When Pesky caught the ball, he had his back to the field and play," Doerr said. "I honestly can't tell you if I yelled at Johnny or what. Even if I did, I don't think he would have heard me because there were 36,000 screaming fans in the stands."

"Culberson played the ball too conservatively," Doerr said. "Dom's out there, Slaughter's out. Instead, he scores and we lose the Series."

According to Baseball-Almanac.com, Slaughter said after the game: "When the ball went into left center, I hit second base and I said to myself, 'I can score.' I didn't know whether the ball had been cut off or not. I didn't know nothin'. It was a gutsy play."

"But you know, two men out and the winning run, you can't let the grass grow under your feet."

Ironically, Slaughter often complained to Cardinal manager Eddie Dyer that Gonzalez, the third base coach, stopped him at third during the season when he felt he could score. The 5-foot-9, 192-pound Slaughter wasn't especially fast, as his 71 stolen bases in 19 seasons indicate, but he was smart, reckless and had tremendous desire. Dyer simply told Slaughter to use his discretion in future games. Game 7 happened to be one of them. Many baseball historians believe "The Mad Dash" was Slaughter's ticket to the Hall of Fame in 1985

Slaughter, an outfielder, was considered one of the game's ultimate hustlers, thanks to a run-in he had with Dyer when the two were with the minor league Columbus (Ga.) Redbirds of the Sally League in 1936. Dyer, the Redbirds' manager, got on Slaughter's case for not hustling enough. Since that day, Slaughter, nicknamed "Country" because of his North Carolina tobacco farming business, promised he would never "walk" on a baseball field again. And he didn't. The 19-year veteran always ran at top speed and scored more than 90 runs in seven seasons. He closed out his career with an even .300 batting average. He played on four World Series championship teams: two with the Cardinals (1942 and 1946) and two with the Yankees (1956 and 1958).

A big factor in the Red Sox's seven-game Series loss was the disappointing play of the MVP Williams, who turned in an anemic 5-for-25 performance at the plate with one run-batted-in. The Cardinals used a defensive shift against Williams which usually involved five or six St. Louis fielders playing to the right of second base. The stubborn Williams, a left-handed hitter, insisted on pulling the ball to the right side instead of hitting to the opposite field.

Doerr, meanwhile, had a superb Series, collecting nine hits for a .409 average. Pesky was 7-for-30.

The Red Sox wouldn't appear in another World Series until 1967, when they lost in seven games to St. Louis. Seven-game Series losses followed in 1975 against Cincinnati and again in 1986 against the New York Mets.

They came close to winning AL pennants in 1948, but lost a one-game playoff to Cleveland, 8-3, and in 1978, when they lost a playoff to the New York Yankees, 5-4. In 1949, they entered the last two games of the season with a one-game lead over the Yankees, but the Sox lost both contests, 5-4 and 5-3, to finish one game behind the New Yorkers.

The Sox's championship drought finally ended in 2004 as a wild-card playoff team. First, they swept the Anaheim Angels, 3 games to 0, in the divisional series, then became the first team in baseball history to overcome a 0-3 deficit to beat the Yankees in a best-of-seven to win the American League crown. A four-game sweep of the National League champion Cardinals followed. DiMaggio, Doerr and Pesky were there to witness their Red Sox's World Series win, but their good friend, Williams, had died two years earlier.

For Pesky, the Red Sox's 2004 World Series victory was redemption for the 1946 loss. "For years I said, 'Before I die, I'd like to see the Red Sox win the World Series going through New York and St. Louis,'" he said. "Now I have."

On April 11, 2005, Pesky, along with former Red Sox great (1961-83) and Hall of Famer Carl Yastrzemski, raised the 2004 World Series Championship banner up the Fenway Park flagpole.

Doerr and Pesky played together for seven-plus seasons. Doerr missed the 1945 season serving in the Army. His middle name, Pershing, is in honor of General John J. Pershing, America's World War I hero.

Pesky served in the Navy from 1943-45.

Doerr has always maintained had Pesky not missed those three seasons, he'd be in the Hall of Fame with himself and their good friend Williams.

Another strike against Pesky's Hall of Fame bid was his move to third base for the 1948-49-50 seasons. Manager McCarthy, who led the Yankees to seven World Series titles in the 1930s and 1940s, made the move, putting Vern Stephens at short. The Sox acquired Stephens following the 1947 season from the St. Louis Browns. He spent five productive seasons with the Red Sox, at one point driving in a total of 440 runs and turning 356 double plays during a three-season period (1948-50). He moved to third in 1951 and was eventually traded to the White Sox, Browns and Orioles before retiring after the 1955 season with a career .286 batting average.

Sox manager Joe Cronin, a shortstop, replaced himself with Pesky in 1942, but then McCarthy came along in 1948 and juggled the left side of the infield, despite the fact Stephens was more suited for third because of his strong body and power. And he didn't have the range Pesky had, an important characteristic for a shortstop, according to Doerr.

McCarthy was fairly gruff, always doing things his way with no questions asked. The Red Sox were used to Cronin, who had joined the Sox in 1935 from Washington and was named Boston's player-manager, and to team owner Tom Yawkey. Cronin and Yawkey were always open to suggestions and pampered their players more so than the average manager and owner.

Cronin spent 13 seasons as the Red Sox's skipper, winning 1,071 games and the 1946 American League pennant. A .301 career hitter, Cronin always believed Pesky was more suited for short, which is why he stepped aside when Pesky joined the Red Sox in 1942.

"Doerr and Pesky were slick .... almost magical," former Tiger, Red Sox and Browns pitcher Elden Auker said several months before his death at the age of 96 in August 2006. "Their first season playing together was my last (1942). It was tough to get anything past those guys. They both could go left and right, and they could turn the double play as well as anyone."

Auker said he followed the game closely after he retired "because baseball took your mind off the war for two or three hours each day." He worked on airplane and naval guns during the war years.

"If I recall right, the Red Sox became a better team when Pesky joined the Red Sox (in 1942) and teamed with Bobby. Pesky made that team's middle defense as strong as anyone's."

Auker was right. In 1940 and 1941, the Red Sox never challenged for the American League crown with 82 and 84 victories, respectively. In 1942, Pesky's rookie season, the Red Sox improved to 93-59. There was improvement in the DP department, too. In 1941, Doerr and Cronin totaled 149 double plays. In 1942, Doerr and Pesky totaled 199. The team's ERA dropped from 4.19 in 1941 to 3.44 in 1942.

When Pesky and Williams were out of the lineup due to the war from

1943-45, the Sox became a second-division team, again. When they returned in 1946, Boston ran away with the AL pennant with 104 wins.

Boston remained contenders through the 1950 season (94-60), then never really challenged for a pennant until 1967, when it defeated Minnesota on the last day of the season to claim the American League flag.

"Losing Williams during the war was a big blow (for the Red Sox)," Auker said. "But I never thought people fully appreciated what Pesky did for that club. He did it all."

In 1946, Doerr and Pesky committed only 38 errors between them. Doerr had 129 double plays, Pesky 96.

"I was better at short because I had good range, whereas at third you don't need as much (range)," said Pesky, who was tagged with the nickname "needle nose" because of his sharp-pointed nose. "And I liked short because you're involved in the action. You're really in the game, plus I liked playing with Bobby."

"We enjoyed playing with one another," Pesky said. "Bobby was great, quick and could make the double play as good as anyone. We were comrades."

"I was disappointed when Johnny was moved to third," Doerr said. "I couldn't understand why McCarthy didn't put Stephens at third. Vern was good, but I think Johnny was better and had better range at short. Had he stayed at short, we would have worked together for at least 9-10 years. You really have to play together 2-3 years to learn each other's habits."

"The big thing was, Johnny and I spent a lot of time working hard together in practice. Practice, practice, practice. We took a lot of pride in the way we played together around second base," Doerr said. "We worked on quickness, a quarter of a step, a half of step. Just when we were getting it together, Johnny got moved. Had we remained a combination, it would have helped him (Pesky) get into the Hall of Fame."

Doerr also believes DiMaggio belongs in the Hall. "I still can't figure that one out," Doerr said.

DiMaggio, nicknamed "The Little Professor" because of his business smarts, finished his 11-year career with a .298 batting average, the same as former Yankee slugger and Hall of Famer Mickey Mantle. DiMaggio was also:

1) A seven-time All-Star selection;
2) Ranked among the top 3 in runs scored 6 times;
3) Ranked among the top 6 in hits 6 times;
4) Ranked among the top 8 in doubles 6 times;
5) Ranked among the top 10 in stolen bases 8 times.

An outstanding defensive player, DiMaggio finished his career with a .978 fielding percentage, which is comparable to Hall of Fame outfielders Roberto Clemente, Willie Mays, Henry Aaron and his own brother, Joe.

DiMaggio shrugs it off, though, realizing he had a great career and, best of all, had the opportunity to play with his friends, Williams, Pesky and Doerr.

"I thought Bobby and Johnny were very good playing together," said DiMaggio, who got a first-hand look playing behind them in center field.

"Bobby was the smoothest fielder I ever saw. They compared him to Joe Gordon (of the Yankees). They called Joe 'Flash Gordon,' but Bobby was every bit as effective. Rizzuto didn't have the arm Johnny had at short, but he did have a quick release."

"You have to be together and know each other to be successful," DiMaggio said. "You have to know your teammates as best as you can. There definitely has to be a chemistry out there and Bobby and Johnny had it."

"As a whole team, we had chemistry. When we played, with Ted (Williams) in left, me in center, Pesky at short and Doerr at second, I can't ever remember an 'Alphonse Gaston' play," DiMaggio continued. "As soon as those three heard my voice, they'd back off and let me make the play. We never had any problems."

Pesky and Doerr still laugh at the French term DiMaggio came up with. At first, Pesky thought it was the name of a player in the Pacific Coast League. "Alphonse Gaston" implies that the four were either being excessively polite or were attempting to divest themselves of responsibility. In other words, when there was a pop fly in short center or left center, the play belonged to DiMaggio.

To this day, Pesky ranks himself third, defensively, behind two of his rival shortstops, Hall of Famers Pee Wee Reese of the Dodgers and the Yankees' Rizzuto. At the plate, though, Pesky ranks himself ahead of those two. The table on the next page proves Pesky right:

**Pesky vs. Reese & Rizzuto**

|  | Reese | Rizzuto | Pesky |
|---|---|---|---|
| Major league seasons | 16 | 13 | 10 |
| Games played per season | 135.4 | 127.8 | 127.0 |
| Career batting average | .269 | .273 | .307 |
| Runs per season | 83.6 | 67.5 | 86.7 |
| Hits per season | 135.6 | 122.2 | 145.5 |
| Doubles per season | 20.6 | 18.4 | 22.6 |
| Triples per season | 5.0 | 4.8 | 5.0 |
| Home runs per season | 7.9 | 2.9 | 1.7 |
| Runs-batted-in per season | 55.3 | 43.3 | 40.4 |
| Double plays per season | 78.4 | 93.6 | 61.6 |
| Errors per season | 25.4 | 20.2 | 17.8 |
| Assists per season | 383.2 | 359.0 | 311.4 |
| Putouts per season | 257.8 | 247.7 | 198.7 |
| Career fielding percentage | .962 | .968 | .966 |

Pesky is the only player in history to lead his league in hits during his first three seasons in the majors (1942, 1946, 1947). After batting .331 his rookie season (205 hits), he came back three years later following his stint in the Navy to hit .335 in 1946 (208 hits) and .324 in 1947 (207 hits). A left-handed contact hitter with little power, he struck out just 218 times in his career. He was also among the top 10 in on-base percentage six times.

"I didn't even know about that hits record," Pesky said. "We didn't worry about records when we played. We just played everyday and had fun."

Pesky was, and still is, a popular figure within the baseball community, especially in New England.

The Fenway Park faithful affectionately call the right-field foul pole "The Pesky Pole," which is just 302 feet from home plate. Six of Pesky's 17 career homers either hit or just cleared the brightly lit yellow pole. Pitcher Mel Parnell came up with the nickname in 1951 when Pesky won a game for the Red Sox hurler with a line-drive homer that hit the pole. The pole was officially dedicated to Pesky on his birthday, Sept. 27, 2006.

A fact baseball observers have overlooked about Pesky was the generosity he showed teammate Billy Goodman during the 1950 season. Pesky produced a fine season with a .312 batting average and 102 runs scored. The 24-year-old Goodman, who played all four infield positions plus the outfield, was challenging for the American League batting championship. In an effort to make sure Goodman had enough at-bats to qualify for the batting crown, Pesky took himself out of the lineup. Goodman gained the necessary at-bats and won the batting title with a .354 mark.

"I went to our manager, Steve O'Neill, and told him to play Billy instead of me so he'd have the opportunity to do something he may never have another chance to do, to win a batting title," Pesky recalled. "Back then, you were more concerned about winning than your own stats."

Pesky and the Red Sox got both: They finished the season in third place, four games behind the Yankees; and Goodman's .354 average led the league, ahead of Detroit's George Kell (.340) and New York's DiMaggio (.328).

"You mention Billy Goodman, it makes me feel good all over," Pesky said. "He was a great player (.300 career average). He wasn't big (5-feet-11, 165 pounds), but boy he could hit. Billy and I had a good relationship. He was a great teammate. It's too bad he died so young (age 58 in 1984)."

Goodman played 16 major league seasons (1947-62), 10 with the Red Sox (1947-56). He also played for the Orioles (1957), the White Sox (1958-61) and Houston (1962). Goodman played a big role in the White Sox's drive to the 1959 American League pennant. Although he ranked among the American League's top 10 hitters five more times, he never came close to winning another batting crown.

Lou Boudreau became skipper of the Red Sox in 1952 after nine seasons guiding the Cleveland Indians as a player-manager. His most-memorable season came in 1948, when the shortstop-manager hit .355, drove in 106 runs, was named the American League's Most Valuable Player and led the Indians to a six-game World Series victory over the Boston Braves.

For Pesky, the fun subsided during the 1952 season, when he was shipped to Detroit in a nine-player deal. Boston sent Pesky, infielder Fred Hatfield, outfielder Don Lenhardt, pitcher Bill Wright and first baseman Walt Dropo to the Tigers in exchange for outfielder Hoot Evers, third basemen George Kell and Johnny Lipon, and pitcher Dizzy Trout.

"I thought my world came to an end," Pesky said of the trade from Boston. "I couldn't believe I was leaving Boston. I didn't want to leave Boston. But once I got there (to Detroit), I was treated well."

At about the same time, it was rumored that Doerr was headed to Detroit. That, Doerr said, "Made me sick to my stomach." As it turned out, it was just a rumor, but trading Pesky "was a big surprise and mystery," the Red Sox second baseman said.

The big trade did little to help the two teams' pennant hopes. The Red Sox finished sixth in the American League with a 76-78 record, while Detroit finished dead last with a 50-104 mark.

Playing second, short and third for the Tigers, Pesky managed one last productive season at the plate in 1953, hitting .292. In 1954, he was traded to Washington, released, signed by Baltimore and released again.

He managed in the Tigers' and Red Sox's minor league systems for seven seasons. He managed the Red Sox in 1963-64, compiling a 146-175 record, but run-ins with first baseman Dick Stuart, nicknamed "Dr. Strangeglove" because of his 25 errors, and with the young outfielder Yastrzemski, who was team owner Yawkey's "favorite son," led to his dismissal.

Pesky also worked in the Yankee organization at Denver under manager Ralph Houk, who eventually guided New York to a pair of World Series titles in 1961 and 1962. In Denver, Pesky tutored the likes of future major league stars Bobby Richardson and Tony Kubek.

"I loved those two kids," Pesky recalled. "Tony and Bobby were one of the best double-play combinations I've ever seen. They both had great instincts. We spent a lot of time together. They'd come over to my house to watch the baseball game of the week on television, then we go out to the ball park for our game that night."

During the 1965-66-67 seasons, Pesky was the first base coach for the Pittsburgh Pirates, who—ironically—were managed by Harry Walker, the same Harry Walker whose bloop double in Game 7 of the 1946 World Series scored Slaughter from first base to give the Cardinals the title.

Pesky then became a popular fixture in the Red Sox's television and radio broadcast booth from 1969-74 as New Englanders enjoyed his wit and wisdom. The next 10 years were spent with the big club, working under managers Darrell Johnson, Don Zimmer and Houk before becoming a special instructor.

Today, the club's official "goodwill ambassador" is a regular in uniform at home games at Fenway Park and is affectionately called "Mr. Red Sox." Pesky also attends spring training in Fort Myers, Fla., where "I help work with the kids and help correct the little things."

Doerr, meanwhile, was called a lot of things by his teammates and rivals, all positive. Former New York Yankee outfielder Tommy Henrich (1937-42 and 1946-50) told the National Baseball Hall of Fame, "Bobby is one of the few who played the game hard and retired with no enemies."

Ted Williams said Doerr was "the silent captain of the Red Sox."

And in 1946, Babe Ruth, 11 years after the home run king's retirement, said "Doerr, and not Ted Williams, (was) the No. 1 player on the (1946 Red Sox) team."

"I was honored to hear stuff like that," Doerr said. "To think Ruth would say that, you had to be flattered."

Doerr was just 19 years old in 1937 when he made his major league debut with the Red Sox. Fifteen years later (minus one for military service), he retired, having played every one of his 1,865 games at second base. A .288 career hitter, Doerr drove home more than 100 runs six times. In the field, he had a streak of 414 chances without committing an error. He turned 1,507 career double plays, nine times exceeding the 100 mark. With Pesky at short, they totaled 805—451 for Doerr, 354 for Pesky.

Doerr was playing for San Diego in the Pacific Coast League where he caught the eye of Red Sox scout and Hall of Famer Eddie Collins, a former second baseman for Philadelphia and the White Sox who compiled a career batting average of .333 in 25 seasons. One of Doerr's teammates was also snatched by Collins at the same time—20-year-old Ted Williams. The two young players bonded immediately and were inseparable.

Meanwhile, a young kid named Pesky was working in the visitors' clubhouse in Portland. His job was to hang up the uniforms of the visiting Pacific Coast League players, who included Doerr and Williams.

Pesky played ball in Portland for several years, then caught the eyes of scouts from the Cardinals and the Red Sox. The Cards were willing to pay Pesky $2,500, but he declined and went with the Red Sox's offer of $500 in 1940 because he and his parents were impressed with Boston scout Earl Johnson and club owner Yawkey.

Dom DiMaggio joined the Red Sox in 1940, then Pesky made it to the big club in 1942. A four-way friendship developed.

"The four of us would hang out together all the time," Doerr recalled.

"Back then, we'd play games at 3 o'clock," Pesky said. "The four of us would have breakfast at 10, then take the 10-minute walk to the park and get there at noon."

"In the locker room we were all in one corner," Pesky continued. "Ted held court and everyone had their say, but Ted never lost an argument."

Once they all retired, the foursome got together many times for fishing trips and a lot of laughs as their bond grew stronger. Then in 2002, the foursome became a threesome.

Williams died on July 5, 2002 of cardiac arrest at the age of 83 in Hernando, Fla., after a long illness. Prior to his passing, Pesky and DiMaggio drove from

Massachusetts to Florida to visit Williams and extend their final good-byes. Doerr, who lives in Oregon, could not make the trip.

"When we saw Ted, it was just awful," Pesky said, "but his mind was still as sharp as it could be. We all loved one another, Ted, Bobby, Dom and myself. I know that might sound corny, but it's true. It was especially true of Ted, who would give you hell one minute, then he'd love you the next."

The journey south, plus their extraordinary friendships as players and retirees, is beautifully documented in the book *"The Teammates: A Portrait of a Friendship"* by the late David Halberstam.

Doerr retired in 1951 because of a bad back, then moved to Oregon. He returned to the organization in 1957 as a minor league instructor, then joined the big club as a coach for the 1967-68-69 seasons. In 1967, he was a member of the coaching staff that helped the 100-to-1 longshot Red Sox win the AL pennant on the final day of the season.

Today, "The three of us keep in touch," Pesky said of his friendships with DiMaggio, who resides in southeast Florida, and Doerr, who fishes the lakes and rivers in Oregon.

"We don't get to see one another as often as we want, but life goes on."

"When we do talk to one another or get together, though," Pesky added, "we feel like we're 25 again."

# DEFENSE BY THE NUMBERS

A look at the individual fielding statistics of Bobby Doerr and Johnny Pesky during the time period they played for the Boston Red Sox at their primary positions, second base and shortstop (PO – putouts; AST – assists; E – errors; DP – double plays; PCT. – fielding percentage):

| | BOBBY DOERR, 2B | | | | | JOHNNY PESKY, SS | | | | |
|---|---|---|---|---|---|---|---|---|---|---|
| YEAR | PO | AST | E | DP | PCT. | PO | AST | E | DP | PCT. |
| 1942 | 376 | 453 | 21 | 105 | .975 | 320 | 465 | 37 | 94 | .955 |
| 1946 | 420 | 483 | 13 | 129 | .986 | 296 | 479 | 25 | 96 | .969 |
| 1947 | 376 | 466 | 16 | 118 | .981 | 251 | 391 | 16 | 90 | .976 |
| 1951 | 303 | 311 | 12 | 99 | .981 | 204 | 340 | 22 | 74 | .961 |
| Totals | 1,475 | 1,713 | 62 | 451 | .981 | 1,071 | 1,675 | 100 | 354 | .965 |

**NOTE:** *Although a large majority of the seasonal and career double plays listed above involved the two keystone partners as a unit playing together at the same time during the noted time period, some were obviously not. The difference is due to many factors, including the number of games played, late-inning substitutions, injuries, a position change, DPs converted independent of each other and, in some cases, games missed due to military service.*

Jackie Robinson (far left) and Pee Wee Reese (far right) strike a pose with the other members of the Dodgers' 1952 starting infield: first baseman Gil Hodges (left), catcher Roy Campanella (center) and third baseman Billy Cox.

## CHAPTER SIX

# 2B JACKIE ROBINSON & SS PEE WEE REESE BROOKLYN DODGERS, 1948-52

**NAME: Jack Roosevelt Robinson**
**Nickname:** Jackie
**Born:** Jan. 31, 1919, Cairo, Ga.
**Died:** Oct. 24, 1972, Stamford, Conn.
**Batted/threw:** Right/right
**Height/weight:** 5-feet-11, 204 pounds
**Major league seasons:** 10 (Brooklyn, 1947-56)
**Major league debut:** April 15, 1947 (**Dodgers 5,** Braves 3)
**Final major league game:** Sept. 30, 1956 (**Dodgers 8,** Pirates 6)
**Position:** Second base (also third base: 256 games; first base: 197; outfield: 162)
**Career games:** 1,382
**Career double plays:** 830
**DPs with Dodgers at second base (1948-52):** 582
**Career errors:** 117
**Career assists:** 2,728
**Career putouts:** 4,007
**Career fielding percentage:** .983
**Gold Gloves:** The Rawlings Gold Glove Award began in 1957
**All-Star:** 6 times
**World Series:** 1-5
**Career batting average:** .311
**Turning two:** Robinson starred as himself in the 1950 movie "The Jackie Robinson Story."
**Hall of Fame:** Class of 1962

**NAME: Harold Henry Reese**
**Nickname:** Pee Wee
**Born:** July 23, 1918, Ekron, Ky.
**Died:** Aug. 14, 1999, Louisville, Ky.
**Batted/threw:** Right/right
**Height/weight:** 5-feet-9, 170 pounds
**Major league seasons:** 16 (Brooklyn Dodgers, 1940-57; Los Angeles Dodgers, 1958)
**Major league debut:** April 23, 1940 (**Dodgers 8,** Boston Bees 3)
**Final major league game:** Sept. 26, 1958 (Cubs 2, **Dodgers 1**)
**Position:** Shortstop (also third base: 115 games)
**Career games:** 2,166
**Career double plays:** 1,255
**DPs with Dodgers at shortstop (1948-52):** 475
**Career errors:** 407
**Career assists:** 6,131
**Career putouts:** 4,124
**Career fielding percentage:** .962
**Gold Gloves:** The Rawlings Gold Glove Award began in 1957
**All-Star:** 10 times
**World Series:** 1-6
**Career batting average:** .269
**Turning two:** Reese was among the top 10 vote-getters for Most Valuable Player eight times during his career
**Hall of Fame:** Class of 1984

The date was May 13, 1947. The site was Crosley Field in Cincinnati, home of the Reds. The opponents were the 12-8 Brooklyn Dodgers.

An event took place on this day that would eventually lead to one of the most-important historic and social events in the United States. For Major League Baseball, it was *THE* most-important event.

As the Dodgers took the field, 28-year-old rookie Jackie Robinson, the grandson of a slave, positioned himself at first base from where he began to hear his daily dosage of obscene remarks and gestures from the Cincinnati crowd. They were the same insults he had heard earlier in the season from his own home fans in Brooklyn, and on the road in New York and Philadelphia.

Robinson had grown accustomed to the racial slurs, but it still hurt this proud and athletic man who was told by Dodger owner Branch Rickey to simply "turn the other cheek."

Suddenly, Dodger shortstop Harold "Pee Wee" Reese trotted across the infield, put his arm around Robinson's shoulders and whispered something into his ear.

"No one knows what Pee Wee said to Jackie, but my guess is he said, 'You think this is tough in Cincinnati, wait until you get to St. Louis,'" said former Dodger pitcher and teammate Carl Erskine with a laugh. "What Pee Wee was really telling the world with that gesture was, 'This man is my teammate.'"

"I'll never forget that day," said former Dodger pitcher Clyde King. "The boos and the ugliness settled down. I know when Pee Wee returned to his home in Kentucky, he took some heat from his friends, but it all eventually died down."

That one incident helped change the way the public, teammates and rival players viewed the talented Robinson, but Reese did so much more for baseball's first major league black player.

The Brooklyn players were split on the idea of having a black player on their team. Many signed a petition to keep Robinson off the roster. Most of them were pulling for Arky Vaughan, a veteran infielder who had missed the 1944-45-46 seasons due to the war, to make a big comeback, thus taking Robinson's roster spot. Vaughan was a consistent .300 hitter with Pittsburgh (1932-41) and Brooklyn (1942-43) before being called to war.

The Dodgers kept Vaughan, but in the role of a utility player who appeared in 129 games in 1947 and 1948 before retiring.

"Pee Wee put an end to that petition among the Dodger players who demanded that Jackie be dismissed from the team," King said. "He was a no-nonsense guy."

And Reese was the first Brooklyn player to shake Robinson's hand to welcome him to the Dodger clubhouse prior to the start of the 1947 season.

"What a decent human being," Robinson told the National Baseball Hall of Fame. "How much he helped me. But he refused to take the credit."

Robinson's wife, Rachel, said many times that Reese's "leadership skills and sensitivity to bring the team together" helped her husband, adding that Reese "was more than a friend. He was a good and decent man."

"Pee Wee had an unbiased response to Jackie's arrival," said Erskine, a right-hander who won 122 games in 12 seasons with the Dodgers

(1948-59), including no-hitters in 1952 against the Cubs and 1956 against the Giants. "Pee Wee knew Jack was a first-class person and a big-league player. He wanted to support Jackie. Pee Wee was as loyal as anyone to Jackie. He did tell Jack he wasn't his 'Great White Father.' He said he was with him 100 percent and that he'd fight for him."

Following the 1947 season, in which he batted .297 and won baseball's first Rookie-of-the-Year Award, Robinson was moved to second base where he teamed with Reese at shortstop to form one of baseball's classic keystone combinations from 1948-52.

But getting through that 1947 season, which saw manager Burt Shotton's Dodgers win the National League pennant only to lose to the New York Yankees in seven games in the World Series, was not an easy task.

Robinson's first major league game was played at home at Ebbets Field on opening day, April 15, 1947, against the Boston Braves. Although he did not get a hit, Robinson did score the eventual winning run in a 5-3 victory.

"Actually, that first game was a very low-keyed event," Erskine said. "The newspapers treated it like any other game."

"There was a handful of people who believed this was right and there was a handful of southern boys who had to be against it because they had to answer to their buddies back home. Most people were neutral. The majority of players and fans were just curious."

"In Cincinnati and St. Louis, they segregated their crowds," Erskine continued. "The score wasn't important. The big thing was, what did Jackie do? If Jackie popped out, the white fans would cheer. If he got a hit, the black fans cheered."

"Jackie, unfortunately, didn't stay with us in our hotels and he couldn't eat with us. That was a real shame. It took seven years for all the hotels we stayed in to accept blacks."

The late, great sports writer Jimmy Cannon called Robinson "the loneliest man I have ever seen in sports."

Born in Georgia in 1919, Jackie, his four siblings and mother moved to Pasadena, Calif., after his father abandoned them. A standout athlete in high school, he enrolled at Pasadena Junior College, where he starred in football, baseball and basketball. In the winter of 1939, he started classes at UCLA, where he became the school's first athlete to letter in four sports in one year—football, baseball, basketball and track. In August 1941, he was selected to the College All-Star Football Team that played Coach George Halas' Chicago Bears of the National Football League. One of his all-star teammates was University of Michigan running back/quarterback and 1940 Heisman Trophy winner Tom Harmon. Drafted by the Bears, Harmon chose acting over football. He also served in the Army Air Corps, then played two seasons (1946-47) professionally for the NFL Los Angeles Rams. He eventually went into sportscasting. ·

Robinson was forced to quit school following his junior year at UCLA so he could go to work to earn money for his mother. He turned to professional football in the fall of 1941, playing for the Los Angeles Bulldogs of the Pacific Coast League.

In 1942, Robinson joined the Army for World War II. He fought for his rights and never backed away from a fight. He was court-martialed when, as a second lieutenant, he refused to "sit in the back of the bus" as ordered. With the help of world heavyweight boxing champion Joe Louis, all charges were eventually dropped and he received an honorable discharge.

In 1944 and 1945, Robinson returned to baseball and played shortstop for the Kansas City Monarchs in the Negro League. The following season, he manned first and second base for the Montreal Royals, Brooklyn's top minor-league club. After batting .349 for the Royals, it was obvious Robinson was ready for the major leagues in 1947.

The "bus incident," however, stuck in Dodger president Branch Rickey's mind and concerned him. Rickey was looking for a black player who had the strength to ignore the hatred and hardships that were certain to come. Could Robinson block out the insults and focus on baseball? Rickey had a gut feeling that Robinson could.

On April 10, 1947, following a spring training game in Havana, Cuba, Rickey purchased Robinson's contract from Montreal.

And with the support of former Kentucky governor and Baseball Commissioner Happy Chandler, who announced to the world, "If they (blacks) can fight and die on Okinawa, Guadalcanal (and) in the South Pacific, they can play ball in America," Rickey and Robinson integrated baseball.

While the Dodgers were courting Robinson, Reese, who played shortstop for the Dodgers from 1940-42, was wrapping up a three-year stint in the Navy (1943-45).

"Pee Wee told us that while he was in the Navy he got word the Dodgers were seriously looking at a player by the name of Jackie Robinson and that he was a shortstop," Erskine recalled. "Well, Pee Wee was ready to come back to fight for his shortstop job."

Reese didn't disappoint the Dodgers in his first season back in 1946, hitting .284 and turning 104 double plays.

With Reese back in the fold at short, manager Shotton played Robinson at first. He replaced Ed Stevens and Howie Schultz, who shared first-base duties in 1946. Both players were average hitters, lacked power and were eventually let go in 1947 when it became apparent Robinson was going to be a Dodger for years to come.

Robinson then moved to second in 1948 when Gil Hodges returned from three distinguished years in the Navy. Before entering the Navy in 1944, Hodges had played in exactly one game for the Dodgers in 1943 as a third baseman. In 1947, Hodges appeared in 24 games as a catcher before moving to first in 1948. He stayed at first until his retirement in 1963.

Hodges, who played 14 full seasons for the Dodgers (16 overall), has always been a "Hall of Fame Mystery." He was a .273 career hitter, belted 370 homers and drove home 1,274 runs. An eight-time All-Star, he was annually among the leaders in slugging percentage and home runs. Defensively, he had a .992 fielding percentage and was involved in 1,632 double plays. He was one of the major reasons why the Dodgers won six National League pennants between 1949 and 1959. He also managed the 1969 New York Mets to the World Series crown, yet he is not in the Hall of Fame.

With Hodges at first and Robinson's move to second in 1948, the Dodgers shipped five-year veteran Eddie Stanky to the Boston Braves.

Stanky, nicknamed "The Brat" for his feisty play, spent 11 years in the majors with the Cubs, Dodgers, Braves, Giants and Cardinals. A .268 career hitter, he later managed the Cardinals for three-plus season (1952-55), posting a record of 260-238. He re-emerged in 1966 in Chicago and nearly led the White Sox to the 1967 American League pennant, but a five-game losing streak the final week of the season knocked them out of contention. He was fired the following season.

Robinson, meanwhile, had found a home. He belonged. In 1949, he was named the National League's Most Valuable Player, thanks to his .342 batting average, 16 homers, 124 runs-batted-in, 122 runs, 37 stolen bases and 119 double plays.

"Baseball had accepted Jackie," Erskine said. "He caused people to buy tickets. He was an attraction."

"Baseball should never be indicted," he continued. "It was society that was slow in accepting him. Jackie once told me, 'Bigots come in all colors.' I told Jackie all people with white skin aren't your enemy."

Both King and Erskine believe that had Rickey selected any other black athlete, "It may have taken another 20 years for the color barrier to be broken in baseball," King said.

"Jackie handled all the ugliness very well," said King, a right-handed relief pitcher who won 29 games for the Dodgers in six seasons (1944-45, 1947-48, 1951-52) before spending his final season with Cincinnati in 1953. "Mr. Rickey picked the right man."

"Jackie did everything well," said King, who is still active in baseball as an advisor for the New York Yankees. "He handled things well when opposing fans threw black cats on the field or when an opposing player would tag him out hard on top of his head."

"It's hard to imagine any other black player who could have handled it the way Jackie did," Erskine said. "Mr. Rickey didn't pick Jackie because he was a great player. Mr. Rickey was a brilliant man. He could read people."

"There were five reasons why Mr. Rickey picked Jackie," Erskine said.

"First, Jackie could play baseball very well."

"Second, Jackie was raised by a single-parent mother who instilled in him strong discipline and respect. Mr. Rickey knew this."

"Third, Jack's mother expected her children to be educated. Jackie was a college man. There were very few college players in baseball at that time," Erskine said.

"No. 4, when Mr. Rickey interviewed us, he encouraged us to be married. He wanted a stable player off the field. When he met Jackie, he was already married to Rachel. When Mr. Rickey met Rachel, he knew this guy had it all."

"And finally, Mr. Rickey wanted someone strong enough not to fight," Erskine said. "You won't find any record of Jackie shoving, spitting, whatever on or off the field. He understood what Mr. Rickey meant when he said, 'Turn the other cheek.'"

Hall of Fame broadcaster Ernie Harwell, who announced major league games on television and radio for 55 years, including the 1948 and 1949 seasons for the Dodgers, said it was Robinson's "spirit and leadership qualities that attracted Mr. Rickey."

"Mr. Rickey was so smart. He knew what was going on," Harwell said. "He knew Jackie was intelligent and had a good idea of what to do (on the baseball diamond). Plus, Jackie had a lot of admiration for Mr. Rickey when he came to Brooklyn."

Harwell pointed out that if Rickey had not signed Robinson, Larry Doby could have been the first black player in Major League Baseball. Instead, Doby became the first black player in the American League, signing with the Cleveland Indians on July 2, 1947.

Rickey wanted to sign Doby in addition to Robinson, but when he heard Cleveland owner Bill Veeck wanted him, he let the second baseman go to the American League. Doby appeared in 29 games for the Indians in 1947, then became a regular in 1948 when he hit .301 for the Tribe. A Hall of Famer and seven-time All-Star, Doby spent nine seasons in Cleveland before he was traded to the Chicago White Sox prior to the 1956 season. He retired after the 1959 season with a career average of .283, plus 253 homers and 973 RBIs.

Like Robinson, Doby had a supporting friend on the Indians in second baseman Joe Gordon, who spent seven years with the Yankees before being traded to Cleveland at the end of the 1946 season for pitcher Allie Reynolds. Like Reese, Gordon took Doby under his wings. It was the acquisition of Gordon that led to Doby becoming an outfielder.

Both Gordon and Doby played major roles in the Indians' 1948 American League pennant and World Series victory over the Boston Braves. Gordon hit .280, plus 32 homers and had 124 runs-batted-in. Doby posted an exceptional first full season with his .301 average, 14 homers and 66 RBIs.

Reese spent 16 seasons playing shortstop for the Dodgers. He had brief minor-league stints in the Pirates and Red Sox organizations before the Dodgers signed him on July 18, 1939.

Harold Reese picked up the nickname "Pee Wee" when he was a marble shooting champion as a youth. He was called "The Little Colonel" when he played minor league ball for the Louisville Colonels, then "The Captain" when he became the Dodgers' team captain.

"Pee Wee was a great captain," Harwell said. "Everyone looked up to him. He was liked by all and he was a gentleman to everyone."

"Pee Wee was a true professional," Erskine said. "He was a little older than everyone else and he had the edge on us. He was a natural captain. He was direct. He could give the younger players 'the look' when necessary. He didn't expect the younger players to miss signs. He led by example. He never said, 'I'm the captain.'"

"Pee Wee was one of the best captains I've ever seen and I've been in baseball for 62 years," King said.

"When you look at the great players on those Dodger teams, players with such leadership qualities like Hodges, (Duke) Snider, (Roy) Campanella, Robinson ..... any one of them could have been a great team captain," Erskine said. "But Pee Wee was the man."

"He was also an extension of his managers on the field," Erskine said. "He played for Leo Durocher, Burt Shotton, Chuck Dressen and Walter Alston. Pee Wee was excellent following their styles. They wanted his input. They all went to Pee Wee."

As a keystone combination from 1948-52, Reese and Robinson were tough to beat.

"They worked together, knew each other's moves," King said. "Jackie had tremendous instincts. He could tell if he could make the throw to first for the double play. Sometimes if there was a runner on second, after taking the toss from Pee Wee to get the runner coming from first, Jackie would throw to third to get a surprised runner."

"Jackie was not afraid of hearing footsteps coming his way, either. He could jump up in the air and throw the ball to avoid getting hit."

"That combination of Pee Wee and Jackie was a real contrast seeing them make the double play," Erskine said. "Pee Wee was very acrobatic like a ballerina. Jackie was big, strong, heavy-legged. He'd take the throw and dare the runner to come into second base. Jackie was like a freight train coming out of a tunnel."

"They always made the plays," Erskine added. "They always got the double play."

During their five years as a keystone combination, Robinson was involved in 582 double plays, Reese 475. Robinson was a superb fielder at second, committing only 67 errors during the five-year period for a fielding percentage of .983. In 1950 and 1951, he was involved in 133 and 137 double plays, respectively.

"They were a pitcher's best friend," Erskine said.

"They were like brothers," said Hall of Famer Ernie Banks, who, in 1953, became the Chicago Cubs' first black player. "And they were real role models. How they took the field, how they played the game with so much passion. They were successful as a double-play combination, as players and throughout their lives."

"Back then, we all traveled by train and that gave Pee Wee and Jackie time to bond, time to sit and chat," Banks said. "That was a big part of Jackie and Pee Wee. Plus, they were just smart, good athletes."

Banks recalls his first major league game on Sept. 17, 1953 against the Dodgers.

"Before the game, Jackie came walking across the field to our dugout and said how thrilled he was that I had made the Cubs," Banks recalled. "He told me, 'Listen and you'll learn.' I'll never forget that."

Reese played in seven World Series with the Dodgers, Robinson six.

In 1941, Reese's second season, the Dodgers won 100 games en route to the National League pennant, but they were quickly disposed of in five games by the New York Yankees, who were led by Joe DiMaggio and Joe Gordon.

Reese, Robinson and the Dodgers won six National League pennants in 1947, 1949, 1952, 1953, 1955 and 1956. Unfortunately, all six pennants meant dates with the mighty Yankees in the World Series. The Yanks won five of those six World Series, three of which went the full seven games. "Those Dodger teams all had outstanding athletes and leaders, and coaches," Banks said.

"They had a lot of pride. They were warriors. They believed in winning. They were more business on the field. On the field they were one unit."

FIRST BLACK PLAYERS: TEAM-BY-TEAM

| Player | Team | Debut |
|---|---|---|
| Jackie Robinson | Dodgers | April 15, 1947 |
| Larry Doby | Indians | July 5, 1947 |
| Hank Thompson | Browns | July 17, 1947 |
| Monte Irvin | Giants | July 8, 1949 |
| Hank Thompson (1) | Giants | July 8, 1949 |
| Sam Jethroe | Braves | April 18, 1950 |
| Minnie Minoso | White Sox | May 5, 1951 |
| Bob Trice | Athletics | Sept. 13, 1953 |
| Ernie Banks | Cubs | Sept. 17, 1953 |
| Curt Roberts | Pirates | April 13, 1954 |
| Tom Alston | Cardinals | April 13, 1954 |
| Nino Escalera | Reds | April 17, 1954 |
| Chuck Harmon | Reds | April 17, 1954 |
| Carlos Paula | Senators | Sept. 6, 1954 |
| Elston Howard | Yankees | April 14, 1955 |
| John Kennedy | Phillies | April 22, 1957 |
| Ozzie Virgil, Sr. | Tigers | June 6, 1958 |
| Pumpsie Green | Red Sox | July 21, 1959 |

(1) traded from Browns to Giants in 1949.

**Note:** *Teams are not listed again if they moved to a new city. Also, since the beginning of expansion in 1961, all expansion teams were already integrated.*

**Source:** *Wikipedia: The Free Encyclopedia*

The Dodgers appeared to have the 1951 National League pennant wrapped up as the season entered its final three weeks, but the New York Giants made up 13.5 games down the stretch to tie Brooklyn and force a three-game playoff.

Brooklyn dropped the opener at home, 3-1, on Oct. 1, then came back the next day in New York to beat the Giants, 10-0, forcing a third and decisive game.

That finale would become one of baseball's most-unforgettable contests as Bobby Thomson delivered the "Shot Heard 'Round the World."

With the Dodgers clinging to 4-2 lead with one out and two Giants on base in the bottom of the ninth inning, Thomson belted an 0-1 pitch from Brooklyn pitcher Ralph Branca into the left field stands to give the New Yorkers a 5-4 win and the National League pennant. The loud radio cry by Giants' broadcaster Russ Hodges— "The Giants win the pennant, the Giants win the pennant!"—is replayed many times on television.

The celebration was short-lived for the Giants, however, as they lost to the Yankees in six World Series games.

The Dodgers finally won the Series from the Yankees in 1955, with Roy Campanella behind the plate, Hodges at first, Jim Gilliam at second, Reese at short and Robinson at third. The outfield featured Duke Snider, Carl Furillo and Sandy Amoros. The pitching staff showcased Erskine, Johnny Podres and Don Newcombe.

"Brooklyn's Bums," as they were called by their fans, ran away with the

1955 National League pennant by 13.5 games over Milwaukee. Snider was named the Major League Player of the Year with a .309 average, 42 homers and 136 runs-batted-in. Campanella won the Most Valuable Player Award thanks to a .318 batting average, 32 homers and 107 runs-batted-in.

Newcombe, the first black pitcher in the major leagues, was the ace of the staff, posting a 20-5 record and 3.20 earned-run-average. Erskine was 11-8, Billy Loes 10-4, Clem Labine 13-5 and Podres 9-10.

The Yankees, meanwhile, narrowly won the American League pennant by three games over Cleveland and five over Chicago, but they were loaded with Mickey Mantle, Yogi Berra, Bill Skowron, Joe Collins, Elston Howard, and pitchers Whitey Ford, Bob Turley and Tommy Byrne.

The Yankees took the opener, 6-5, but the play of the game took place when Robinson stole home on starting pitcher Ford and catcher Berra. To this day, Berra insists Robinson was out. But it was academic.

After dropping the second game, 4-2, the Dodgers rattled off three straight wins behind the arms of Podres, Erskine and Roger Craig to take a 3-2 Series lead. The Yankees took Game 6 with a 5-1 win behind the splendid pitching of Ford.

In Game 7, Podres pitched an eight-hit, complete game as the Dodgers posted a 2-0 win and their first World Series title since 1900 when they were known as the Brooklyn Superbras. Hodges provided all the offense Podres and the Dodgers needed with a run-scoring single and a sacrifice fly. For the Series, Hodges batted .292 and drove in five runs.

Reese had a solid Series at the plate, going 8-for-27 for a .296 average. In seven World Series (44 games), Reese batted .272. Three times he hit above .300. For Robinson, who stumbled to .182 in the 1955 Series, he posted a disappointing .234 batting average in six World Series (38 games).

In 1956, Robinson was bounced around the infield from first to second to third. He did hit a respectable .275. On Dec. 13, 1956, he was traded to the Giants for Dick Littlefield and $30,000 cash, but he refused to report to his new team and the trade was voided. Two weeks later, the 37-year-old Robinson announced his retirement in *"Look"* magazine.

Robinson often said, "The way I figured it, I was even with baseball and baseball with me. The game had done much for me, and I had done much for it."

Littlefield, a pitcher, played for 10 major league teams during a nine-year career which saw him post a 33-54 record.

"I was surprised that the Dodgers tried to trade Jackie," Harwell said. "I always thought he'd be a Dodger his entire career, that he would never be traded. Those things happen, though, especially with aging stars."

"I think every player who played with Jackie had a special bond with him," Erskine said. "I know I'll never forget him."

Erskine wrote a book, *"What I Learned From Jackie Robinson"* (McGraw-Hill Publishing), that chronicles his friendship with Robinson.

Following his retirement, Robinson became vice-president of the restaurant and coffee company Chock Full O' Nuts until 1964. He was then an aide to New York Governor Nelson Rockefeller. He also began speaking out for civil rights, but his life was cut short by diabetes. He died of a heart attack in Stamford, Conn., in 1972 at the age of 53.

The Reverend Jesse Jackson gave the eulogy at Robinson's funeral on Oct. 23, 1972, saying in part: "When Jackie took the field, something within us reminded us of our birthright to be free."

Jackson also said, "He didn't integrate baseball for himself. He infiltrated baseball for all of us, seeking and looking for more oxygen for black survival, and looking for new possibility."

In 1973, Robinson's widow, Rachel, founded the Jackie Robinson Foundation (JRF), a not-for-profit national organization to perpetuate the memory of her husband and his achievements. The Foundation assists minority youths by granting four-year college scholarships. Through 2006, more than 1,200 students had received scholarships totaling $14.5 million. JRF scholars have posted a graduation rate of 97 percent, more than twice the national average for minority students.

In 1997, Major League Baseball dedicated the season to Robinson on the 50th anniversary of his big-league debut. His No. 42 uniform number was retired in perpetuity by all major league teams.

Reese, meanwhile, spent one last full season (1956) at short, then was moved between third and shortstop in 1957 and 1958 before retiring.

Following his retirement, Reese, a .269 career hitter, coached for the Dodgers in 1959, the club's second year in Los Angeles and a season that saw the team win the World Series in six games over the Chicago White Sox.

He then spent nearly 20 years as a broadcaster on "Baseball's Game of the Week" on the CBS and NBC television networks during the 1960s and 1970s.

He teamed with fellow Hall of Famer Dizzy Dean on the television broadcasts and the two always gave viewers an entertaining and amusing program as this dialogue printed in *"Baseball Digest"* in 1974 indicates:

**Reese:** "Diz, you've watched this pitcher out there for four innings, and he's doing a great job. What would you say he's been throwing out there?"

**Dean:** "Well Pee Wee, I have been watching him for four innings and I believe that's a baseball he's throwin.' "

Reese died in 1999. At his funeral, Joe Black, a pitcher for the Dodgers from 1952-55, said: "Pee Wee helped make my boyhood dream come true to play in the majors, the World Series. When Pee Wee reached out to Jackie, all of us in the Negro Leagues smiled and said it was the first time that a white guy had accepted us."

"When I finally got up to Brooklyn, I went to Pee Wee and said, 'Black people love you. When you touched Jackie, you touched all of us.' With Pee Wee, it was No. 1 on his uniform and No. 1 in our hearts."

# DEFENSE BY THE NUMBERS

A look at the individual fielding statistics of Jackie Robinson and Pee Wee Reese during the time period they played for the Brooklyn Dodgers at their primary positions, second base and shortstop (PO – putouts; AST – assists; E – errors; DP – double plays; PCT. – fielding percentage):

| | JACKIE ROBINSON, 2B | | | | | PEE WEE REESE, SS | | | | |
|---|---|---|---|---|---|---|---|---|---|---|
| YEAR | PO | AST | E | DP | PCT. | PO | AST | E | DP | PCT. |
| 1948 | 308 | 315 | 13 | 80 | .980 | 335 | 453 | 31 | 93 | .962 |
| 1949 | 395 | 421 | 16 | 119 | .981 | 316 | 454 | 18 | 93 | .977 |
| 1950 | 359 | 390 | 11 | 133 | .986 | 282 | 398 | 26 | 94 | .963 |
| 1951 | 390 | 435 | 7 | 137 | .992 | 292 | 422 | 35 | 106 | .953 |
| 1952 | 353 | 400 | 20 | 113 | .974 | 282 | 376 | 21 | 89 | .969 |
| Totals | 1,805 | 1,961 | 67 | 582 | .983 | 1,507 | 2,103 | 131 | 475 | .965 |

**NOTE:** *Although a large majority of the seasonal and career double plays listed above involved the two keystone partners as a unit playing together at the same time during the noted time period, some were obviously not. The difference is due to many factors, including the number of games played, late-inning substitutions, injuries, a position change, DPs converted independent of each other and, in some cases, games missed due to military service.*

## CHAPTER SEVEN

# 2B NELLIE FOX & SS LUIS APARICIO CHICAGO WHITE SOX, 1956-62

**NAME: Jacob Nelson Fox**
**Nickname:** Mighty Mite
**Born:** Dec. 25, 1927, St. Thomas, Pa.
**Died:** Dec. 1, 1975, Baltimore, Md.
**Batted/threw:** Left/right
**Height/weight:** 5-feet-9, 150 pounds.
**Major league seasons:** 19 (Philadelphia, 1947-49; Chicago White Sox, 1950-63; Houston, 1964-65)
**Major league debut:** June 8, 1947 (Indians 2, **Athletics 0**)
**Final major league game:** July 24, 1965 (**Astros 4,** Reds 2)
**Position:** Second base
**Career games:** 2,367
**Career double plays:** 1,621
**DPs with White Sox at second base (1956-62):** 791
**Career errors:** 209
**Career assists:** 6,385
**Career putouts:** 6,102
**Career fielding percentage:** .984
**Gold Gloves:** 3
**All-Star:** 12 times
**World Series:** 0-1.
**Career batting average:** .288
**Turning two:** Fox led the American League in singles seven consecutive seasons (1954-60), a major league record.
**Hall of Fame:** Class of 1997

Luis Aparicio, who named his first son "Nelson" after Fox, brought the stolen base back to baseball.

**NAME: Luis Ernesto Aparicio**
**Nickname:** Little Looie
**Born:** April 29, 1934, Maracaibo, Venezuela
**Died:** Still throwing as of October 1, 2007
**Batted/threw:** Right/right
**Height/weight:** 5-feet-9, 160 pounds
**Major league seasons:** 18 (Chicago White Sox, 1956-62, 1968-70; Baltimore, 1963-1967; Boston, 1971-73)
**Major league debut:** April 17, 1956 (**White Sox 2,** Indians 1)
**Final major league game:** Sept. 28, 1973 (**Red Sox 5,** Brewers 3)
**Position:** Shortstop
**Career games:** 2,601
**Career double plays:** 1,553
 **DPs with White Sox at shortstop (1956-62):** 658
**Career errors:** 366
**Career assists:** 8,016
**Career putouts:** 4,548
**Career fielding percentage:** .972
**Gold Gloves:** 9
**All-Star:** 10 times
**World Series:** 1-1.
**Career batting average:** .262
**Turning two:** Aparicio led the AL in stolen bases nine consecutive seasons, including a career-high 57 in 1964. He's credited with bringing the stolen base back to the game as an offensive weapon.
**Hall of Fame:** Class of 1984

**Nellie Fox gets set to fire to first to complete a double play after receiving the toss from his keystone partner, Luis Aparicio.**

The "go go" in the "Go Go Chicago White Sox" of the late 1950s and early 1960s was provided by two of baseball's smallest and scrappiest players ever to play the game.

Both stood just 5-feet-9, but for seven seasons (1956-62), second baseman Nellie Fox and shortstop Luis Aparicio formed one of baseball's greatest keystone combinations with their fiery brand of play, both offensively and defensively. They were always on the move, always running, always talking and always making the key plays up the middle of the White Sox's defense.

"I don't see how the White Sox could have won the 1959 (American League) pennant without them," said Hall of Fame catcher Yogi Berra, whose mighty Yankees finished third that season, 15 games behind the Sox.

"Luis had such a great arm and could run like heck," Berra continued, "and Fox had his best all-around year."

The Yankees had won four straight American League pennants and a pair of World Series crowns prior to 1959.

With Fox, the first White Sox player to win the league's Most Valuable Player Award, batting .306 with 191 hits, and Aparicio spraying the ball to all fields for a .257 average and a league-high 56 stolen bases, the White Sox posted a 94-60 record, five games ahead of second-place Cleveland.

Ironically, the White Sox clinched their first pennant since the 1919 Black Sox Scandal on—what else?—a double play in Cleveland on Sept. 22.

"The White Sox led (4-2) in the bottom of the ninth," recalled former Chicago sports writer Jerome Holtzman, baseball's "official" historian and a member of the National Baseball Hall of Fame. "With a runner on first, Vic Power hit the ball to Aparicio, who ran over, tagged second and threw to first for the double play" to end the game.

The Sox, who were built around defense, speed and pitching, fell short in the World Series against Los Angeles, the first Series to be played on the west coast. The Sox walloped the Dodgers, 11-0, in the opener behind big right-handed pitcher Early Wynn, and first baseman Ted Kluszewski's two home runs and fives RBIs.

The White Sox then lost the next three games by narrow margins: 4-3 behind the pitching of Johnny Podres and second baseman Charlie Neal's three RBIs; 3-1 behind fireballer Don Drysdale and pinch-hitter Carl Furillo's two-run single in the seventh; and 5-4, thanks to Gil Hodges, who had a solo homer and RBI single, and starting pitcher Roger Craig.

Dodger relief specialist Larry Sherry appeared in all three games, picking up a victory and two saves while working seven innings, allowing one run, four hits and striking out four.

The White Sox won Game 5, thanks to Bob Shaw's 1-0 gem. The lone run scored on—what else? —a double play. Fox scored from third base in the fourth inning when teammate and catcher Sherm Lollar grounded into a double play off a 23-year-old pitcher named Sandy Koufax.

Koufax pitched well enough to win Game 5, allowing five hits over seven innings. Three years later, he became one of the game's all-time greatest pitchers. In his final four seasons (1963-66), he posted a 97-27 record, led the National League in earned-run-average each year, won three Cy Young Awards and one Most Valuable Player honor. The lefty also garnered numerous awards in the postseason, won three of four World Series (including 1959), and posted a 4-3 mark and an earned-run-average of 0.95. He also hurled four no-hitters, including a perfect game in 1965. He was elected to the Baseball Hall of Fame in 1972.

The White Sox failed to tie the Series in Game 6, losing, 9-3, at Comiskey Park, as Sherry shut down the Chicago bats again in 5-plus innings of scoreless relief. In four relief appearances, the powerful, 6-feet-2, 204-pound righty allowed one earned run in 12.2 innings on eight hits en route to being named the Series' Most Valuable Player.

Fox and Aparicio did their parts, though, hitting .375 and .308, respectively.

"Aparicio was the best shortstop in his generation," said Holtzman, who spent more than 60 years writing for the *Chicago Sun-Times* and *Chicago Tribune*. "He was a ballerina out there."

"I thought Fox was an ordinary second baseman, but he was colorful and appealed to the fans and he always had that wad of tobacco in his jaw."

Thanks to Fox's 93 double plays and Aparicio's 87, and only 33 errors between them, both won The Rawlings Gold Glove Award in 1959, an honor given to the top defensive player at his position. In 1960, the tandem took top honors again, marking the first time in baseball history that a second baseman and shortstop from the same team won back-to-back Gold Gloves. During the seven seasons they played side-by-side, they totaled 1,449 DPs—791 for Fox, 658 for Aparicio. Fox had a streak of nine straight seasons (1950-58) of 100 or more double plays, including a career-high 141 in 1957.

Fox, nicknamed "Mighty Mite" after a popular brand of vacuum cleaner, always credited his success in the field to Aparicio, claiming a good second baseman needs to play with a great shortstop.

"Looie covered so much ground and had such a great arm," said former Yankee, Tiger and Red Sox manager Ralph Houk. "He'd reach sharp groundballs hit up the middle behind second base and throw the runner out."

Hall of Fame shortstop Phil Rizzuto of the Yankees also thought highly of "Little Looie." According to the National Baseball Hall of Fame, Rizzuto said, "Luis Aparicio is the only guy that I ever saw go behind second base, make the turn and throw Mickey Mantle out. He was as sure-handed as anyone,"

"Fox had a good arm and could handle the (double play) pivot at second very well," Houk said. "Plus he was a great leader."

Casey Stengel, who managed the Yankees to seven World Series crowns and 10 American League pennants, once told *The New York Times:* "That little feller, Fox, he ain't so big, but he's all fire."

"Nellie and Looie were simply great in the field," former White Sox pitcher Billy Pierce said. "They provided wins with their defense. Looie could go left and right, and Nellie could go back on pop flies. Between the two, they could cover everything behind short and second."

The left-handed Pierce spent 18 years in the majors, 13 in Chicago where he posted back-to-back 20-win seasons. For his career, he won 211 games and had an impressive 3.27 earned-run-average.

"As a pitcher, I knew anytime a ball went to Looie or Nellie, we had an out or a double play," Pierce said. "It was a pleasure to be a pitcher for that club."

Another pitcher on the 1959 team, the right-handed Shaw, credits his 18-6 record to the White Sox's keystone combo.

"I was a sinkerball pitcher, so I counted on Looie and Nellie," said Shaw, who won 108 games during his 11-year career. "They were great team players, hard-nosed. They hung in there and made the double play."

White Sox center fielder Jim Landis remembers a time when Fox may have "hung in there" a bit too long.

Playing in Kansas City on Sept. 4, 1960, big Bob Cerv of the Athletics, all 200-plus pounds of him, "ran into Nellie pretty hard," Landis said. "Nellie didn't say a word. He went back to his position, but you could tell he was hurting. About five innings later, he went to Skip (manager Al Lopez) and said he had to come out. The next day, Nellie couldn't play and it stopped one of Nellie's streaks."

Fox had played in 798 consecutive games up to that point. Following his day off, he played in another 274 straight games. That's 1,072 out of a possible 1,073 games.

Cerv, a former University of Nebraska baseball and basketball player who spent his first five seasons (1951-56) with the Yankees in a limited role, was purchased by Kansas City only to be traded back to the New Yorkers in 1960 for Andy Carey. The following season, he shared an apartment with Mickey Mantle and Roger Maris, both of whom were in pursuit of Babe Ruth's single-season record of 60 home runs in 1961. Cerv and Maris were credited with "toning down" Mantle's off-field antics which, in turn, made the switch-hitting slugger a better player. Maris passed the mighty Babe in the 162nd and final game of the season with his 61st homer at Yankee Stadium. Mantle suffered an injury late in the season and finished with 54.

Cerv won a pair of World Series rings, first in 1956 when the Yankees beat the Dodgers in seven, and again in 1961, a five-game win over Cincinnati. What's interesting about his two rings is the fact he made just one plate appearance in the 12 Series games, banging out a sole single, that coming in 1956. An injury forced him to miss the entire 1961 Series. He did play in two other Series with the Yankees—both seven-game losses to the Dodgers in 1955 and to the Pirates in 1960 when he hit .357. Cerv, a 12-year vet, had a .276 career batting average.

Landis said Fox did not have the natural abilities to be a great player, but "I admired how well Nellie worked to develop himself to be a great player. I give Nellie 150 percent credit for the way he played," Landis said. "He worked hard everyday to be the very best he could be."

Landis remembered how popular Fox was with the fans, at the stadium and around town.

"We were riding around once in Nellie's jeep and everyone—and I mean everyone—stopped and yelled at Nellie. They loved him," Landis said.

On the field, Landis recalled how Lopez would "bawl me out" for allowing Fox to take all the pop flies in short center.

"Nellie wanted all the balls," Landis said. "But Skip (Lopez) would come up to me and say, 'Damn it, Jim, you're the center fielder. You're the boss out there. Call Fox off.'"

"I was young, so I told Skip, 'You tell him yourself.' Nellie was just a go-go-goer," Landis said. "Looie was the same way. He never wanted a ball to get past him."

Lopez was considered a "player's manager." He could easily relate to his players' problems, whether they were professional or personal. He always said he couldn't get too close to his players, but he knew how to get the most out of them and it showed in his record as a manager.

He managed just two teams, the Cleveland Indians (1951-56) and the White Sox (1957-65). In 1968, he helped the White Sox by finishing the season after Eddie Stanky and Les Moss had been fired. In 1969, he started the season as manager as a favor to the club, then retired after 17 games, giving way to Don Gutteridge.

In the 15 full seasons he managed, the Hall of Famer never experienced a losing record. His 1954 and 1959 teams were the only non-Yankee clubs to win the American League pennant between 1949 and 1964.

His 1954 Indians won a then-record 111 games and lost just 43 en route to the World Series, where they were surprisingly swept four straight by the New York Giants. The 1998 Yankees broke the Indians' record of 111 wins with 114 in 1998, then Seattle topped that mark with 116 victories in 2001. Overall, Lopez posted a 1,410-1,004 career record.

Prior to becoming a manager, the Hall of Famer spent 19 seasons in the majors as a catcher with the Dodgers, Braves, Pirates and Indians. He had a career batting average of .261 and hit just 51 home runs. Defense was his forte, posting an impressive .984 fielding percentage behind the plate.

One of his best managerial moves was putting two fiercely competitive players like Fox and Aparicio together at second and short.

"They were a team," Shaw said. "They were very close to one another."

"Looie and Nellie always got along great," Shaw said. "I never saw a rift between them. Everything was on the plus side. They played hard together. They talked to one another. They always knew what they were going to do if the ball came to them."

Aparicio, who finished second to Fox in the 1959 Most Valuable Player voting, named his first son "Nelson" after his double-play partner.

"It's important for an entire team to be close," Shaw continued. "Probably more so for the second baseman and shortstop, who have to be on good terms or they won't be successful."

"Back then, we didn't have those situations that you see now in the NFL where players bad-mouth one another."

"When we played, there was respect for one another and respect for the game," Shaw said. "When someone hit a home run, they simply ran the bases. They didn't jump up and down like they do today."

Fox's play caught the attention of the late, great poet Ogden Nash, who penned the following poem titled *"The Holler Guy."* It appeared in *LIFE Magazine* on Sept. 5, 1955.

*This holler guy who we are follering,*
*What does he holler when he is hollering?*
*You can hear him clean to hell and gone,*
*C'mon there baby, c'mon, c'mon!*
*Or he will change his holler, maybe,*
*To let's go, baby, baby, baby!*
*He uses a plug of tobacco per game,*
*And has never lost or swallowed same.*
*Nellie Fox so lives to play*
*That every day's a hollerday.*

"Fox was our sparkplug," Lopez said shortly before his death at the age of 97 in October 2005 after the White Sox won the World Series over Houston, their first since 1917 when they beat the Giants in six games. "He couldn't stand still and he was always talking. He was one of the toughest and most-reliable defensive players I ever saw. At the plate, he was one of baseball's toughest outs and one of the best clutch hitters."

In 9,232 career at-bats, Fox struck out just 216 times.

"Nellie was the toughest out for me," Hall of Fame pitcher (236 career wins) and former Yankee Whitey Ford (1950, 1953-67) once said. "In 12 years, I struck him out once and I think the umpire blew the call."

"With Looie, no one could get anything past him," Lopez said. "If there was anything hit to the left side (of the infield), Looie would get it, he was that quick. And he had a rifle of an arm."

Fox started his career in the Philadelphia Athletics' organization (1947-49). Team owner, general manager and manager Connie Mack realized Fox was a strong defensive player at second, but questioned his abilities offensively, so he traded him to the White Sox for catcher Joe Tipton following the 1949 season. It didn't take long for Mack to realize he had made a mistake. Tipton, a catcher, spent seven seasons in the big leagues and never batted higher than .239.

Fox was an immediate starter for the Sox in 1950, replacing the traded Cass Michaels, the White Sox's regular second baseman from 1945-49. He eventually returned to the Sox in 1954 as a third baseman after stops in Philadelphia, Washington and St. Louis.

Fox appeared in 130 games his rookie season (1950) and struggled at the plate (.247), but he stepped it up the following season with a .313 average, 189 hits and near-flawless play at second base (17 errors and 112 double plays).

During his 14 years with the Sox, Fox batted over .300 six times and was named to 12 All-Star Teams. In 2,367 career games, he collected 2,663 hits, more than one hit per game.

"Fox had this big, bottle bat and he'd hit the ball to left," historian Holtzman recalled.

Aparicio, who was being scouted by Cleveland, signed with the Sox as an amateur free agent in 1954 for $5,000. Two years later, he found himself starting at shortstop alongside Fox. He replaced the popular Chico Carrasquel, another Venezuelan star who urged Sox general manager Frank Lane to sign the speedy shortstop. Carrasquel had replaced Hall of Famer Luke Appling after being purchased from the Brooklyn Dodgers. Appling, a Hall of Famer and two-time American League batting champion, played short for the White Sox for 20 seasons and had a career batting average of .310.

The popular Carrasqual played six seasons (1950-55) with Fox and the White Sox. He was a solid player in the field and at the plate. He had an exceptional rookie season, hitting .282 and turning 113 double plays. When Aparicio arrived, Carrasqual, who had problems controlling his weight, was traded to Cleveland, where he spent three season before ending his career in Kansas City (1958) and Baltimore (1959).

Aparicio came from a baseball family. Luis Sr., his father, was a prominent shortstop in Venezuela and owned a Winter League team. A stadium and many streets in Venezuela are named after the Aparicio family.

Aparicio, just 22, hit .266, drove home 56 runs and stole 21 bases en route to American League Rookie-of -the-Year honors in 1956, beating out another fine rookie, Cleveland slugger Rocky Colavito. Aparicio also proved he could turn the double play with 91.

Offensively, Aparicio and Fox, who batted first and second, respectively in the White Sox batting order, did a solid job setting the table for the club's big guns like Billy Goodman, Al Smith, Minnie Minoso and Lollar.

"Looie and Nellie were a great one-two punch," Pierce said. "Looie would get on and he'd be a threat to steal. Nellie was a threat to bunt or get Looie around home. They always made contact with the ball and they gave us a chance to get a run early in the game."

"With that strong pitching staff of Wynn and Pierce and their defense and speed, you couldn't let the White Sox get a jump on you," said former Yankee shortstop Tony Kubek (1957-65). "You weren't going to score many runs against guys like Wynn."

Wynn, who won 300 career games, is a Hall of Famer. He came up with the Senators in 1939, then moved to Cleveland in 1949. In nine seasons with the Tribe, he won 20 or more games four times. In 1958, he moved to Chicago, where he won 22 games and the American League Cy Young Award in 1959. In 1963 at the age of 43, he returned to Cleveland where he finally won his 300th game after numerous attempts.

Wynn shocked a lot of fans when he talked about "knocking down" his own mother "if she was crowding the plate" or "digging in."

Mickey Mantle once said of Wynn: "That S.O.B. is so mean, he would knock you down in the dugout."

Following third, fourth and fifth-place finishes between 1960 and 1962, the White Sox shocked their fans and shipped Aparicio to Baltimore for knuckleballer Hoyt Wilhelm and three young prospects—third baseman Pete Ward, shortstop Ron Hansen and outfielder Dave Nicholson.

The trade was a gamble on the White Sox's part. During his seven years (1956-62) in Chicago, Aparicio led the American League in stolen bases seven consecutive seasons, was a five-time All-Star, won five Gold Gloves and led the league in fielding percentage and assists five straight years. Public-relations-wise, it was a disaster because the trade meant the end of the White Sox's beloved Fox-Aparicio keystone combination.

Aparicio, who was only 28 at the time of the trade, didn't take too kindly to the move, especially when the Sox gave Nicholson his number 11 (it has since been retired in Aparicio's name). He planted a curse, saying the White Sox would not win another pennant for 40 years. As it turned out, it was 44.

The trade actually benefited both teams and Aparicio: the White Sox got immediate results from Wilhelm and the three young players, and challenged for the AL pennant the next several seasons.

In 1963, with Hansen now Fox's keystone mate, the White Sox won 94 games and finished second in the American League behind the Yankees.

"I was surprised by the trade," said Hansen, who was 25 years old at the time and coming off back-to-back 110-double-play seasons. "It was a good trade for me because I was going to a good club, but a little difficult because I was replacing Looie, who was so popular in Chicago."

"My first year started out rough, but by the end of the season, things worked out. People came over to my side."

"What was helpful was Nellie and Jim (Landis) took me under their wings," said Hansen, who has worked the past 18 years as a major league scout, the past four with the Philadelphia Phillies. "My locker space was next to them and I have a lot to thank them for."

"Nellie, of course, was toward the end of his career, but he helped me whenever he could as far as positioning me for players. He was such a good teammate."

At 6-feet-3 and 200 pounds, Hansen played 15 seasons and converted 783 total double plays. He is one of 12 players in major league history to pull off one of the game's rarest plays—an unassisted triple play. It came on July 30, 1968 in Cleveland when he was a member of the Washington Senators. An unassisted triple play is about as rare as a pitched perfect game. During the modern era through 2006, there were 15 perfect games pitched.

On Dec. 10, 1963, the White Sox dropped another bombshell on their fans by trading the 35-year-old Fox to the Houston Colt .45s for pitchers Jim Golden and Danny Murphy. Golden never appeared in a White Sox game. Murphy was 4-4 in two seasons with the Sox.

The following season (1964), with Al Weis (.247) and Don Buford (.262) sharing the second-base duties, the White Sox nearly overtook the Yankees in the American League pennant race, but came up one game short despite 98 victories.

"We just couldn't overtake the big guys," Hansen said, referring to the Yankees.

Following another second-place finish in 1965 and a fourth in 1966, the White Sox were involved in a wild four-team race that came down to the final weekend of the 1967 season between Boston, Detroit and Minnesota. The White Sox stumbled badly the last week of the season, though, finishing fourth, three games behind the AL-pennant winning Red Sox, who lost a seven-game World Series to St. Louis.

Aparicio, meanwhile, never lost a step and was an instant hit in Baltimore. In 1966, he joined Brooks Robinson, Frank Robinson and a young Orioles pitching staff led by Jim Palmer and Dave McNally in a four-game sweep of the Los Angeles Dodgers in the World Series. Aparicio hit .250 in the Series.

From 1963 to 1965, his double-play partner in Baltimore was Jerry Adair, then Davey Johnson in 1966 and 1967. During his five seasons with the Orioles, Aparicio was involved in 432 double plays.

In 1968, the Orioles decided to make Mark Belanger their regular shortstop and traded Aparicio back to Chicago, where he continued to excel in the field and at the plate (.313 in 1970). He played with several keystone mates from 1968-70, including Sandy Alomar, Bobby Knoop and Tim Cullen. The White Sox, though, lost more than 90 games all three seasons. He then spent the final three years (1971-73) of his career with American League East contender Boston, where he played alongside a reliable second baseman, Doug Griffin.

Through the 2006 season, Aparicio still held the all-time record for games played at shortstop at 2,583 (he appeared in 18 games as a pinch-hitter for a total of 2,601), ranked fourth in the major leagues in double plays by a shortstop (1,553), and still owned American League shortstop records for putouts (4,548) and total chances (12,564). He never played a single inning at any other position.

When it was announced in 1984 that he had become the first player from Venezuela to be elected to the National Baseball Hall of Fame, play was halted during a game in Caracas, Venezuela. Newspaper accounts said it was the most impressive showing of pride in a national sports hero.

Fox, meanwhile, made an immediate impact in Houston with the expansion Colt .45s in 1964. In the first game played in the Astrodome, an exhibition, Fox drove home the winning run in a 12-inning, 2-1 win over the Yankees. In that game, the first played on Astroturf and indoors, the Yankees' Mantle hit the first home run in Astrodome history.

Fox lasted a year and one-half in Houston, playing in 154 games at second, third and first while hitting .265 and .268. During his stay in Houston, he spent a great deal of time tutoring a young second baseman by the name of Joe Morgan, who later played for the Cincinnati Reds in the 1970s, won back-to-back Most Valuable Player Awards (1975-76) and is a member of the Hall of Fame.

Fox retired on July 31, 1965 with a career batting average of .288 and a strong fielding percentage of .984. In 19 professional seasons, he committed just 209 errors. He led the American League in hits four times, in games played five times and in singles seven times. Defensively, he led in fielding percentage six times and in double plays five.

In 1968, he became a coach for the Washington Senators under manager Ted Williams, who had always admired the little second baseman.

"I just loved him," Williams said, according to Baseball-Almanac.com. "As a person, as an individual, you couldn't possibly not love him."

Williams credited Fox for helping his Senators rise from a 65-96 record in 1968 to 86-76 the following year. Fox stayed with the club when it moved to Texas, then retired for good in 1972.

He died in 1975 at the age of 47. When he was first diagnosed with cancer in 1973, Bill Veeck visited Fox and told him to get better because the controversial owner was planning to purchase the White Sox and he wanted the retired second baseman to manage the club. He never had that chance.

Fox's enshrinement into Baseball's Hall of Fame was a long, drawn-out affair. Ten years after his death, he received 74.6 percent of the votes, four-tenths shy of the required 75 percent necessary to earn a spot in the Hall. As years passed, his percentage dropped. Finally in 1997, the Veterans Committee voted him in.

At his Hall of Fame induction ceremony on Aug. 3, 1997, his widow, Joanne, said: "He played the game with all his heart, all his passion and with every ounce of his being."

According to the Baseball Hall of Fame, former White Sox manager Paul Richards (1951-54; 1976) said of Fox: "I've never seen anybody who wanted to play more than Fox did. In spring training you had to run him off the field to get him to rest, and I mean literally run him off."

Richards' best season in Chicago came in 1954 when the White Sox posted a 91-54 mark. He later managed Baltimore for seven seasons (1955-61). His career record: 923-901, no pennants.

Aparicio is alive and well, periodically managing baseball teams in his native Maracaibo, Venezuela. Now 73, Aparicio keeps to himself, enjoying his privacy. He threw out the first ball prior to Game 1 of the 2005 World Series between the White Sox and Houston Astros.

"It was great seeing Looie that night (in Chicago)," Landis said. "But after exchanging a few words, he disappeared and we never saw him again."

Aparicio did address the media briefly prior to Game 1, saying he was "proud of his fellow countryman," manager Ozzie Guillen, who guided the White Sox to the four-game sweep of Houston in the Series. "I'm very glad for the Sox and congratulate Ozzie because he is a hard worker. He's doing a tremendous job, and the White Sox and the people of Chicago deserve it."

Guillen spent 16 seasons (1985-2000) in the majors, 13 as the White Sox's shortstop (1985-97). A .264 career hitter, Guillen was involved in 1,094 double plays as a shortstop. He was the American League's Rookie of the Year in 1985 and the third base coach for the 2003 World Champion Florida Marlins. He's the first native of Venezuela to manage a Major League Baseball team. To this day Guillen maintains that if it had not been for his mentor, Aparicio, he probably wouldn't have played baseball.

Today, White Sox fans have a monument to remember their beloved Fox and Aparicio. On July 23, 2006, the White Sox paid tribute to their key-stone combination by unveiling life-size sculptures of the two at U.S. Cellular Field in Chicago.

"The double-play combination of Aparicio and Fox was one of the most popular and talented middle infield combinations baseball has ever seen," White Sox chairman Jerry Reinsdorf said at the ceremony. "Their style of play resonated with a city that loved the intensity they brought to the field everyday, so it's only appropriate to acknowledge them for the memories they gave to the people of Chicago."

DEFENSE BY THE NUMBERS

A look at the individual fielding statistics of Nellie Fox and Luis Aparicio during the time period they played for the Chicago White Sox at their primary positions, second base and shortstop (PO – putouts; AST – assists; E – errors; DP – double plays; PCT. – fielding percentage):

| | NELLIE FOX, 2B | | | | | LUIS APARICIO, SS | | | | |
|---|---|---|---|---|---|---|---|---|---|---|
| YEAR | PO | AST | E | DP | PCT. | PO | AST | E | DP | PCT. |
| 1956 | 478 | 396 | 12 | 124 | .986 | 250 | 474 | 35 | 91 | .954 |
| 1957 | 453 | 453 | 13 | 141 | .986 | 246 | 449 | 20 | 85 | .972 |
| 1958 | 444 | 399 | 13 | 117 | .985 | 289 | 463 | 21 | 90 | .973 |
| 1959 | 364 | 453 | 10 | 93 | .988 | 282 | 460 | 23 | 87 | .970 |
| 1960 | 412 | 447 | 13 | 126 | .985 | 305 | 551 | 18 | 117 | .979 |
| 1961 | 413 | 407 | 15 | 97 | .982 | 264 | 487 | 30 | 86 | .962 |
| 1962 | 376 | 428 | 8 | 93 | .990 | 280 | 452 | 20 | 102 | .973 |
| Totals | 2,940 | 2,983 | 84 | 791 | .986 | 1,916 | 3,336 | 167 | 658 | .969 |

NOTE: *Although a large majority of the seasonal and career double plays listed above involved the two keystone partners as a unit playing together at the same time during the noted time period, some were obviously not. The difference is due to many factors, including the number of games played, late-inning substitutions, injuries, a position change, DPs converted independent of each other and, in some cases, games missed due to military service.*

A few years after he retired, Atlanta tried to sign Bobby Richardson, but he declined, saying, "Once a Yankee, always a Yankee."

CHAPTER EIGHT

# 2B BOBBY RICHARDSON & SS TONY KUBEK NEW YORK YANKEES, 1957-65

**NAME: Robert Clinton Richardson**

**Nickname:** Bobby (also known as one of "The Milkshake Boys")

**Born:** Aug. 19, 1935, Sumter, S.C.

**Died:** Still throwing as of October 1, 2007

**Batted/threw:** Right/right

**Height/weight:** 5-feet-9, 170 pounds

**Major league seasons:** 12 (N.Y. Yankees, 1955-66)

**Major league debut:** Aug. 5, 1955 (**Yankees 3,** Tigers 0)

**Final major league game:** Oct. 2, 1966 (**Yankees 2,** White Sox 0)

**Position:** Second base (also third base: 38 games; shortstop: 21)

**Career games:** 1,412

**Career double plays:** 977

**DPs with Yankees at second base (1957-65):** 869

**Career errors:** 150

**Career assists:** 3,540

**Career putouts:** 3,159

**Career fielding percentage:** .978

**Gold Gloves:** 5

**All-Star:** 7 times.

**World Series:** 3-4

**Career batting average:** .266

**Turning two:** Richardson led the American League in base hits with 209 in 1962 when he batted a career-high .302

**Hall of Fame:** No

Tony Kubek turned down football scholarships from Notre Dame and Michigan State to play pro baseball.

**NAME: Anthony Christopher Kubek**

**Nickname:** Tony (also known as one of "The Milkshake Boys")

**Born:** Oct. 12, 1936, Milwaukee, Wisc.

**Died:** Still throwing as of October 1, 2007

**Batted/threw:** Left/right

**Height/weight:** 6-feet-3, 191 pounds

**Major league seasons:** 9 (N.Y. Yankees, 1957-65)

**Major league debut:** April 20, 1957 (**Yankees 10,** Red Sox 7)

**Final major league game:** Oct. 3, 1965 (**Yankees 11,** Red Sox 5)

**Position:** Shortstop (also outfield: 145 games; third base: 55)

**Career games:** 1,092

**Career double plays:** 583.

**DPs with Yankees at shortstop (1957-65):** 569

**Career errors:** 162

**Career assists:** 2,850

**Career putouts:** 1,808

**Career fielding percentage:** .966

**Gold Gloves:** None

**All-Star:** 3 times.

**World Series:** 3-3

**Career batting average:** .266

**Turning two:** Kubek was the American League's Rookie of the Year in 1957 when he batted .297 at the age of 20. He collected 23-of-24 first-place votes.

**Hall of Fame:** No

Off the field they were nicknamed "The Milkshake Boys" because of their clean living and early-to-bed lifestyle.

On the field, second baseman Bobby Richardson and shortstop Tony Kubek were as sure-handed as they came and two of the major reasons why the New York Yankees dominated Major League Baseball in the late 1950s and early 1960s.

During the nine years they played side-by-side, the Yankees won seven American League pennants and three World Series crowns. In the field, they led the American League in double plays four times. Combined, they totaled 1,438 double plays—869 for Richardson, 569 for Kubek—before back and neck injuries forced Kubek to retire after the 1965 season.

Richardson turned more than 100 double plays six times in the eight seasons he played in 100 or more games, including a career-best 136 in 1961 and 121 in 1965. Kubek's best year was 1961 when he was involved in 107.

"Both were sure things...as dependable as you can get," recalled former teammate and Hall of Fame catcher Yogi Berra. "They were a terrific double-play combination."

"Down the middle, you're looking for great defense, and that includes the shortstop and second baseman who really have to know one another," explained Ralph Houk, who managed both players in the minors in Denver, then guided the Yankees to three AL pennants (1961-63) and a pair of World Series titles over Cincinnati (1961) and San Francisco (1962). "They have to live like twins."

"Tony and Bobby were the best I had," Houk said. "They ate together and hung out together. As a result, they really got to like each other and they got used to each other."

They knew how to play the hitters. They played each hitter a little differently. You have to have the mind and skills (to do that)."

"Tony and Bobby were key parts of our club. Of course, we had some guys named (Mickey) Mantle, Roger (Maris), Yogi and Whitey (Ford) and others who were important, too," Houk added with a chuckle.

"They really clicked on the field and were good friends," Berra said. "And they were just good players."

Richardson credits his father, Robert Sr., "for affording me all the opportunities to play baseball," he said. "I used to spend hours hitting stones with a bat."

He also used to spend hours throwing a tennis ball against the Richardson's home's chimney, honing his skills catching groundballs on the rebounds.

From the very beginning, Richardson wanted to be a New York Yankee.

First, the Yankees had a minor league team from Norfolk of the Class B Piedmont League spring train in Richardson's hometown of Sumter, S.C. The team was managed by Mayo Smith, who later went on to lead the Detroit Tigers to the 1968 World Series title over St. Louis. During the team's stay in Sumter, Richardson, playing shortstop for the local American Legion team, gained the attention of Smith.

Second, Richardson idolized New York shortstop and Hall of Famer Phil Rizzuto, who was showcased on the cover of recruiting brochures the Yankees spread around town.

Third, after Richardson's American Legion team won a regional championship, the coaches took the players to see the 1942 motion picture "The Pride of the Yankees," starring Gary Cooper as Lou Gehrig. The big first baseman died June 2, 1941 of Amyotrophic Lateral Sclerosis (ALS), a degenerative muscle disease. It is now known as "Lou Gehrig's Disease."

"After I saw that movie, I knew then I wanted to be a Yankee," Richardson said. "The Yankees had so much class."

"Mayo said he'd like to sign me when I graduated from high school. Back then, you didn't have the draft. There was a rule that all teams could offer you the same amount of money ($4,000). Twelve teams offered me contracts, but I chose the Yankees."

On the day of his high school graduation in 1953, H.P. Dawson of the Norfolk club visited the Richardson home and signed the shortstop.

The Yankees then sent Richardson by train to New York's Yankee Stadium—"I had a fear of flying, so I took a Pullman," he said—where he spent four days working out with the major leaguers. He took batting practice and fielding, and had the opportunity to meet the likes of Mickey Mantle, Gil McDougald, Jerry Coleman and Rizzuto, all of whom showed a genuine interest in the new signee, Richardson said.

"It was a thrill," Richardson recalled. "I came home to a hero's welcome."

After splitting his first pro season at Norfolk, Va., and Olean, N.Y., Richardson spent the 1954 season at Binghamton, N.Y., where he batted an impressive .310 in 141 games. In 1955, he played a full season at Denver, the Yankees' highest-ranking farm club, hit .296 in 119 games, was promoted to New York for 11 games, then demoted to Richmond.

In 1956, it was back to Denver as a second baseman. It was in Denver where he met then-manager Houk and a strong, 6-feet-3 farmboy by the name of Kubek from Milwaukee, Wisc.

Kubek "was a great athlete," Richardson recalled. "He could do anything."

And he did, lettering in every sport in high school. His play on the football field brought scholarship offers from Notre Dame and Michigan State, but he wanted to play professional baseball. Kubek's hero, his father Tony Sr., played in the 1930s for the Milwaukee Brewers of the old American Association. Managing the rival Toledo Mud Hens was a "gentleman" by the name of Charles "Casey" Stengel, who had just completed a 14-year major league career (.284 average) as an outfielder with the Dodgers, Pirates, Giants, Phillies and Braves.

Stengel's Mud Hens eventually went bankrupt in 1931, which was a blessing in disguise for the fiery skipper as he began his 25-year managerial career in the majors in 1934 with the Brooklyn Dodgers, then the Boston Braves, New York Yankees and New York Mets.

"My dad ended up playing in industrial leagues and I started playing when I was 14 or 15 years old," Kubek said.

Stengel, then in his fifth season as manager of the Yankees and coming off four straight World Series titles (1949-52), remembered the Kubeks from the early days, so he invited Tony, a senior in high school, to a tryout in 1953 at old Comiskey Park in Chicago.

"Rizzuto was getting a little old at short for the Yankees, so they were taking a look at young players," Kubek recalled. "There were a bunch of scouts at Comiskey and Frank Crosetti was pitching batting practice."

Crosetti played 17 seasons (1932-48) at shortstop for the Yankees and was a member of six world championship teams. He is one of the few Yankees to have played with Babe Ruth, Lou Gehrig, Joe DiMaggio and Yogi Berra.

The Yankees liked what they saw and signed Kubek to a $3,000 contract, plus a $1,500 bonus. Until Kubek arrived, most shortstops were under 6-feet tall, so he was somewhat of a novelty.

He began his pro career in the Kitty League in 1954 with Owensboro (Ky.), where he batted .344. In 1955, he played at Quincy, Ill., a Class B team.

In 1956, Richardson and Kubek came together in Denver, where they immediately became best friends and shared the same Christian values. "How could anyone not like Bobby?" Kubek asked.

Both players were named All-Stars that season under Houk, with Kubek at short hitting .331 and Richardson at second batting .328.

During their minor league careers, Richardson, Kubek and approximately 50 other young prospects would report to the Yankees' spring training camp in St. Petersburg, Fla., for what Stengel called his "fundamental camp."

"Casey would have scouts and the minor league managers there and we'd spend three weeks working on fundamentals," Kubek said. "We'd work on offensive routines and defensive routines over and over again. They'd teach defense and running and bunting."

"People don't realize how fundamentally sound Casey was," Kubek said. "Oh sure, he did all that double talk, but people didn't know how much he thought of defense and base running."

All of Stengel's wisecracking remarks to the media led to his nickname, "The Ol' 'Perfesser.' "

In 1957, Richardson and Kubek joined the big-league club for good, and roomed together on the road until Kubek's retirement after the 1965 season.

Kubek played the outfield, short, third and even one game at second in 1957 as Gil McDougald was still manning the shortstop position. He did appear in 127 games and hit .297 en route to American League Rookie-of-the-Year honors.

Richardson appeared in 97 games at second, sharing the position with old reliables Jerry Coleman and Billy Martin.

Most of Richardson's starts came after June 15, 1957, the day Stengel traded his favorite son, Martin, to the Kansas City Athletics. Martin had joined the Yankees in 1950 and played mostly second, but he did see action at short, third and the outfield. He later managed the Yankees for eight years on four different occasions and won two of three World Series.

Richardson knew something was cooking the day he won the second baseman's job.

New York had just beaten the Athletics, 9-2, and the players and coaches, minus Stengel and Martin, were waiting on the bus to take them back to their Kansas City hotel.

"We all knew something was going on," Richardson recalled. "Finally, Billy came onto the bus, sat next to me and said, 'The position is yours, kid.'"

Richardson also inherited Martin's beloved No. 1 uniform jersey. Until then, Richardson had been wearing No. 29. The No. 1 has since been retired under Martin's name.

With Martin gone, Coleman, who spent his entire nine-year career with New York playing second, short and third, took Richardson under his wings.

"I thought Jerry Coleman was the best at turning the double play and he spent a lot of time working with me," Richardson said. "He taught me to position myself, to straddle the bag and how to hold your position at second."

"I was hit only one time turning the double play," Richardson said. "It was Frank Robinson (of Baltimore). I got a low throw from (third baseman) Clete Boyer and Frank knocked me down. I always thought Clete was the best defensive third baseman at that time, but I've never let him forget it."

Having played short earlier in his career, Richardson was well aware of the differences between his position and Kubek's.

"At short, you have to field the ball cleanly and get rid of it quick," Richardson explained. "At second, you have time to knock the ball down and still get your double play."

"A shortstop has to be a good athlete with a strong-and-quick throwing arm," Kubek said. "He has to be able to change directions, have baseball smarts and visualize plays before they happen. You should always be ready."

"You have to have agility. Because of my height (6-feet-3), I had to think more on my feet. At Denver, Ralph (Houk) hired (former Red Sox shortstop) Johnny Pesky, who was an excellent teacher. He preached to me the need for good footwork. He kept telling me, 'You're a big guy. You have to have footwork, footwork, footwork.' To help, I played a lot of handball, which is excellent for hand-and-eye coordination."

Their success as a keystone combination can be attributed to several factors.

"We roomed together and warmed up to each other right away," Richardson said. "A tremendous chemistry developed. On the field, we knew what to expect from each other."

"Bobby was just a great defensive player," Kubek said. "That's something you learn to become. Casey had a rule that the shortstop and second baseman always had to play catch with each other before a game and they'd have to take groundballs together during infield practice."

"Crosetti always said you don't win pennants unless you can catch the ball and, believe me, Bobby and I took a lot of groundballs."

"When I was (TV and radio) broadcasting," Kubek continued, "I saw teams put in less time on their defensive skills. I think fans don't appreciate a good defensive player."

No one is really sure how the nickname "The Milkshake Boys" originated, although it did fit the bill for these two clean-living players who loved to play ball and get their eight hours of sleep.

Berra's reasoning is that the two "liked milkshakes, but we all liked milkshakes. Tony and Bobby would go out at night, but they just got home earlier."

Richardson and Kubek think the media pinned the nickname on them "because we didn't drink," Kubek said. Houk also thinks Stengel may have helped plant the nickname. One of Stengel's most-famous quotes about Richardson was: "Look at him. He don't drink, he don't smoke, he don't chew (tobacco), he don't stay out too late and he still don't hit .250!"

Actually, Richardson, the club's lead-off batter, had a career batting average of .266, plus an impressive .305 mark in seven World Series. Twice during the regular season he hit above .300—.301 in 1959 and .302 in 1962.

Ironically, Kubek, who batted second, concluded his nine-year career with the same .266 batting average.

The two set the table for the famed "Bronx Bombers," which featured Roger Maris in the third spot, Mantle at cleanup, catcher Elston Howard, first baseman Bill "Moose" Skowron, outfielder-catcher Berra and third baseman Boyer.

On the bench they had the likes of Tom Tresh, Hector Lopez, Johnny Blanchard and Bob Cerv.

The pitching staff during the Yankees' pennant runs included Whitey Ford, Al Downing, Ralph Terry, Luis Arroyo, Art Ditmar and Jim Coates.

The roster was a wild bunch. The Yankee dressing room was no place for children. That's why the lockers of Richardson and Kubek were strategically located at one end of the dressing room, out of earshot of cursing teammates who may have had rough days at the plate. Yet, on the field, the Yankees did their jobs and did them well, winning American League pennants in 1957, 1958, 1960, 1961, 1962, 1963 and 1964 with Richardson and Kubek on board.

They lost to Milwaukee in seven games in 1957, as Braves outfielder Henry Aaron batted .393 with three homers and seven runs-batted in, and pitcher Lew Burdette's three complete-game victories and 0.67 earned-run-average.

In 1958, it was the Braves and Yankees, again, but this time, the New Yorkers rallied from a 3-games-to-1 deficit to take the Series in seven. The big blow in Game 7 came from Skowron, who broke open a 3-2 game with a three-run homer in the top of the eighth en route to a 6-2 Yankee victory.

The Chicago White Sox took the AL pennant in 1959, losing to the Los Angeles Dodgers in six, but the Yankees were back in the Fall Classic in 1960 against a surprising Pittsburgh Pirate club. In 1959, the Pirates finished in fourth place in the National League with a 78-76 mark, but in 1960, manager Danny Murtaugh's club improved 17 games in the win column to finish 95-59, seven games ahead of second-place Milwaukee.

Most baseball observers figured the Yankees would dispose of the Pirates in four or five games. The Pirates did have some talent, including National League Most Valuable Player and shortstop Dick Groat (.325), outfielder Roberto Clemente (.314) and a young second baseman named Bill Mazeroski (.273 and 127 double plays). The pitching staff included Vernon Law (20-9), Bob Friend (18-12), Vinegar Bend Mizell (13-5), Harvey Haddix and Roy Face.

Power-wise, the Pirates were no match as first baseman Dick Stuart led the club with 23 homers. For the Yankees, Mantle had 40, Maris 39 and Skowron 26.

Stengel surprised everyone, including his players, by starting Ditmar in Game 1 instead of the lefty Ford, the ace of the staff. Ditmar lasted a third of an inning as the Pirates took the opener, 6-4, behind Mazeroski's two-run homer. The Yankees came back the next day behind pitcher Bob Turley to win, 16-3. Mantle belted two homers and drove in five runs.

Ford finally got the call for Game 3 and shut down the Pirates, 10-0, on four hits. Richardson got the Yanks rolling in the first with a grand slam homer. Ironically, Richardson hit just one homer during the 1960 regular season. When he went to the plate with the bases loaded in the first inning, he was originally given the bunt signal. He fouled off the first pitch, then was told to swing away. At first, Richardson thought Pirate left fielder Gino Cimoli was going to catch the ball, but instead it flew over the fence.

"The full realization of what happened didn't sweep over me until I crossed home plate," Richardson recalled.

Later in the game, he came up with the bases loaded again, but this time he hit a two-run single, giving him a World Series single-game record six runs-batted-in.

Despite being outscored 45-17 in the first six games by the Yankees, the Pirates forced a memorable seventh game at Forbes Field in Pittsburgh on Oct. 13.

The Yankees led, 7-4, entering the bottom of the Pirates' eighth, but the Buccos put up a five spot to take a 9-7 lead. The key play of the inning came when a hard, tailor-made double-play groundball was hit by Bill Virdon to Kubek at short. The ball took one of the game's most-famous bad hops and hit Kubek in the throat, knocking the shortstop to the ground. Kubek was forced to leave the game, being replaced by backup Joe DeMaestri.

With two runs already in to make the score 7-6, the Pirates' Hal Smith, who was inserted late in the game in place of starting catcher Smokey Burgess, belted a three-run homer to give Pittsburgh the 9-7 lead.

The Yankees tied it at 9 in the ninth, but Mazeroski put an end to it leading off the bottom of the inning, taking a 1-0 pitch from Terry over the head of a frustrated Berra and over the left-field wall for a 10-9 World Series win. It marked the first time in baseball history that a home run had decided a World Series.

Richardson was named the Series' Most Valuable Player based on his .367 average and seven-game World Series-record 12 runs-batted-in, a mark that still stood through 2007. Kubek hit .333.

"Boy, we should have won that World Series," recalled Houk, then the team's general manager.

"You take the hop away and we turn two and probably win the Series," Richardson said. "Baseball games are won and lost just like that. That's why double plays are so important."

Kubek still has a couple observations about the 1960 Series.

"First, we (the players) were all surprised that Whitey (Ford) didn't start Game 1, which would have given him three starts in the Series," Kubek said. "As it turned out, he started two games, completed both of them and didn't allow an earned run."

"Second, as we were headed out of the dugout for the bottom of the eighth (of Game 7) with the lead (7-4), I looked over at Casey figuring he'd want me to go to left field and have Joe DeMaestri go to short. Yogi was still a great player, but he had lost a step in the outfield."

DeMaestri appeared in 49 games for the Yankees that season at second and short and committed just one error.

"Nothing was said, so I took my position at short," Kubek said. "You never know what might have happened had DeMaestri been at short. He may have played a little deeper and would have been able to handle Virdon's groundball."

Stengel got fired after the 1960 Series after guiding the Yankees to 10 pennants and seven world titles, and was replaced by Houk. Two years later, Stengel took over the expansion New York Mets, but experienced zero success with four last-place finishes and a .302 winning percentage.

Under Houk, the Yanks rolled past Cincinnati in five games in the 1961 Series. It was the year of the great home run chase to break Babe Ruth's single-season record of 60 home runs. Maris broke the mark with his 61st homer in the 162nd and final game of the season, while an injured Mantle finished with 54. Ruth achieved his 60 in 154 games.

The Yankees won the AL pennant again in 1962 despite the fact Kubek played in only 62 games due to National Guard duty. He returned late in the season for the World Series against the powerful San Francisco Giants. The Series went to a seventh game at Candlestick Park in San Francisco and the outcome wasn't decided until Richardson made a game-saving catch with two outs in the bottom of the ninth.

With Yankee pitcher Terry nursing a 1-0 lead in the bottom of the ninth, the Giants put the tying and winning runs on second and third with two outs. Up to the plate came slugger Willie McCovey, a future Hall of Famer (1986) who belted 521 career homers.

"During a conference on the mound, Tony came over to me at second and said, 'You've already made an error in the Series. You better hope he (McCovey) doesn't hit it to you,'" Richardson said. "Willie Mays (of the Giants) was standing on second base and he just started laughing."

McCovey ripped a hard line drive to the right of Richardson that appeared headed to right center. Richardson nabbed it.

"Mantle used to hit balls like that," Richardson said of McCovey's shot. "It was hit high, but because of the overspin, it came right down to me."

The Yankees advanced to the World Series the next two years. In 1963, Houk's final year as Yankee manager until 1966, the Los Angeles Dodgers swept New York four straight as pitchers Sandy Koufax, Don Drysdale and Johnny Podres limited the Bombers to four runs and a team batting average of .171. That was the last Series Kubek would play in, as back and neck injuries forced him to the bench.

In 1964, with Berra managing the Yankees and Houk back in the front office, St. Louis beat New York in seven games, thanks to pitcher Bob Gibson's 7-5, complete-game victory in the finale. Lou Brock and Ken Boyer both hit homers for the Cards.

Richardson collected 13 hits for a .406 average in the Series, but Kubek was unable to play due to back and neck injuries. Replacing him was Phil Linz, a steady fielder, but weak hitter.

Although his Yankees won 99 games during the regular season and he took the Cardinals to seven in the Series, Berra was fired after the season and replaced by Johnny Keane, the Cardinals' manager.

New York's dominance in the American League had weakened in 1964, as the Chicago White Sox and Baltimore Orioles both made serious bids to overtake the Yankees. However, the White Sox finished one game behind the Yankees, the Orioles two.

One of the more-memorable—and comical—events of the 1964 season came on Aug. 20 following a four-game series loss in Chicago to the White Sox. The four-game sweep dropped the Yankees 4.5 games behind the Sox.

The night before the fourth straight loss in Chicago, batting practice coach Spud Murray bought a harmonica and joined Richardson and Kubek for a night of singing. Prior to the Chicago series, the Yankees had been in Minnesota, where Richardson and Kubek visited the Rev. Billy Graham's headquarters. Kubek had purchased a chorus book in Minnesota and the three of them spent most of the evening in their Chicago hotel singing to Murray's attempts to play the harmonica. Richardson and Kubek both enjoyed reading the Bible and they found the religious songs uplifting.

"The next day, the (Yankee) players were complaining about the drunks who kept them up all night singing," Richardson recalled with a laugh. "Tony picked up a couple of extra harmonicas, so we gave one to Tom Tresh and one to Phil Linz."

Following the fourth straight loss in Chicago the next day, "Phil was playing his on the bus. Yogi told Phil to put the harmonica away in so many words, but Phil didn't hear him clearly, so he asked, 'What did he say?' Mantle, sitting a few rows in front of Phil, turned and said, 'Yogi wants you to play it louder,' so Phil kept playing," Richardson said. "Yogi came to the back of the bus, grabbed the harmonica and threw it. It hit (first baseman) Joe Pepitone in the head. Phil was fined $200."

The Yankees went on to lose two straight to Boston, then won 29 of their last 40 games to nail down the 1964 pennant.

The 1964 pennant and World Series would be the last for Richardson and the Yankees for quite some time.

The Yankees stumbled badly under Keane in 1965, finishing in sixth place with a 77-85 record. Kubek gutted out the season, playing in 109 games, and planned his retirement. Richardson also had retirement on his mind.

"Tony and I had played nine years together and we thought it was time to make our families our priorities," Richardson said. "The Yankees asked us not to retire in the same year. Tony was hurting pretty bad and couldn't play, so he retired."

"Ralph (Houk) gave me a five-year contract, one to play and four to decide what I wanted to do. After my final year (1966), I could have been a coach with the Yankees, a broadcaster or a minor league manager, but I didn't want all that travel."

During his final season at second for the Yanks, Richardson was teamed with several shortstops, including Horace Clarke, Ruben Amaro and Dick Schofield. The Yankees finished last that season under Houk, who replaced the fired Keane.

Houk stayed with the Yankees through 1973 and got the club back on track before moving on to Detroit (1974-78), where he managed another classic keystone combination in second baseman Lou Whitaker and shortstop Alan Trammell, and the Boston Red Sox (1981-84).

Richardson returned to the Yankees in 1967 to play in his first old-timers game. "I was only 31," Richardson said. "Three years later, I played in another old-timers game in Atlanta at the age of 34 and the Braves actually made a pitch for me."

Richardson declined the Braves' contract offer, saying, "Once a Yankee, always a Yankee. Team loyalty...you don't see much of that anymore."

Richardson eventually got into college coaching at the University of South Carolina (1970-76), where he led the Gamecocks to a second-place finish behind Texas in the 1975 College World Series with a 51-6-1 record. In 1974, his Gamecocks finished 48-8. Overall, he was 220-91-2. Among his players were the sons of Phil Rizzuto and Whitey Ford.

Richardson later became the baseball coach and athletic director at Coastal Carolina College from 1984 to 1986, then the athletic director and assistant to the chancellor at Liberty University from 1987 to 1990 before retiring for good.

"After I retired, I started speaking at American Legion, Babe Ruth, Dixie Youth and prayer breakfasts," Richardson said.

Today, he's in demand around the country as he and his wife, Betsy, travel to speaking engagements, many of them for the Fellowship of Christian Athletes.

He spoke at the funerals of former teammates Maris and Mantle. At both services, he read a poem written by Walt Huntley, who had mailed it to Richardson in the 1960s. *It's called "God's Hall of Fame:"*

*Your name may not appear down here*
*On this world's Hall of Fame.*
*In fact, you may be so unknown*
*That no one knows your name;*
*The headlines here may pass you by,*
*The neon lights of blue*

*May never come your way,*
*But if you love and serve the Lord,*
*Then I have news for you.*
*This Hall of Fame is only good*
*As long as time shall be;*
*But keep in mind, God's Hall of Fame*
*Is for eternity.*
*This crowd on earth they soon forget*
*The heroes of the past.*
*They cheer like mad until you fail*
*And that's how long you last.*
*But in God's Hall of Fame*
*By just believing in His Son*
*Inscribed you'll find your name.*
*I tell you, friend, I wouldn't trade*
*My name however small,*
*That's written there beyond the stars*
*In that Celestial Hall,*
*For all the famous names on earth,*

*Or glory that it shares;*
*I'd rather be an unknown here*
*And have my name up there."*

Richardson was one of the last people to see and speak to Mantle before his death on Aug. 13, 1995 in Dallas, following a failed liver transplant. Maris had died 10 years earlier on Dec. 14, 1985 of cancer in Houston.

Kubek became a popular radio and TV broadcaster, spending nearly three decades on network television doing the color commentary for "The Game of the Week," playoffs and more than a dozen World Series.

He's been out of broadcasting for 10 years and has not been to a major league game since.

"I didn't like what I was seeing," Kubek said. "I didn't like the attitude of the players. They were getting selfish, which was affecting the quality of play."

Today, he and his wife, Margaret, enjoy spending time with their five grandchildren in Appleton, Wisc., and working with the local Lutheran Church.

"We go and listen to first graders read," Kubek said. "We also work with the Hispanics Outreach Program. We enjoy teaching people more about Jesus."

And Kubek spends many summer nights at the youth baseball league parks, watching his grandsons play the game he loved and played so well.

## DEFENSE BY THE NUMBERS

A look at the individual fielding statistics of Bobby Richardson and Tony Kubek during the time period they played for the New York Yankees at their primary positions, second base and shortstop (PO – putouts; AST – assists; E – errors; DP – double plays; PCT. – fielding percentage):

| | BOBBY RICHARDSON, 2B | | | | | TONY KUBEK, SS | | | | |
|---|---|---|---|---|---|---|---|---|---|---|
| YEAR | PO | AST | E | DP | PCT. | PO | AST | E | DP | PCT. |
| 1957 | 206 | 223 | 9 | 60 | .979 | 74 | 108 | 6 | 26 | .968 |
| 1958 | 104 | 110 | 6 | 35 | .973 | 242 | 453 | 28 | 98 | .969 |
| 1959 | 256 | 292 | 17 | 85 | .970 | 121 | 317 | 11 | 42 | .976 |
| 1960 | 312 | 337 | 18 | 103 | .973 | 228 | 443 | 22 | 84 | .968 |
| 1961 | 413 | 376 | 18 | 136 | .978 | 261 | 449 | 30 | 107 | .959 |
| 1962 | 378 | 451 | 15 | 116 | .982 | 71 | 117 | 9 | 27 | .954 |
| 1963 | 335 | 424 | 12 | 105 | .984 | 227 | 403 | 13 | 80 | .980 |
| 1964 | 400 | 410 | 15 | 108 | .982 | 186 | 307 | 11 | 52 | .978 |
| 1965 | 372 | 403 | 15 | 121 | .981 | 134 | 237 | 14 | 53 | .964 |
| Totals | 2,776 | 3,026 | 125 | 869 | .979 | 1,544 | 2,834 | 144 | 569 | .967 |

NOTE: *Although a large majority of the seasonal and career double plays listed above involved the two keystone partners as a unit playing together at the same time during the noted time period, some were obviously not. The difference is due to many factors, including the number of games played, late-inning substitutions, injuries, a position change, DPs converted independent of each other and, in some cases, games missed due to military service.*

Bill Mazeroski made plays look easy, according to his keystone mate Gene Alley, who added, "He won or saved a lot of games for the Pirates because of his defense."

### CHAPTER NINE
# 2B BILL MAZEROSKI & SS GENE ALLEY PITTSBURGH PIRATES, 1965-71

**NAME: William Stanley Mazeroski**

**Nickname:** Maz, No Touch

**Born:** September 5, 1936, Wheeling, W. Va.

**Died:** Still throwing as of October 1, 2007

**Batted/threw:** Right/right

**Height/weight:** 5-feet-10, 183 pounds

**Major league seasons:** 17 (Pittsburgh, 1956-72)

**Major league debut:** July 7, 1956 (Giants 3, **Pirates 2**)

**Final major league game:** Oct. 4, 1972 (Cardinals 4, **Pirates 3**)

**Position:** Second base

**Career games:** 2,163

**Career double plays:** 1,706

**DPs with Pirates at second base (1965-71):** 667

**Career errors:** 204

**Career assists:** 6,694

**Career putouts:** 4,976

**Career fielding percentage:** .983

**Gold Gloves:** 8

**All-Star:** 7 times

**World Series:** 2-0

**Career batting average:** .260

**Turning two:** Mazeroski made a cameo appearance in the 1968 movie "The Odd Couple" in which he hits into a game-ending triple play against the New York Mets. The scene was filmed prior to the Pirates' June 27, 1967 game at Shea Stadium. It only took two takes.

**Hall of Fame:** Class of 2001

Gene Alley said part of his success was knowing where Pittsburgh pitchers were going to pitch opposing hitters, so he had a good idea where to play each batter.

**NAME: Leonard Eugene Alley**

**Nickname:** Gene

**Born:** July 10, 1940, Richmond, Va.

**Died:** Still throwing as of October 1, 2007

**Batted/threw:** Right/right

**Height/weight:** 6-feet, 165 pounds

**Major league seasons:** 11 (Pittsburgh, 1965-73)

**Major league debut:** Sept. 4, 1963 (Braves 1, **Pirates 0**)

**Final major league game:** Sept. 27, 1973 (Phillies 3, **Pirates 2**)

**Position:** Shortstop (also second base: 130 games)

**Career games:** 1,195

**Career double plays:** 805

**DPs with Pirates at shortstop (1965-71):** 554

**Career errors:** 166

**Career assists:** 3,641

**Career putouts:** 1,879

**Career fielding percentage:** .971

**Gold Gloves:** 2

**All-Star:** 2

**World Series:** 1-0

**Career batting average:** .254

**Turning two:** The Pirates thought so highly of Alley while he was in the minors, they traded perennial All-Star shortstop Dick Groat to St. Louis after the 1962 season. In his second full season with the Pirates, Alley hit .299.

**Hall of Fame:** No

It's ironic that the player generally recognized as the greatest defensive second baseman in the game is best remembered for one swing of the bat.

That swing came in the bottom of the ninth inning of Game 7 of the 1960 World Series at Forbes Field in Pittsburgh. The date was Oct. 13. The score was tied at 9. The opponents were the heavily favored New York Yankees, who were expected to sweep the Series. Their lineup of Mantle, Maris, Skowron, Berra, Howard, Richardson, Kubek and Boyer appeared unbeatable.

The hitter was 25-year-old Bill Mazeroski, the eighth batter in the Pittsburgh Pirates' lineup. On the mound was the reliable Ralph Terry, who had entered the game in the eighth for the New Yorkers to put an end to a rally that saw the Pirates score five runs.

Terry's first pitch to Mazeroski was a ball. The second pitch was a strike. Mazeroski took a hard, but smooth cut at the ball and sent a towering drive to left field. Yankee left fielder Yogi Berra thought he had a play on the ball, but he ran back to the warning track, ran out of room and helplessly watched the ball clear the wall and disappear into the trees. World champion Pirates 10, Yankees 9.

Through 2007, Mazeroski was the only player in the history of the game to end a World Series with a Game 7 home run. The only other home run to end a World Series game came off the bat of Toronto Blue Jay Joe Carter, but his ninth-inning, three-run blast in 1993 against Philadelphia came in Game 6 of that Series.

Despite being outscored 55-27 and out-hit 91-60 by the Yankees, the Pirates had won their first World Series since 1925, when they dropped the Washington Senators in seven games. They appeared in the 1927 World Series, but quickly went down in four against the Yankees.

"Every day of my life I think of that home run," Mazeroski said years later. "I suppose it must be the most-important thing I've ever done. Every kid dreams of hitting a home run to win a World Series. I got to live that dream."

After he hit the walk-off, World Series-winning homer, Mazeroski believed people would eventually forget about it. Not true. To this day, it's replayed frequently on many of the all-sports, cable-television networks.

"I never looked at myself as a hero," the always-modest Mazeroski said. "It was just another home run to win a game."

"That home run probably made him a legend," said former Chicago sports writer Jerome Holtzman, who is now Major League Baseball's official historian.

"They don't talk about his sure-handed fielding, his quick throws, his quick flips to second base on double plays," said Holtzman, who covered baseball for the *Chicago Sun Times* and *Chicago Tribune* for 60 years. "They remember the home run."

Pirate fans definitely remember it and future generations will be told about it. Every Oct. 13, Pirate fans gather on the campus of the University of Pittsburgh where a plaque marks the spot where Mazeroski's homer cleared the left field wall. A portion of the wall remains. Home plate remains in its original location, encased in the floor of a University of Pittsburgh building. The Pirate faithful also listen to a tape

recording of the Game 7 radio broadcast, which featured an error by the great broadcaster Chuck Thompson. In reporting Mazeroski's ninth-inning at-bat, Thompson stated that the Yankee pitcher was Art Ditmar instead of Terry.

In Game 1 of the Series, Mazeroski had another "big blow" that helped lift the Pirates past the Yankees. His two-run homer propelled the Pirates to a 6-4 victory at Forbes Field. Mazeroski, always known for his clutch hitting, went 8-for-25 in the Series (.320 average) with a pair of homers and five runs-batted-in. Based on his performance, Mazeroski won the "Babe Ruth Award," which, at that time, was the World Series' Most Valuable Player Award. His counterpart on the Yankees, Bobby Richardson, made it a "battle of the second basemen" with a .367 average, eight runs and 12 runs-batted-in. Through 2006, Richardson's 12 RBIs still stood as a World Series record.

During his 17-year career, Mazeroski was a steady performer at the plate, finishing with a batting average of .260 and 138 home runs. He never hit .300, never hit more than 20 homers or drove in more than 85 runs in a season. He had only 27 career stolen bases and never scored more than 75 runs in a season.

What Mazeroski did possess were "good range, good hands, a lightning-flash release and a terrific work ethic," according to former Pirate coach Clyde King, who is now in his 62nd year in baseball as an advisor for the Yankees.

"I've never seen a better second baseman turn a double play," King said. "There were others like Bobby Richardson (Yankees) and Jackie Robinson (Dodgers), but Maz was the best. He was so quick with his hands it was hard to tell if he even touched the ball."

That's where the nickname "No Touch" came from.

"I played catch with Maz many times," said Bill Virdon, the Pirates' center fielder for 11 seasons and a member of the 1960 world championship team. "He always played with a small glove. I'd throw him the ball. He'd take his glove hand, the ball would hit the heal of his glove and deflect to his throwing hand. He'd get his right hand in position and deliver the ball back immediately."

Shortstop Gene Alley, Mazeroski's "classic" keystone partner from 1965-71, still laughs at the small glove "Maz" used. "It was so small," Alley said, "a tee-ball player would probably throw it away. He was a magician with that glove, though."

"Maz never really caught the ball, never closed his glove," Alley continued. "He turned his glove at an angle and held his right hand just so. Then the ball would slide out of his glove and into his hand and the ball would explode to first base. It was a wonder the ball stayed in there. He was the only one I ever saw do it like that."

"The first time I saw Maz when I joined the Pirates, I was so impressed with his quickness and how well he played the infield," Alley added. "I didn't think I'd make it (in the majors), but then I learned there was only one Mazeroski."

"Maz is the best I've seen, period," said Virdon, who also managed for 13 seasons (1972-84) with the Pirates, Yankees, Astros and Expos and won three division titles. "I backed him up for 10 years in center field and never got a ball."

"Maz had the natural ability, yet he worked at it every day. I never saw hands so sure in all the time I played," Virdon said.

"The only other player close to the hands of Maz was Ozzie Smith (St. Louis shortstop, 1982-96). I've never seen anyone more consistent at his position."

Mazeroski signed with the Pirates as a shortstop at the age of 17 in 1954 right out of high school in Tiltonsville, Ohio. He was immediately moved to second base by the Pirates' Branch Rickey, who joined the Pirates from the Dodgers. Rickey was so good at finding talent, the late great sports writer Jim Murray once wrote: "He could recognize a great player from the window of a moving train."

Mazeroski spent 2.5 seasons in the minors, bouncing back and forth between Williamsport (Pa.) of the Class A Eastern League and Hollywood (Calif.) of the Triple-A Pacific Coast League. He struggled, both at the plate and in the field. He opened the 1956 season back in Hollywood, where his average climbed to .306 in 80 games. At the halfway mark of the Pacific Coast League season, he was promoted to Pittsburgh at the age of 19.

He replaced a carousel of Pittsburgh second basemen, including Johnny O'Brien and Gene Freese, who also played some third base.

Through 2007, Mazeroski was the king of career double plays for a second baseman with 1,706, including a record-high 161 in 1966. He committed just 204 career errors, an average of 12 per season. During one 11-year stretch (1958-1968), Mazeroski participated in more than 100 double plays per season. He led the league in assists nine times, fielding percentage three times and double plays eight times.

His first keystone partner was Dick Groat (1956-62), who was traded to St. Louis, then Dick Schofield (1963-64), a 19-year veteran who played for seven teams.

Groat was a solid defensive player (1,237 career double plays and a .961 fielding percentage) and a solid hitter (.286 career average). In 1960, the year the Pirates won the National League pennant by seven games over the Milwaukee Braves with a 95-59 record and beat the Yankees in the Fall Classic, he was named the NL's Most Valuable Player based on his .325 batting average.

That 1960 Pirate team, managed by Danny Murtaugh, had a strong supporting cast around its keystone combination. Dick Stuart was at first and Don Hoak played third. Bob Skinner was in left, Virdon in center and Roberto Clemente in right.

The 25-year-old Clemente, the first Latino player in the majors, had an MVP season himself with a .314 average, 16 homers and 94 runs-batted-in. Many believed he was the National League's MVP, but he finished a surprising distant eighth in the voting.

Groat batted above .300 four times in his 13 full seasons and won a second World Series ring in 1964 when the Cardinals beat the Yankees in seven games.

The Pirates' 1960 pitching staff was led by 20-game winner Vernon Law, Bob Friend (18-12), Harvey Haddix (11-10) and Vinegar Bend Mizell

(13-5). Roy Face (10-8, 24 saves) was the closer. Catchers Smokey Burgess (.294) and Hal Smith (.295) combined for 18 homers and 94 runs-batted-in.

Alley was signed by the Pirates in 1959 right out of high school and spent five seasons in the minors before being called up to the major leagues. His final minor-league stop was in 1963 at Grand Forks, N.D., where he was a teammate of future Hall of Famer Willie Stargell.

Playing behind the reliable Dick Schofield, Alley saw limited action in 1963 and 1964 with the Pirates, appearing in a total of 98 games at second, third and short. A month into the 1965 season, the Pirates were so sure about Alley's ability to play shortstop fulltime and team with Mazeroski on the double play, they traded Schofield to the Giants. Alley stayed at short on a permanent basis until the end of the 1972 season.

During his first full season (1965) with the Pirates, Alley was constantly being compared to fan-favorite Groat.

"Dick (Groat) was a great leader on the field and was one of those people who was limited in natural talent," Virdon said. "But he got the most out of his natural ability. He really didn't have power, speed or range, but his knowledge and know-how was above everyone else. He knew how to win."

"Dick (Groat) was a good hitter and he had great knowledge of the opposing hitters," said Friend, a righty who won 191 games in 15 seasons for the Pirates.

"Alley had more range than Dick or anyone else I saw in a long time, for that matter," Friend continued. "Alley had a great arm. He was quick and rangy."

"Maz and Alley took us out of some big innings because of their ability to turn the double play. I was a sinkerball pitcher, so I needed that double play," Friend said. "You have to be strong up the middle. That's the key for any pitcher if you want to win."

Murtaugh once said that Mazeroski and Alley took away five runs a week from their opponents because of their air-tight defense up the middle.

Dave Giusti, a pitcher who spent 15 years in the majors—seven with the Pirates (1970-76)—was amazed at the wizardry of Mazeroski and Alley while he was playing for Houston (1962-68).

In a game at the Astrodome, the Pirates held a 7-6 lead with one out in the bottom of the ninth, but the Astros had loaded the bases. Houston catcher Ronnie Brand hit a sharp grounder into the hole to the left of Alley.

"We're all thinking the game's going to at least be tied," Giusti told Paul Meyer of *Baseball Digest*, "because there's no way Alley can get the guy at the plate. And there's no way they can turn a double play."

"Then the game was over. Double play. So quick. From Alley to Maz to first. We're thinking, 'What happened?'"

Giusti eventually became the ace of the Pirates' bullpen, especially during the 1971 postseason when he recorded four saves and failed to allow a run in 11 innings of work against the Giants and the Orioles. He concluded his career with exactly 100 wins and 145 saves.

"Gene was just an outstanding defensive shortstop," King said. "That's why he was able to make plays like that. I think that helped Maz a lot. He threw the ball to Maz perfectly all the time."

"Alley also got rid of the ball quickly. It was something they both worked on. They both had great work ethics. They took a lot of infield practice. They took a lot of time preparing for each game."

"Some of their talent came from hard work, some of it was instincts and some of it was God-given ability," King said.

"They were just fabulous," said former Chicago Cubs shortstop Don Kessinger, who played in the same era. "They were simply great players and great people. We had great respect for them and we admired them every time we played them."

During their seven seasons as a keystone combination, Mazeroski turned 667 double plays, Alley 554. In 1966, Mazeroski was involved in 161 double plays, which was still a record through the 2006 season. As a team, the Pirates turned 215 double plays that season, which was still a major league record through 2006.

It wasn't until the 1966 season when Alley became comfortable and confident playing shortstop in the big leagues. In 1965, his first full season, he was forced to play 40 games at second while Mazeroski was nursing a broken foot. When Maz returned, Alley moved back to short where he played 110 games. Between the two positions, he was involved in 113 double plays. Ironically, Maz also turned 113 DPs when he returned.

"I really liked playing shortstop," Alley said. "It was just the feeling of being out there and playing defense. Things really turned around that season (1966). We set the team double-play record (215), which is something I'm proud of, and we just had a lot of fun. I really hadn't done much prior to that season, and the people in Pittsburgh really got behind us and came out to see us make double plays."

During that record-breaking season, Alley had 128 double plays.

At the plate, Alley's batting average rose from .252 in 1965 to .299 in 1966. He was a good hit-and-run man and an excellent bunter. In 1966, he was second in the National League with 20 sacrifice hits. He was also tough to double-up, grounding into only 95 double plays during his 11-year career. A .254 lifetime hitter, he collected 999 career hits.

The 1966 Pirates had the National League's most-feared lineup with an outfield of Matty Alou (.342), Clemente (.317) and Stargell (.315). First baseman Donn Clendenon batted .299 and Mazeroski added a .262 average, plus a career-high 82 runs-batted-in.

Late in the season, when the Pirates were battling the Dodgers and the Giants for the National League flag, Alley was nearly lost for the season. In a game against the Mets on Aug. 10, 1966 at Forbes Field, a pitch by New York's Bob Shaw hit Alley on the left side of his face. The injury knocked Alley unconscious and required nine stitches above his left eye. Alley, the "gamer" that he was, somehow came back three days later against Cincinnati at Crosley Field with a badly bruised face and a half swollen-shut left eye. As the Pirates' lead-off hitter, Alley took a swing at Reds pitcher Milt Pappas' first pitch and ripped a line-drive single. He collected another single to spark the Pirates to a come-from-behind 4-2 victory.

That win put the Pirates at 69-47 for the year, two games ahead of the Giants and 3.5 ahead of the Dodgers.

The NL pennant race went down to the final days, but Los Angeles prevailed, taking the crown by 1.5 games over San Francisco and 3 games over the Pirates. Los Angeles was then swept by Baltimore in the World Series.

The Pirates didn't contend for postseason play again until 1970, when they won the National League East title with an 89-73 mark, only to be swept in three games by Cincinnati for the NL pennant. Cincinnati then got walloped in five games by Baltimore

Meanwhile, Mazeroski and Alley continued to set the standard for turning double plays.

In 1966 and 1967, they became only the second keystone combination to win two Gold Glove Awards in the same years. The first duo to achieve that feat was Nellie Fox and Luis Aparicio (1959 and 1960) of the Chicago White Sox.

"There was no secret to our success," Alley said. "We just had a lot of opportunities to make the double play and we didn't mess up too many times. We turned the double plays we were supposed to turn."

"We knew the hitters and their speed. When we caught the ball, we got rid of it pretty quick. Maz was really good at catching the ball and getting rid of it. I can't ever remember him giving me a bad throw."

"Maz made plays look easy," Alley continued. "He made the tough plays without flair. He won or saved a lot of games for the Pirates because of his defense."

Alley said knowing their own pitchers benefited the infield defense.

"Maz and I learned our pitchers and what they planned to throw to certain hitters," Alley said. "We had a meeting with the pitcher before every game. He'd tell us how he'd pitch a batter so we had a good idea of where to play each hitter."

Very few base runners racing from first to second were able to break up an Alley-to-Mazeroski double play, not only because of their quickness, but because of Maz's muscular "tree-stump" legs.

Former Pirates, including Alley, remember one play in particular when Ron Stone, a rookie for Philadelphia, tried to impress his teammates by trying to take Mazeroski out of a double play. At first base, Stone was warned not to try to take out the "tree stump."

Stone didn't listen. He attempted to take Maz out and failed. The Pirate second baseman easily made the relay throw to first to complete the double play, then he reached down to help Stone up. After Mazeroski dusted off Stone's uniform, the rookie got back to the dugout and discovered he had broken ribs. A first baseman and outfielder, Stone lasted five seasons in the majors, played in 388 games and batted .241.

"Maz was so durable," Friend said. "Nobody took him out (on a double play)."

"You didn't want to slide into Maz," Alley said with a laugh. "I saw a few people try and they usually got hurt."

"Maz made so many great plays, you really didn't notice him," Virdon said. "Some players tried to break up the double play. They seldom succeeded. Maz would look down at the opposing player and say, 'Are you OK?'"

As active as he was on the field, "Maz was basically a quiet person," recalled Virdon, who roomed with him for five seasons. "He barely said 'boo' to you. He had a good sense of humor and everyone enjoyed him. You never heard a bad word come out of his mouth. You just couldn't ask for a better player."

Alley also roomed with Mazeroski for five seasons in the late 1960s and early 1970s. "Maz talked a lot more than people thought," Alley said. "I was the quiet one. I just sat there in the room and listened to him. He talked about everything."

Alley and Mazeroski were members of the Pirates' 1971 National League championship team (97-65 mark) that defeated the Baltimore Orioles in seven games in the World Series. Unfortunately, both were nursing injuries. Alley, who appeared in 114 games that season despite shoulder and knee problems, appeared in two Series games. Mazeroski, who played 70 regular-season games because of a variety of ailments, only appeared once as a pinch-hitter.

Dave Cash started at second for the Pirates, while Jackie Hernandez took over at shortstop for the Series. Bob Roberston was at first, while Jose Pagan played third. The outfield had Stargell in left, Gene Clines in center and Clemente in right. Manny Sanguillen was the catcher.

Dock Ellis (19-9), Bob Johnson (9-10), Steve Blass (15-8), Luke Walker (10-8), Nelson Briles (8-4) and Bob Moose (11-7) were the pitchers.

Managing the Pirates was Murtaugh, who came out of retirement to lead the club to the National League East title and a 3-1 series victory over the San Francisco Giants in the National League Championship Series.

The Orioles were led by four pitchers, all 20-game winners, in 1971: Jim Palmer, Dave McNally, Pat Dobson and Mike Cuellar. Their potent offense was paced by first baseman Boog Powell, third baseman Brooks Robinson and outfielder Frank Robinson.

The Birds took the first two games in Baltimore: 5-3 behind McNally's complete-game, three-hitter and Merv Rettenmund's three-run homer; and 11-3 behind Palmer's strong eight innings, and Brooks Robinson's three hits and three runs-batted-in.

The Pirates then swept three straight at home. In Game 3, Blass twirled a brilliant three-hitter and Roberston blasted a three-run homer for a 5-1 victory.

In Game 4, the first World Series contest played at night (Oct. 13, 1971), pinch-hitter Milt May's single in the seventh inning proved to be the difference in a 4-3 Bucco win.

Game 5 was all Briles, who hurled a two-hit, 4-0 victory. Clemente, Robertson and Briles drove in all the runs the Pirates needed.

Baltimore knotted the series at 3 with a 3-2 victory, setting the stage for a dramatic Game 7. Brooks Robinson knocked home Frank Robinson with a single in the bottom of the 10th inning for the Game 6 winner.

Clemente gave the Pirates a 1-0 lead in the fourth inning of Game 7 in Baltimore with a tape-measure shot, then Pittsburgh ran the count to

2-0 in the eighth when Pagan doubled home Stargell. The Orioles managed a run off starter Blass in the bottom of the eighth on a fielder's choice grounder that scored Frank Robinson. After that, Blass slammed the door shut for a 2-1 Pittsburgh win, giving the Pirates their fourth World Series title. Pittsburgh won a fifth Series in 1979, this time coming back from a 3-1 deficit against the same Orioles.

"Winning the 1971 World Series that year was a big thrill for me and the team," Alley said, "but I didn't have a very good year (.227 average) and it was disappointing for both Maz and myself that we couldn't play bigger roles because of the injuries. But it was a team thing. Everyone contributed."

The 37-year-old Clemente was the overwhelming choice for Most Valuable Player of the 1971 Series with his .414 average, two homers and four runs-batted-in. A lost fact about Clemente's post-season brilliance was that he hit in all seven World Series games in 1960 and in all seven in 1971. His World Series line: 14 games, 58 at-bats, 21 hits, .362 average, three homers and seven RBIs.

Fourteen months later (Dec. 31, 1972), "The Great One," as he was called by teammates, perished in a plane crash off the coast of Isla Verde, Puerto Rico, at the age of 38 while delivering aid to earthquake victims in Nicaragua.

In his eulogy, then-Baseball Commissioner Bowie Kuhn said of Clemente: "He gave the term 'complete' a new meaning. He made the word 'superstar' seem inadequate. He had about him the touch of royalty."

For Mazeroski, his career came to an end after the 1972 season when he was used sparingly and in a utility role. He had major league coaching stints with the Pirates in 1973 and with Seattle in 1979-80.

Alley retired after the 1973 campaign due to a pair of knee operations which limited him to 76 games.

Today, Mazeroski is a private person. He declines interviews, is extremely modest and doesn't like to talk about himself nor the past. Former teammate Blass once said of Mazeroski, "He was a player, not a speaker."

Alley was a soft-spoken person as a player and remains that way today, but not to the extent of Mazeroski. He's proud of the 11 seasons he played with the Pirates and the seven years he played shortstop next to Mazeroski at second.

Alley still enjoys the game, although he hasn't attended a major league contest in person in approximately 30 years. He says he gets enough baseball on television from his Glen Allen, Va., home.

Mazeroski is a regular at the Pirates' spring training camp in Bradenton, Fla., and lives in Florida and Pennsylvania. After he retired, he still had a stake in baseball: the Hall of Fame.

From 1978 through 1992, Mazeroski failed to muster enough votes from the Baseball Writers Association of America to gain entry into the National Baseball Hall of Fame. Finally, he was selected by baseball's Veterans Committee in 2001.

As far as former Pirate general manager Joe Brown was concerned, it was a long time coming. He pointed out that no modern middle infielder ever led the league in as many fielding categories as Mazeroski did and that "showed quality over a long period of time. You don't get those statistics by accident," he said.

Brown, who was the Pirates' GM from 1956 to 1976 and saw his club win two World Series and five divisional titles, was a baseball genius. He pieced together the team that shocked the Yankees in the 1960 World Series.

## MAZ: MR. DURABILITY

To show Mazeroski's durability, he was just one of two major league players to man second base on a regular basis during the entire 1960s. The table below includes the year and the number of double plays by Mazeroski and Julian Javier:

| Player (1960-69) | '60 | '61 | '62 | '63 | '64 | '65 | '66 | '67 | '68 | '69 | Total |
|---|---|---|---|---|---|---|---|---|---|---|---|
| Bill Mazeroski (a) | 127 | 144 | 138 | 131 | 122 | 113 | 161 | 131 | 107 | 46 | **1,220** |
| Julian Javier (b) | 71 | 82 | 96 | 93 | 97 | 40 | 89 | 72 | 68 | 70 | **778** |

(a)   Mazeroski appeared in 2,104 games defensively during his career, all but 10 at second base.

(b)   Javier played for the Cardinals (1960-71), Reds (1972) and had 907 career DPs as a second baseman. He appeared in 1,577 games defensively, all but 25 at second base.

The fact that he was never voted in by the Baseball Writers didn't bother Mazeroski. But once he was elected by the Veterans Committee, he did tell MajorLeagueBaseball.com, "When you say Hall of Fame, it means something. It means you have accomplished something."

On Aug. 5, 2001, Mazeroski's day had come. Full of emotion, he addressed his family, fans and fellow Hall of Famers in Cooperstown (transcript provided by the National Baseball Hall of Fame):

"I've got 12 pages here. That's not like me. I'll probably skip half of it and get half way through this thing and quit anyhow. It's getting awful hot out here, so that's a good excuse to make it short," Mazeroski said.

"So, but anyhow, I think defense belongs in the Hall of Fame. Defense deserves as much credit as pitching and hitting. And I'm proud and honored to be going into the Hall of Fame on the defensive side and mostly for my defensive abilities. I feel special."

"This is gonna be hard, so I probably won't say about half of this stuff. I want to thank the Veterans Committee for this great, great honor. The highest honor in baseball. I thought when the Pirates retired my number (9) that that would be the greatest thing to ever happen to me. It's hard to top this. I don't think I'm gonna make it. I think you can kiss these 12 pages down the drain."

"I just want to thank everybody. I want to thank the Hall of Fame, I want to thank the Veterans Committee, I want to thank all the friends and family that made this long trip up here to listen to me speak and hear this crap. Thank you very, very much. Thanks everybody. That's enough."

Also inducted that day were Dave Winfield (22 seasons, .283 average, 465 homers) and Kirby Puckett (12 seasons, 207 homers, .318 average).

Following the Hall inductions, master of ceremonies George Grande said of Mazeroski: "I think Bill's speech lasted 30 seconds .... and in those 30 seconds you knew everything you needed to know about Bill Mazeroski—what a sensitive man he was, what a great person he was."

## DEFENSE BY THE NUMBERS

A look at the individual fielding statistics of Bill Mazeroski and Gene Alley during the time period they played together at their primary positions, second base and shortstop (PO – putouts; AST – assists; E – errors; DP – double plays; PCT. – fielding percentage):

| | BILL MAZEROSKI, 2B | | | | | GENE ALLEY, SS | | | | |
|---|---|---|---|---|---|---|---|---|---|---|
| YEAR | PO | AST | E | DP | PCT. | PO | AST | E | DP | PCT. |
| 1965 | 290 | 439 | 9 | 113 | .988 | 163 | 376 | 18 | 79 | .968 |
| 1966 | 411 | 538 | 8 | 161 | .992 | 235 | 472 | 15 | 128 | .979 |
| 1967 | 417 | 498 | 18 | 131 | .981 | 257 | 500 | 26 | 105 | .967 |
| 1968 | 319 | 467 | 15 | 107 | .981 | 162 | 394 | 15 | 86 | .974 |
| 1969 | 134 | 192 | 4 | 46 | .988 | 36 | 66 | 5 | 17 | .953 |
| 1970 | 227 | 325 | 7 | 87 | .987 | 202 | 381 | 15 | 84 | .975 |
| 1971 | 95 | 121 | 3 | 22 | .986 | 187 | 316 | 22 | 55 | .958 |
| Totals | 1,893 | 2,580 | 64 | 667 | .986 | 1,242 | 2,505 | 116 | 554 | .968 |

**NOTE:** *Although a large majority of the seasonal and career double plays listed above involved the two keystone partners as a unit playing together at the same time during the noted time period, some were obviously not. The difference is due to many factors, including the number of games played, late-inning substitutions, injuries, a position change, DPs converted independent of each other and, in some cases, games missed due to military service.*

### CHAPTER TEN

# 2B GLENN BECKERT & SS DON KESSINGER, CHICAGO CUBS, 1965-73

**NAME: Glenn Alfred Beckert**

**Nickname:** Bruno

**Born:** October 12, 1940, Pittsburgh, Pa.

**Died:** Still throwing as of October 1, 2007

**Position:** Second base

**Batted/threw:** Right/right

**Height/weight:** 6-feet-1, 190 pounds

**Major league seasons:** 11 (Chicago Cubs, 1965-73; San Diego, 1974-75)

**Major league debut:** April 12, 1965 (**Cubs 10,** Cardinals 10, tie)

**Final major league game:** April 27, 1975 (Braves 4, **Padres 1**)

**Career games:** 1,320

**Career double plays:** 758

**DPs with Cubs at second base (1965-73):** 742

**Career errors:** 179

**Career assists:** 3,719

**Career putouts:** 2,712

**Career fielding percentage:** .973

**Gold Gloves:** 1

**All-Star:** 4 times

**World Series:** 0-0

**Career batting average:** .283

**Turning two:** Beckert topped the 180-hit mark three times, including 1971 when he hit a career-high .342, third-best in the National League.

**Hall of Fame:** No

**NAME: Donald Eulon Kessinger**

Nickname: Don

Born: July 17, 1942, Forrest City, Ariz.

Died: Still throwing as of October 1, 2007

Position: Shortstop (also second base: 78 games; third base 28 games)

Batted/threw: Both/right

Height/weight: 6-feet, 175 pounds

Major league seasons: 16 (Chicago Cubs, 1964-75; St. Louis, 1976-77; Chicago White Sox, 1977-79)

Major league debut: Sept. 7, 1964 (Braves 8, **Cubs 7**)

Final major league game: July 31, 1979 (Yankees 7, **White Sox 3**)

Career games: 2,078

Career double plays: 1,215

DPs with Cubs at shortstop (1965-73): 794

Career errors: 350

Career assists: 6,453

Career putouts: 3,292

Career fielding percentage: .965

Gold Gloves: 2

All-Star: 6

World Series: 0-0

Career batting average: .252

Turning two: Kessinger ranked among the top 10 in the National League in singles five times and in sacrifice hits six times.

Hall of Fame: No

One of baseball's "classic"—and "classiest"— keystone combinations performed their magic for nine seasons, yet never advanced to postseason play.

From 1965 through 1973, second baseman Glenn Beckert and short-stop Don Kessinger of the Chicago Cubs were as steady and competitive as they came.

"Glenn and Don had great passion for the game," said the great former Cub and Hall of Famer Ernie Banks, who played a "mean" shortstop himself from 1953-61 before moving to first base in 1962. "They were real professionals and they had great passion for the team, the city, their families and their friends."

"We were fortunate to have Don and Glenn for as long as we did," Banks added, "because the keystone combination is the heart."

Beckert and Kessinger both joined the Cubs fulltime in 1965, when Chicago posted a 72-90 mark. That was followed by an embarrassing 59-103 record in 1966.

Beginning in 1967, though, under the leadership of veteran manager Leo Durocher, things began to fall into place as the Cubs fielded one of the most-talented teams in the National League. Durocher had Banks at first, Beckert at second, Kessinger at short and Ron Santo at third. The outfield featured regulars Billy Williams and Adolfo Phillips. Catcher Randy Hundley managed a pitching staff that included Ferguson Jenkins (20-13), Rich Nye (13-10) and Joe Niekro (10-7).

In 1967 and 1968, the Cubs produced back-to-back third-place finishes in the 10-team National League. Chicago fans were growing excited. Hopes were high for 1969, when the NL split into two six-team divisions due to expansion—the East and the West.

The Cubs broke out of the gate fast in 1969, winning 11 of their first 12. By late July, the Cubs were seven games ahead of the Mets in the NL-East.

Chicago still featured one of the league's most-potent lineups from top to bottom, led by Santo (.289 average, 29 homers, 123 RBIs), Banks (.253, 23, 106), and outfielders Williams (.293, 21, 95) and Jim Hickman (.237, 21, 54), and catcher Hundley (.255, 18, 64).

Beckert and Kessinger batted .291 and .273, respectively, and totaled 172 double plays.

The pitching staff had a pair of 20-game winners in Jenkins and Bill Hands, a 17-game winner in fireballer Ken Holtzman, and a bull pen led by Phil Regan (12-6, 17 saves).

The excitement in Chicago, however, slowly turned into a death march.

"I don't know what it was that led to our downfall," Beckert said. "I know Leo never changed the lineup unless there was an injury. We'd come in every day and see the same lineup. He never juggled things around. Never changed the lineup. Wrigley Field didn't have lights back then, so we played a lot of day games and that wore us out."

Years later, Durocher admitted he pushed his players too hard that season. During the late-season swoon, he was quoted in the papers as saying, "Show me a good loser and I'll show you an idiot."

Statements like that didn't sit well with the Cubs.

"We began to feel the pressure," said Beckert, who picked up the nickname "Bruno" after former professional wrestler Bruno Sammartino for his habit in the minor leagues of knocking down teammates in pursuit of pop flies. "The pressure comes from trying to play hard to win."

"It's amazing how they still remember the 1969 Cubs in Chicago," Beckert said. "I'm in my mid-60s now. I hope they win one before I go."

Through 2007, the Cubs hadn't been in a World Series since 1945, when they lost to the Detroit Tigers in seven games. Their last World Series title came in 1908 when they swept Detroit in four.

Durocher, who coined the phrase "Nice guys finish last," didn't panic during his team's slump. He was accustomed to tight pennant races during his 23-year managerial career that featured stints with the Dodgers (1939-46, 1948), Giants (1948-55), Cubs (1966-72) and Astros (1972-73). After all, it was Durocher who brought the Giants back from a 13.5-game deficit in August of 1951 to catch the Dodgers on the final day of the season to force a three-game playoff, which ended with Bobby Thomson's ninth-inning "Shot Heard 'Round the World" homer off Ralph Branca. And it was Durocher who guided the Giants to a four-game sweep of the seemingly unbeatable Cleveland Indians (111 regular-season victories) in the 1954 World Series.

When Durocher was managing the Dodgers in 1941, his club outlasted the St. Louis Cardinals by 2.5 games the final week of play to capture the NL flag.

With history and "baseball smarts" on his side, Durocher was confident his Cubs could hang on in 1969 and send him to his fourth World Series as a manager.

History took a strange turn, though.

On Sept. 2, the Cubs were in first place with an impressive 84-52 record, five games ahead of manager Gil Hodges' New York Mets. The Cubs, however, stumbled badly, finishing the season 8-20, including a 1-11 mark at the start of September. During that horrifying stretch, the Cubs were outscored 31-69.

The Mets, meanwhile, rattled off 13 wins in 16 games, then won nine of their last 10 games to seal the NL-East title.

The Cubs' collapse was painful to watch. Kessinger, the lead-off batter, went 9-for-50. Beckert, who batted second, was 10-for-48. The heart of the Cubs' order also struggled, offensively, with Banks going 5-for-41, Santo 7-for-34 and Hickman 6-for-38. Only Williams hit during the streak, going 14-for-48.

Pitching-wise, Jenkins and Holtzman both went 0-3, while Hands posted a 1-2 mark,

The turning point to the Cubs' season came on Sept. 8-9 when they traveled to Shea Stadium in New York for a crucial two-game series against the Mets. The Cubs arrived in New York 2.5 games ahead of the Mets.

With a crowd of 43,274 on hand for the first game, Tommie Agee gave the Mets a 2-0 lead in the third with a two-run homer off Hands. The

Cubs came back in the sixth and tied it at 2 off Jerry Koosman on an RBI-single by Williams and a sacrifice fly by Santo.

In the bottom half of the sixth, the Mets scored the winning run—a controversial one at that—when Wayne Garrett singled home Agee in a close play at the plate. Photographs of the play show Hundley, the Cubs' catcher, applying the tag before Agee touched home.

"There's no question Agee was out," Beckert said. "Later that night, even Agee told us he was out."

Agee, the Mets' centerfielder, spent five seasons (1968-72) with the Mets and enjoyed three productive seasons, including in 1969 when he belted 26 homers, scored 97 runs, drove home 76 and batted .271. Prior to joining the Mets, he spent three years with the Indians and three with the White Sox. He passed away in 2001 at the age of 59.

With the Cubs' lead in the NL-East down to 1.5 games, 51,448 showed up the next night to watch the Mets' Tom Seaver hurl a five-hit, complete-game, 7-1 victory. During the contest, with Santo in the on-deck circle, a black cat appeared on the field. The cat crossed Santo's path, then ran in front of the Cubs' dugout.

"To tell you the truth, we realized a black cat meant bad luck, but we really didn't pay too much attention to it," Beckert recalled. "What we were thinking about was just how tough of a pitching staff the Mets had."

In addition to the 24-year-old Seaver, who was 25-7 in 1969, and the 32-year-old Koosman (17-9), the Mets also had Tug McGraw (9-3, 12 saves), Nolan Ryan (6-3), Cal Koonce (6-3, 7 saves) and Ron Taylor (9-4, 13 saves).

With the 7-1 win, the Mets stood just one-half game behind the Cubs.

"Had we gone into Shea Stadium and won those two games, I think the outcome of our season would have been different," Kessinger said.

It didn't get any better for the Cubs.

During the next week, the Mets won six straight over the Expos and Pirates, while the Cubs lost two to the Phillies and two-of-three to the Cardinals.

The race was pretty much over. The Mets concluded the season with 100 victories. The Cubs, who were in first place for 155 days, won 92.

## PAINFUL FALL FROM FIRST
*A look at the NL-East standings on Aug. 15, Sept. 2 and Sept. 15, 1969:*

| 8/15 | W | L | GB | 9/2 | W | L | GB | 9/15 | W | L | GB |
|------|----|----|-----|------|----|----|-----|------|----|----|-----|
| Cubs | 74 | 44 | — | Cubs | 84 | 52 | — | Mets | 89 | 58 | — |
| Mets | 62 | 51 | 9.5 | Mets | 77 | 55 | 5.0 | Cubs | 85 | 63 | 4.5 |

New York went on to sweep the Braves in three games in the NL playoffs, then took down the Baltimore Orioles in five World Series game.

"The Mets just had the best team in baseball that year," Beckert said. "Man, it must have been tough being a (Cubs) fan that season."

"It wasn't meant to be," said Banks, who never played minor league ball, jumping straight from the Kansas City Monarchs of the Negro League to the Cubs at the tail end of the 1953 season. "Certain things are meant and some aren't. No matter how hard you try, it's just not meant to be."

"We had the players, we had the manager, we had a nice stadium, a great city and great fans, but it just wasn't meant to be. You have to let it go."

"You don't have to win to be a winner," Banks concluded.

"You have to give those Mets credit," Beckert said. "They had a remarkable team. We couldn't do too much with them. Everything they did was right. We cooled off at the wrong time and they got hot at the right time. Our collapse was a team effort."

During the season, the Cubs went 8-10 against the Mets.

"That season was the best of times and the worst of times," said Kessinger, who had a streak of 54 errorless games that year. "I never had more fun that season, except at the end."

"I do think we had the best team in baseball (in 1969). Our greatest regret was we couldn't bring a pennant to our fans and Chicago."

"Had we held on and won in 1969, I think we could have won a couple more pennants," Kessinger concluded.

The Cubs had a legitimate shot at the 1970 division title, but a 14-14 record in September wasn't good enough to catch the Pirates, who went 18-10, including victories in 13 of their final 18 contests, to finish five games ahead in the National League East.

Chicago managed to finish third behind Pittsburgh in the NL East in 1971 after a slow start in April and May, and a weak finish in September.

The Cubs finished second behind the Pirates in 1972, again getting off to a slow start. With the team sitting at 46-44 in late July, Durocher was fired as manager and replaced by Whitey Lockman, who guided the club to a 39-26 mark the rest of the way.

Durocher had a winning record with every club he managed, including a 535-526 mark with the Cubs. Overall, he won 2,008 games and lost 1,709 for a winning percentage of .540. His lone World Series title in three attempts as a manager came with the Giants in 1954 against the Indians.

Durocher had a 17-year playing career (.247 batting average), primarily as a shortstop. He was a member of two World Series championship teams as a player ——- the 1928 Yankees and the 1934 Cardinals. He spent only two seasons with the Yankees (1928-29) because he had constant run-ins with Babe Ruth, who nicknamed him "The All-American Out." As his career went on, both as a player, coach and manager, he picked up the name "Leo the Lip" for his constant jockeying from the bench. He was inducted into the Hall of Fame in 1994, three years following his death at the age of 86.

When he managed a half season in Brooklyn before being fired in 1948, Durocher played a major role in erasing the color line in baseball by making it perfectly clear to his players that Jackie Robinson would be a member of the Dodgers and that he wouldn't tolerate any dissent. Durocher admired Robinson, who in 1947 became the first black player to play in the major leagues. Durocher would later have an impact on another young black player, Willie Mays, in the early 1950s when he was with the Giants.

Following the 1972 season, the Cubs and their fans suffered through 11 straight losing seasons under seven different managers. In 1984, under the leadership of Jim Frey, Chicago won the NL-East with an impressive 96-65 record. The Cubs, though, lost to San Diego in the NL playoffs, 3 games to 2. The magic was short-lived as the Cubs stumbled to 77-84 in 1985 and 70-90 in 1986 under Frey, John Vukovich and Gene Michael.

Despite the club's ups and downs during their nine productive seasons together, Beckert and Kessinger played steady baseball through the 1973 season.

Beckert, who originally signed with Boston as an amateur free agent in 1962 because he liked Fenway Park, but months later was drafted by the Cubs, was a shortstop by trade, but a tragedy forced him to move to second.

Ken Hubbs was the Cubs' second baseman of the future. He played two solid seasons (1962-63) for Chicago and was named the National League's Rookie of the Year with a .260 batting average. The 20-year-old also became the first rookie in baseball history to win a Gold Glove that 1962 season, at one point playing 78 consecutive errorless games. Hubbs, a California native, was also among the National League leaders in at-bats, singles, triples and sacrifice hits in 1962. His offensive numbers dropped slightly in 1963, but the Cubs weren't concerned.

Hubbs was deathly afraid of flying, so he took flying lessons after the 1963 season with the hope that would overcome his fear. Two weeks after earning his pilot's license, he died in a plane crash in Provo, Utah. The crash was attributed to poor weather conditions.

"Losing Kenny was just terrible," Beckert said. "It's strange how things worked out, though. Leo (Durocher) moved me to second."

The Hall of Famer Banks, meanwhile, had already moved to first in 1962 after spending his first eight seasons at short (1954-61). Andre Rogers took over at short for the 1962-63-64 seasons, with Jimmy Stewart manning second in 1964.

"Moving to first base was not a big issue for me," Banks said. "You move, but the spirit goes with you. Moving to first, the spirit was moving within me. You develop a passion for it and do it."

During those eight full seasons at shortstop, Banks pounded out 296 homers, drove in 752 runs, batted above .285 five times and was involved in 715 double plays. He is, by far, the most popular Cub in history— the reason for his nickname "Mr. Cub." He also became well known for his popular phrase, "Let's play two."

Banks was a two-time National League Most Valuable Player (1958 and 1959) and is a member of the exclusive 500-Home Run Club with 512.

In 1965, Beckert took over at second and Kessinger became the regular shortstop. Kessinger, who was attending the University of Mississippi, signed with the Cubs in 1964 for a $25,000 bonus.

At Mississippi, Kessinger was an All-American baseball and basketball player in 1964. An All-Southeastern Conference basketball selection three times (1962-64), he ranks ninth in Ole Miss scoring with 1,553 points.

"I felt relieved that I wasn't the guy who replaced a legend at short," Kessinger said of Banks. "Andre (Rogers) was between me and Ernie."

Rogers spent 11 seasons (1957-67) in the majors with the Giants, Cubs and Pirates. He was a .249 career hitter and his fielding was suspect as his .956 percentage at short indicates.

During their nine years together with the Cubs, Beckert and Kessinger totaled 1,536 double plays—794 for Kessinger, 742 for Beckert. Their best season came in 1968 when they totaled 204.

Beckert, who played in the shadows of Pittsburgh's Bill Mazeroski during his early years and Cincinnati's Joe Morgan in his later years, was second in the National League in assists from 1966 to 1969. In 1971, he won a Gold Glove.

Kessinger actually led the National League in errors his first season (28), but then established himself as a six-time All-Star and two-time Gold Glove winner (1969 and 1970). He led National League shortstops in assists and double plays four times, and in putouts three. He also had an amazing streak of 500-plus assists for six consecutive seasons (1968-73).

"We were fortunate to play together as long as we did," Kessinger said. "We played well together and had a great friendly situation."

The entire Cubs' infield played well together for nine years. From 1965 to 1970, the infield had Banks, Beckert, Kessinger and Santo. From 1971 to 1973, the Cubs started Hickman at first, Beckert, Kessinger and Santo. Banks played in 39 games in 1971, then retired.

"We all had good communications with each other," Beckert said. "Especially Don and myself. Don was religious and everything was in order. I was a bit wild, but we worked hard together, talked to each other often. If we had problems, we'd talk together to work them out, just like any other business."

"When I was traded to San Diego in 1974, I played with a shortstop (Enzo Hernandez) who couldn't speak English and I couldn't speak Spanish," Beckert added with a laugh. "Now that was interesting. That shows you how important communication is."

Kessinger said what made he and Beckert a "reliable" double-play combination was the fact they spent hours taking infield practice together.

"Glenn and I would spend hours fielding balls and tossing the ball to each other in the exact same spot on every play," Kessinger said. "Your double-play partner needs to know where the ball is coming. Throwing the ball in a general area isn't good enough. It has to be in the same spot every time."

"Glenn and I knew exactly where we wanted the ball. All that practice paid off."

Beckert caught the baseball bug as a child when his father used to take him to old Forbes Field in Pittsburgh to see the Pirates play.

"When the Cubs came to town, I remember seeing Ernie (Banks) playing short," Beckert recalled. "I never imagined one day I'd be playing second base for the Cubs next to Ernie, who was playing first base at the time. That was quite a thrill."

"I was really fortunate to play in the major leagues," Beckert continued. "I thought there were better players in the majors. Leo (Durocher) told Don that if we were going to make it in the majors, we'd have to become switch-hitters, which Don was and I wasn't, so I was fortunate."

"I really admired (Pittsburgh second baseman) Bill Mazeroski, who taught me many things. There was no one better at second," said Beckert. "And (former Pittsburgh shortstop) Dick Groat helped me with my hitting."

Beckert, who attended Allegheny College in Meadville, Pa., completed his 11-year major league career with a batting average of .283 and a fielding percentage of .973. He was a contact hitter as he struck out just once every 21.5 at-bat. In comparison, perennial All-Star shortstop and future Hall of Famer Derek Jeter of the New York Yankees, a .317 career hitter, had struck out once every 5.7 plate appearance through the 2006 season.

Beckert's final two major league seasons (1974-75) with the San Diego Padres saw him appear in 73 total games due to knee and heel injuries.

Before retiring, Beckert set a "not-so-distinguishing" major league record that stood by itself until 1998 when Todd Helton of Colorado tied it. On Sept. 16, 1972 at Wrigley Field, Beckert not only went 0-for-6 against the Mets, but he left a record 12 runners stranded on base. The Cubs won the game, 18-5.

Helton tied Beckert's record in a game played on April 11, 1998 at Coors Field in Colorado against Cincinnati. Helton's Rockies lost, 12-5, but he did manage to drive in one run with a sacrifice fly.

Beckert, who lives in Englewood, Fla., considers himself retired, although he is still a member of the Chicago Board of Trade.

Kessinger, who runs a successful real estate business in the Chicago area, was "a special person," according to Banks.

"Don brought to our team the Fellowship of Christian Athletes, which held us together," Banks said. "It wasn't Leo or anyone else. It was Don Kessinger. He held the team together. He had tremendous spirit."

"Bobby Richardson (of the Yankees) was that way," Banks continued. "Cal Ripken (Orioles) was that way. Pee Wee Reese and Jackie Robinson (Dodgers) were both that way."

"It seems like the second baseman or shortstop is a very spiritual guy....the guy who holds the team together," Banks said. "One or both tend to hold the team together. They are the spirit."

"When you talk about success, you talk about spirit. It holds the team together on the field and off the field. Today, a lot of people don't stay together for a long time. There's no loyalty."

Kessinger said he never set out to be a spiritual leader.

"What Ernie said is very humbling," Kessinger said. "The Lord has been good to Don Kessinger. He gives each of us abilities. I'm grateful he gave me the opportunity to play baseball and with friends and in Chicago in front of great fans. My relationship with the Lord has been and is a great part of my life."

"Leaders are born," Kessinger continued. "You lead by example. The way to get people to follow you is to do the best you can everyday. Use what you have and use it to the fullest everyday."

Kessinger was traded prior to the 1976 season to St. Louis, where he played both second and short while accounting for 105 double plays. He was then traded to the Chicago White Sox midway through the 1977 season. He had a fairly productive 1978 season, hitting .255 while adding 62 double plays.

In 1979, his 16th in the majors, he became player-manager of the White Sox. He replaced Larry Doby, the second black person to hold a managerial job in the major leagues. Frank Robinson was the first in 1975 with Cleveland.

Kessinger's Sox posted a 46-60 record. He didn't have a great deal to work with as Sox owner Bill Veeck was producing more of a circus at the time with players wearing old-fashioned black uniforms and short pants.

Following the 1979 season, he retired with a .252 batting average and 1,932 hits. Through the 2006 season, he is only one of four Cubs to collect six hits in a game, that coming on June 17, 1971 in a 7-6 win over St. Louis. The other three are Frank Demaree (1937), Bill Madlock (1975) and Jose Cardenal (1976).

Tony LaRussa, who replaced Kessinger, enjoyed some success during his seven full seasons as manager of the White Sox. In 1983, he guided Chicago to the AL-West title with a 99-63 mark, but lost to Baltimore in the AL Championship Series. Baltimore went on to beat Philadelphia in the World Series.

LaRussa went on to enjoy great success managing Oakland (1986-95) and St. Louis (1996-present) with five pennants and a pair of World Series crowns, those coming in 1989 with the Athletics and 2006 with the Cardinals. Through 2007, he was just one of two managers to win World Series championships in both leagues. The first was Sparky Anderson, who won Series titles with the Cincinnati Reds in 1975 and 1976, and the Detroit Tigers in 1984.

Kessinger returned to the University of Mississippi to coach the school's baseball team from 1991 to 1996, compiling a 185-153 record.

As far as the Cubs were concerned, they've given their fans false hopes on several occasions, first in 1989 when they won the National League East title, only to lose to San Francisco in the NL Championship Series. In 1998, they were swept by Atlanta in the NL Division Series.

In 2003, they outlasted Atlanta in five games in the NL Division Series, then dropped a heartbreaking seven-game series to Florida in the NL Championship Series. The Cubs grabbed a 3-1 NLCS lead, dropped Game 5, then appeared headed for the National League pennant and their first World Series in 59 years until the club "pulled a 1969" and totally collapsed.

With the Cubs ahead, 3-0, after seven innings in Game 6 at Wrigley Field, the Marlins scored eight times in the top of the eighth.

Two plays enabled the Marlins to keep their inning alive: left fielder Moises Alou appeared to have a foul ball in the left field stands on the radar screen, but fan Steve Bartman, along with several others, prevented him from making the catch; the second was a costly error by shortstop Alex Gonzalez on a potential, inning-ending double-play ball hit by Miguel

Cabrera. So instead of limiting the Marlins to one run, the Cubs allowed Florida to put up an eight spot for an 8-3 win.

Bartman, the fan? He was simply a scapegoat. The Cubs lost focus in the eighth inning and failed to overcome adversity.

Florida won Game 7 by a 9-6 count, then defeated the New York Yankees in six games in the World Series.

In 2007, Chicago hoped to get a fresh start with new manager Lou Piniella, who has now been a skipper for 20 seasons with the Yankees, Reds, Mariners, Devil Rays and Cubs. His 1990 Reds won the World Series with a four-game sweep of Oakland, while his 2001 Mariners won a major-league-record 116 games. He spent 19 years in the majors as a player, mostly with the Royals and Yankees, and compiled a lifetime batting average of .291. He was a member of two World Series championship teams: the 1977 and 1978 Yankees.

Player-wise, the Cubs were active in the free-agent market following the 2006 season, which saw the team finish 66-96 under former manager Dusty Baker. It paid off as the Cubs won the NL's Central Division with an 85-77 mark. The club's biggest signee was five-time All-Star outfielder Alfonso Soriano, who became just the fourth player in baseball history to produce a 40-40 season (46 homers and 41 stolen bases) to go along with his .277 average in 2006 while with Washington. He was also a 40-40-40 man as he pounded out 41 doubles. In 2007 with the Cubs, he hit .299 with 33 homers and 70 RBIs.

The Cubs also re-signed third baseman Aramis Ramirez, who posted big numbers in 2006 (.291, 38, 119). In 2007, his average jumped to .310 to go along with his 26 HRs and 101 RBIs. First baseman Derrek Lee, who broke his wrist and appeared in just 50 games in 2006, had a solid 2007 with a .317 average, 22 homers and 82 RBIs.

Pitching-wise, Carlos Zambrano won 18, Ted Lilly 15, Jason Marquis 12 and Rich Hill 11. Ryan Dempster led the bull pen staff with 28 saves.

In the division playoffs, the Cubs fell in three games to Arizona, but 2007 served as a stepping stone for a successful 2008.

DEFENSE BY THE NUMBERS

A look at the individual fielding statistics of Glenn Beckert and Don Kessinger during the time period they played together at their primary positions, second base and shortstop (PO – putouts; AST – assists; E – errors; DP – double plays; PCT. – fielding percentage):

| | GLENN BECKERT, 2B | | | | | DON KESSINGER, SS | | | | |
|---|---|---|---|---|---|---|---|---|---|---|
| YEAR | PO | AST | E | DP | PCT. | PO | AST | E | DP | PCT. |
| 1965 | 326 | 494 | 23 | 101 | .973 | 176 | 338 | 28 | 69 | .948 |
| 1966 | 373 | 402 | 24 | 89 | .970 | 202 | 474 | 35 | 68 | .951 |
| 1967 | 327 | 422 | 25 | 89 | .968 | 215 | 457 | 19 | 77 | .973 |
| 1968 | 356 | 461 | 19 | 107 | .977 | 263 | 573 | 33 | 97 | .962 |
| 1969 | 262 | 401 | 24 | 71 | .965 | 266 | 542 | 20 | 101 | .976 |
| 1970 | 302 | 412 | 22 | 88 | .970 | 257 | 501 | 22 | 86 | .972 |
| 1971 | 275 | 382 | 9 | 76 | .986 | 263 | 512 | 27 | 97 | .966 |
| 1972 | 256 | 396 | 16 | 71 | .976 | 259 | 504 | 29 | 90 | .965 |
| 1973 | 163 | 262 | 7 | 50 | .984 | 274 | 526 | 30 | 109 | .964 |
| Totals | 2,640 | 3,632 | 169 | 742 | .974 | 2,175 | 4,427 | 243 | 794 | .964 |

**NOTE:** *Although a large majority of the seasonal and career double plays listed above involved the two keystone partners as a unit playing together at the same time during the noted time period, some were obviously not. The difference is due to many factors, including the number of games played, late-inning substitutions, injuries, a position change, DPs converted independent of each other and, in some cases, games missed due to military service.*

> When Joe Morgan was traded to Cincinnati, Sparky Anderson told team president Bob Howsan he had just given the Reds the pennant "on a silver platter."

## CHAPTER ELEVEN
# 2B JOE MORGAN & SS DAVE CONCEPCION, CINCINNATI REDS, 1972-79

**NAME:** Joe Leonard Morgan

**Nickname:** Little Joe, The Little General

**Born:** September 19, 1943, Bonham, Texas

**Died:** Still throwing as of October 1, 2007

**Batted/threw:** Left/right

**Height/weight:** 5-feet-7, 160 pounds

**Major league seasons:** 22 (Houston, 1963-71, 1980; Cincinnati, 1972-79; San Francisco, 1981-82; Philadelphia, 1983; Oakland, 1984)

**Major league debut:** Sept. 21, 1963 (Phillies 4, **Astros 3**)

**Final major league game:** Sept. 30, 1984 (**Athletics 8**, Royals 2)

**Position:** Second base

**Career games:** 2,649

**Career double plays:** 1,505

**DPs with Reds at second base (1972-79):** 694

**Career errors:** 245

**Career assists:** 6,969

**Career putouts:** 5,758

**Career fielding percentage:** .981

**Gold Gloves:** 5

**All-Star:** 10 times

**World Series:** 2-2

**Career batting average:** .271

**Turning two:** In 303 games during the 1972 and 1973 seasons, Morgan committed just 17 errors.

**Hall of Fame:** Class of 1990.

Opposing players considered Reds shortstop Dave Concepcion a "hot dog" on the field, so it was common to hear "dog barks" coming out of the rival team's dugout.

**NAME: David Ismael Concepcion**

Nickname: Davey

Born: June 17, 1948, Maracay, Venezuela

Died: Still throwing as of October 1, 2007

Batted/threw: Right/right

Height/weight: 6-feet-1, 180 pounds.

Major league seasons: 19 (Cincinnati, 1970-88)

Major league debut: April 6, 1970 (**Reds 5,** Expos 1)

Final major league game: Sept. 5, 1988 (Astros 3, **Reds 0**)

Position: Shortstop (also second base: 130 games; third base: 120; first base: 62)

Career games: 2,488

Career double-plays: 1,390

DPs with Reds at shortstop (1972-79): 700

Career assists: 7,024

Career putouts: 4,245

Career errors: 326

Career fielding percentage: .972

Gold Gloves: 5

All-Star: 9 times

World Series: 2-2

Career batting average: .267

Turning two: In five National League Championship Series, Concepcion batted .351 in 34 games. He also scored the 1,000,001$^{st}$ run in baseball history in 1975.

Hall of Fame: No

When a young Major League Baseball player has the benefit of being tutored by three future Hall of Famers, chances are he'll become a pretty good player himself.

That young player was second baseman Joe Morgan of the Houston Astros. Today, he's a member of Baseball's Hall of Fame.

The three future Hall of Famers were longtime Chicago White Sox second baseman Nellie Fox, Pittsburgh second baseball Bill Mazeroski and outfielder-first baseman Willie Stargell, also of Pittsburgh.

"I cannot emphasize enough what Nellie and these other older players gave to me," Morgan once said. "From them, I learned not only technique, but a kind of artistry that only comes with a real love of the game."

"Catch the ball with two hands, they emphasized. 'Feel the ball,' they'd say, 'Feel the ball.' Nellie would emphasize this over and over again," Morgan said, according to Baseball-Almanac.com.

Fox, who was traded to the Colt .45s from the White Sox after the 1963 season following a brilliant 14-year career in Chicago, also told Morgan he'd be better off using a smaller glove at second base.

"At the beginning, Joe was a rookie just trying to learn the game," recalled outfielder Jimmy Wynn, who was Morgan's close friend and teammate in Houston from 1963-71. "When Joe first started at second base, he used a glove similar to an outfielder's glove. When the .45s got Nellie Fox, Nellie spent all kinds of time with Joe."

"Nellie told Joe that with a smaller glove, he'd get the ball out of his glove more quickly and, as a result, have a better chance of making the double play," Wynn said. "Nellie was one of the best and Joe knew it, so he listened to Nellie."

Offensively, it was Fox who suggested to the left-handed hitting Morgan that he flap his left arm like a chicken while at the plate. This, Fox insisted, would work as a timing mechanism. Morgan tried it, liked it, stuck with it and it became his trademark.

When it came to turning a double play, it was Stargell who urged Morgan to watch Mazeroski take infield practice at second base.

"Joe studied the play of Mazeroski a lot," Wynn recalled. "Maz was the best at that time, so what better person to look at and copy? Maz made it look so easy and Joe was so impressed. Maz would simply step across the (second base) bag and make the throw to first."

"He (Mazeroski) was, and remains, the unchallenged king of the DP," Morgan explains in his book, *"Baseball For Dummies."* (1)

"Like Maz, I would catch my shortstop's throw out in front of my body. While crossing second, I would step on the center of the bag with my left foot. Then I would pivot and throw from wherever I caught the ball," Morgan writes. "If you step on the center of the bag, your motion continues uninterrupted. This also helps build some momentum behind your throw to first base." (1)

Morgan's uncanny ability to "turn two" was the result of hours of practice. That practice eventually made him half of baseball's finest keystone combination of the 1970s, teaming with shortstop Dave Concepcion in Cincinnati from 1972 through 1979.

In their first season together, they totaled 167 double plays and just 26 errors (only eight by Morgan). In their eight seasons playing side-by-side, Morgan (694) and Concepcion (700) were involved in 1,394 DPs. The also won five Gold Gloves apiece.

From Stargell, Morgan learned that the game of baseball was supposed to be fun. Stargell often said, "The man says, 'Play Ball,' not 'Work Ball.'"

Stargell became Morgan's role model, which is why the young second baseman chose to change his uniform number from 18 to 8, the same number as the Pirate superstar. The two remained close friends until Stargell's death at the age of 61 in 2001.

Morgan was signed by the Colt .45s in 1962 as an amateur free agent. He played in only 18 major league games in 1963 and 1964 before winning the starting second base job away from his mentor, Fox, in 1965.

Even at the age of 21, Wynn knew there was something special about Morgan.

"As a young player, Joe had the knowledge of baseball," said Wynn, who spent 11 seasons in Houston and 15 overall, hitting a career .250 with 291 homers. "As he got older, that knowledge became more profound."

"Joe could also run, field and play second with the best of them," Wynn said. "He could hit and hit with power. It was obvious he had a bright future."

Morgan had several keystone partners with the young Colt .45s, who changed their name to "Astros" in 1965: Bob Lillis (1965), Sonny Jackson (1966-67), Denis Menke (1969-70) and Roger Metzger (1971).

As Morgan became a better player, so did the young Astros, who finished the 1969 season—their eighth in the league—with a record of 81-81 under manager Harry Walker. Morgan batted only .236, but he did score 94 runs, hit 15 homers and drew 110 base-on-balls. Defensively, he committed only 18 errors for a fielding percentage of .972 and turned 79 double plays with Menke as his keystone mate.

In 1970 and 1971, the Astros produced back-to-back 79-83 records, serving notice that they were no longer pushovers in the National League. Morgan's performance at the plate those two seasons improved to .268 and .256.

With the Astros gaining ground, they pulled off a surprising trade with the Cincinnati Reds after the 1971 season. Houston sent Morgan, outfielders Ed Armbrister and Cesar Geronimo, and pitcher Jack Billingham to Cincinnati in exchange for first baseman Lee May, and infielders Tommy Helms and Jimmy Stewart.

"Alex Grammas, my coach in Cincinnati, said if we could get Joe, we'd be set," explained then-Cincinnati manager Sparky Anderson. "The day the trade was announced (Nov. 29, 1971), I walked over to our team president, Bob Howsan (1967-78 and 1983-84), and said he had just given us the pennant on a silver platter."

"Joe really didn't want to leave because he had so many friends in Houston," Wynn said. "I was disappointed he got traded because we had a nucleus of a good team and we were very close friends. We were coming together as a team. We thought we had a chance to win our division (NL-West)."

"Someone got the idea to trade Joe to Cincinnati and he became what I thought he would be—a superstar," Wynn said. "But the trade was good for Joe. Look what happened to him (in Cincinnati). It all worked out well. He became a Hall of Famer."

Morgan, who was replacing the traded Helms at second, was going to a Cincinnati team that had won 102 games in 1970 under first-year manager Anderson, but lost to Baltimore in five World Series games. In 1971, the team stumbled to 79-83 and a fifth-place finish in the National League's West Division.

After the Reds' disappointing 1971 season, they believed Morgan and Billingham were the missing ingredients to challenge for division titles throughout the 1970s.

"Getting Joe was a tremendous boost to our team," said Anderson, who managed the Reds to 1,450 victories in nine seasons and World Series titles in 1975 and 1976. "Morgan's greatest asset was his abilities, but the thing that stood out was his intelligence."

"In my 26 years of managing, he is the only player I never gave a sign to," Anderson said. "When he first joined us, I set him down and said, 'I hear you're so smart. The only time you'll get a sign from me is when you ask for one.' Joe never needed a sign because he understood the game inside and out. That's why he had more than 600 stolen bases (actually 689) in his career."

Morgan's batting average took a dramatic hike when he joined the Reds. A .250-.260 hitter in Houston, Morgan climbed to the .290-300 range, including a career-high .327 in 1975. In four of his eight seasons in Cincinnati, he hit 20 or more homers.

"Ted Kluszewski noticed that Joe was generating his power during the last half of his swing," Anderson explained. "Ted worked with Joe on that and, as a result, he started hitting more homers. If Joe had a flaw, he'd go straight to Ted."

Kluszewski was on the Reds' coaching staff from 1970-78. He spent 14 season in the majors, 11 with the Reds (1947-57) when he was considered one of the game's top sluggers. During his stay with the Reds, he hit more than 35 homers four times and drove in more than 100 runs five times. In 1959 with the Chicago White Sox, he hit a pair of homers in the first game of the World Series against the Los Angeles Dodgers.

At the same time Morgan was making a name for himself in Cincinnati, the club was breaking in a scrawny, 22-year-old shortstop by the name of Davey Concepcion, who signed with the club as a pitcher in 1967. He was moved to shortstop in the minors, allowing him to follow in the footsteps of his childhood heroes who were also from Venezuela, Chico Carrasquel and Luis Aparicio, both of the White Sox.

Anderson brought Concepcion along slowly, playing him sparingly in 1970 and 1971 behind Woody Woodward. Concepcion was a workhorse, always fielding at least 80 grounders before every game.

In 1972, Morgan and Concepcion, who wore the unlucky No. 13 on his jersey, started at second and short, respectively. It was a keystone combination that would play together for eight seasons.

"Davey could do things that no other shortstop could do," Anderson said. "He could throw from anyplace on the field. He had tremendous range. He developed going deep into the hole and getting the ball to first on a skip."

"Davey just loved fielding groundballs. Everything came so natural to him. He had great rhythm."

That rhythm and timing were important in turning two.

"Davey Concepcion liked to take the throw on the outfield side of second," Morgan writes in "*Baseball for Dummies.*" "So I would give it to him chest-high (the easiest ball to handle and throw while on the move) on the bag's outside edge. I've also played with some shortstops who wanted my toss on the inside of the bag. However, no matter what your shortstop prefers, you shouldn't wait to make the ideal throw. If you're off-balance, get the ball to your partner any way you can and let him make the adjustment. If your double-play partner hasn't reached the bag, feed the ball to him wherever he is. Never make him wait for the ball or you can disrupt his timing."

"The double play is the greatest play in baseball," Morgan writes. "When you turn a double play in a crucial situation, you immediately become the most popular guy on your club. Nothing short of a win is more pleasing to a fielder than getting two outs with one ball." (1)

One pitcher who benefited from the Reds' classic keystone combo was Billingham, who won 145 games during a 13-year career, including 87 victories in six years in Cincinnati.

"Being a sinkerball pitcher made it more comfortable for me having Joe and Davey behind me," said Billingham, who had back-to-back 19-win seasons in 1973 and 1974. "Without Joe and Davey, my record wouldn't have been as good as it was. It helped my game."

"In my 13 years (1968-80), Davey was the best shortstop I saw," Billingham continued. "Joe was a better overall player, but I think they made each other a little bit better."

"Concepcion had great range and a great arm," said former Houston manager Bill Virdon (1975-82), who won division crowns in 1972 with Pittsburgh and 1980 with Houston. "Davey just did his job consistently well everyday. Nothing flashy. He made the tough plays look routine."

"Joe was limited somewhat, but he didn't make mistakes," Virdon said. "His arm was so-so, but he was sure handed and he could hit a ton. His hitting made him a second baseman."

"They weren't like (Bill) Mazeroski or (Gene) Alley (of Pittsburgh), but fundamentally, they were solid," said Chicago Cub shortstop Don Kessinger, who formed a classic DP combination with Glenn Beckert (1965-73).

"Joe did so many things right," Kessinger said. "Plus he was such a great offensive player. Concepcion was a one-handed type player who made tough plays look routine."

"Joe and Dave formed an excellent double-play combination," said Jerome Holtzman, Major League Baseball's official historian who covered the game for 60 years for the *Chicago Tribune* and *Chicago Sun Times.*

"Joe was no (Bill) Mazeroski, but he was a good, all-around player. Concepcion was no (Luis) Aparicio, but he had good range at short and got the job done."

Concepcion has always believed that shortstops are born. "You can't learn it," he has preached over the years. "I think being able to play the infield, especially shortstop, is something you are born with."

Opposing players considered the easy-going Concepcion a "hot dog" on the field, especially after the shortstop would make a spectacular play, so it was common to hear "dog barks" coming out of the rival team's dugout.

"They had the knack and instincts to play their positions well and they worked hard to keep those things," said Billingham, who posted a 2-0 record in World Series play for the Reds. "They worked well together and they became two of the top middle infielders in the game."

They worked so well together that they are just one of nine keystone combinations to win Gold Glove Awards in the same season, doing so a record-tying four consecutive years (1974-77).

## GOLD GLOVE KEYSTONE COMBINATIONS

| | |
|---|---|
| 2 | Luis Aparicio and Nellie Fox, White Sox, 1959-60 |
| 2 | Gene Alley and Bill Mazeroski, Pirates, 1966-67 |
| 1 | Jim Fregosi and Bobby Knoop, Angels, 1967 |
| 2 | Mark Belanger and Dave Johnson, Orioles, 1969, 1971 |
| 4 | Mark Belanger and Bobby Grich, Orioles, 1973-76 |
| 4 | Dave Concepcion and Joe Morgan, Reds, 1974-77 |
| 2 | Alan Trammell and Lou Whitaker, Tigers, 1983-84 |
| 3 | Omar Vizquel and Roberto Alomar, Indians, 1999-2001 |
| 1 | Edgar Renteria and Fernando Vina, Cardinals, 2002 |

**Note:** The baseball glove manufacturer *Rawlings* invented the award in 1957 to honor the best-fielding players at their positions in the American and National leagues. Each league has three outfielders, as opposed to a left fielder, center fielder and right fielder.

Although they enjoyed great success as a keystone combination, Morgan and Concepcion weren't especially close like a Robinson-Reese of the Dodgers or a Fox-Aparicio of the White Sox or a Richardson-Kubek of the Yankees. Concepcion was more laid back, while Morgan was more intense. They went about their business seriously on the diamond, then went their separate ways off the field.

With Morgan and Concepcion in place up the middle of the Cincinnati defense, the 1972 Reds won the National League West by 10.5 games over the up-and-coming Astros. The Reds were solid at every position, including catcher Johnny Bench, first baseman Tony Perez, and out-fielders Pete Rose and Bobby Tolan, plus a pitching staff that featured Gary Nolan (15 wins) and Ross Grimsley (14).

Anderson's Reds outlasted Pittsburgh in a dramatic five-game National League Championship Series in which the winning run scored on a wild pitch. In the bottom of the ninth inning of the fifth-and-deciding game, the Pirates held a 3-2 lead, but Bench quickly tied it with a lead-off homer off relief pitcher Dave Giusti. Following back-to-back singles by Perez and Denis Menke, the Pirates replaced Giusti with flame-thrower Bob Moose. George Foster, running for Perez, advanced to third on a deep fly ball. With pinch-hitter Hal McRae at the plate and the count 1 ball and 2 strikes, Moose uncorked a wild pitch in the dirt to score Foster from third to give the Reds the NL flag.

In the World Series against Oakland, six of the seven games were decided by one run. Gene Tenace's two-run double in the sixth inning of Game 7 proved to be the difference in Oakland's 3-2 win and world championship, the first of three straight for the Athletics.

In 1973, the Reds won another National League Western Division title with a 99-63 record. Morgan batted .290 with 26 homers, 82 runs-batted-in, 111 walks and 116 runs scored. Concepcion, who was named team captain, found his stroke with a .287 average. Pitching-wise, Billingham won 19 and Don Gullett 18.

The Reds lost to the New York Mets (82-79) in the National League playoffs in five games. This series was marred by a bench-clearing brawl and a near forfeit due to the riotous behavior of Shea Stadium fans during a "wrestling" match at second base between base runner Rose and Mets shortstop Bud Harrelson. Both benches participated in the Game 3 melee that lasted nearly 10 minutes. Anderson pulled his team off the field until order was restored. No one knows why the tussle started, but the Mets won the game, 9-2, and the series, then lost to Oakland in seven in the World Series.

In 1974, the Reds won 98 games, but finished four games behind the Dodgers in the NL-West to miss the playoffs. The 98 wins were the second most in all of baseball that season.

Anderson's club hit its stride and was unbeatable in 1975 and 1976. The Reds were called "The Big Red Machine" as they won National League pennants in 1975 and 1976 with 108 and 102 regular-season victories, respectively. Anderson had by far the best team in baseball with Bench, Perez, Morgan, Rose and Concepcion in the infield; Cesar Geronimo,

Foster and Ken Griffey in the outfield; and starting pitchers Billingham, Nolan and Gullett.

In 1975, they won the NL-West by a whopping 20 games over the Dodgers. At one point during the season, they won 41 of 50 games. The Reds swept the Pirates three straight in the NL playoffs, then were set to meet the American League champion Boston Red Sox in what would turn out to be one of the most-memorable and most-dramatic World Series ever played.

The Red Sox won the AL-East by 4.5 games over Baltimore with a 95-65 mark, then took down Oakland in three games in the AL playoffs, ending the Athletics' string of three straight World Series titles (1972-73-74).

Boston, managed by Darrell Johnson, had a solid lineup as well, with rookie outfielders Fred Lynn (.331, 21, 105) and Jim Rice (.309, 22, 102), a young catcher named Carlton Fisk (.331, 10, 52), and veteran captain, Carl Yastrzemski (.269, 14, 60), who had moved from left field to first base with the arrival of Rice.

Luis Tiant (18-14), Rick Wise (19-12), Bill Lee (17-9), Roger Moret (14-3) and Reggie Cleveland (13-9) formed a solid starting pitching rotation.

Red Sox fans weren't accustomed to their club playing in the Fall Classic. Prior to 1975, the Sox lost seven-game Series to St. Louis in 1946 and 1967. Prior to that, the Sox won five Series titles between 1903 and 1918. Three of those championship teams featured a young pitcher by the name of George Herman Ruth.

With Rice out of the lineup due to an arm injury, Yastrzemski was forced back to left field with the reliable Cecil Cooper (.311, 14, 44) starting at first.

The Series opened at Boston's Fenway Park where Tiant twirled a five-hit, complete-game 6-0 victory. Third baseman Rico Petrocelli had two RBIs, while shortstop Rick Burleson added three singles and an RBI.

In Game 2, the Sox held a 2-1 lead in the ninth, but then Concepcion took over. He singled home the tying run, stole second, then scored on Ken Griffey's single for a 3-2 Cincinnati victory.

The two teams traded one-run victories in Games 3 and 4. In the third contest in Cincinnati, the Reds won, 6-5, thanks to homers by Concepcion, Bench and Geronimo. In Game 4, Tiant again went the distance in a 5-4 Red Sox win.

Perez had a pair of homers and four RBIs in Game 5 to give the Reds a 6-2 victory and 3-games-to-2 lead in the Series.

The powerful Reds were anxious to return to Boston and put the Sox away in Game 6, but the rain Gods got in the way, forcing a four-day break between Games 5 and 6. This concerned Anderson, who believed his club had the momentum following his club's Game 5 win.

Game 6 at Fenway ranks as one of the greatest World Series contests played. It ran 12 innings, lasted more than four hours, ended after midnight and saw 12 pitchers take the mound, eight by the Reds.

The Red Sox jumped to a 3-0 lead in the first inning of Game 6, then found themselves trailing 6-3 in the bottom of the eighth, thanks to Griffey and Foster, who had two RBIs each against a well-rested Tiant.

Sox fans were prepared for the worse.

Enter Boston pinch-hitter Bernie Carbo, who was Cincinnati's No. 1 draft pick ahead of Bench in the 1965 player draft. The left-handed batter was named Rookie of the Year by *The Sporting News* in 1970 after hitting .310 with 23 homers and 63 RBIs, but he slumped the next two seasons, was shipped to St. Louis, then ended up in Boston in 1974. A good contact hitter with some power, Carbo was a solid fielder, but he couldn't break into Boston's starting outfield of Dwight Evans, Lynn and Rice.

Sent to the plate with two runners on and two outs, Carbo stepped into a Rawley Eastwick 0-2 pitch and walloped a towering drive into the center-field bleachers to tie the game at 6. Carbo's shot is still considered one of the most-dramatic pinch-hits in World Series history. He also became only the second player in Series history to hit two pinch-hit homers in one Fall Classic. His first came in the Sox's 6-5 loss in Game 3. Chuck Essegian of the Dodgers was the first to accomplish the feat in 1959 against the White Sox.

Morgan came close to ending the contest well after midnight in the 11th inning when he hit a deep fly to right. Sox right fielder Evans dove into the stands, caught the ball, then fired a strike to first base to double-up base-runner Griffey, who was running on the play.

Still tied at 6 in the bottom of the 12th, Fisk led off against the Reds' eighth pitcher of the night, Pat Darcy. After taking a ball, Fisk lifted a high drive down the left-field line toward the corner of Fenway Park's famed "Green Monster." As Fisk took several short steps toward first, waving his arms to the right in a heavenly effort to prevent the ball from going foul, the ball hit the foul pole for a home run and a 7-6 Red Sox win. Fisk's homer ranks among the greatest in Series history.

"I knew it was going out," a modest Fisk said afterward. "It was just a question of it being fair or foul. The wind must have carried it 15 feet toward the foul pole. I just stood there and watched. I didn't want to miss seeing it go out."

The Reds put away the Sox the next night in Game 7, overcoming a 3-0 first-inning deficit to win 4-3 on Morgan's run-scoring single in the top-half of the ninth inning.

Although Morgan hit just .259 and Concepcion .179 in the Series, both were responsible for driving home key runs, especially in Games 2 and 7.

In 1976, the Reds coasted to another NL-West crown with 102 victories, then swept three straight from Philadelphia in the National League playoffs.

Next came the Yankees (97-62), who easily won the American League East title by 10.5 over Baltimore and outlasted Kansas City in the AL playoffs, 3 games to 2, on Chris Chambliss walk-off homer in the ninth-inning of Game 5.

New York had not been in a World Series in 12 years, when it lost to St. Louis in seven games, but new owner George Steinbrenner brought in some outstanding talent with his check book and hired Billy Martin to lead the troops.

The Yankees had a strong offensive attack, led by catcher Thurman Munson (.302, 17 homers, 105 RBIs), third baseman Graig Nettles (32, 93), the first baseman Chambliss (.293, 17, 96), and outfielders Oscar Gamble (17, 57) and Roy White (14, 65).

Ed Figueroa led the pitching staff with a 19-10 record, followed by Jim "Catfish" Hunter (17-15).

The Yankee bats went silent, though, as the Reds' pitching staff held the New Yorkers to an anemic .222 average and eight runs in the four-game sweep. Bench led the Reds with a .533 batting average, a pair of homers and six RBIs, while Foster pounded out a .429 mark. Concepcion hit .357 in the Series, Morgan .333.

Pitchers Pat Zachey, Billingham, Nolan and Gullett picked up the wins for the Reds.

With their second straight Series title, the Reds became the first National League team to win back-to-back championships since the 1921-22 New York Giants defeated the cross-town Yankees. Through 2007, the Reds were the only team to sweep through the modern-day playoff system undefeated, going 7-0.

Six teams have gone through the postseason by losing just one game— the 1969 Mets, 1970 Orioles, 1984 Tigers, 1989 Athletics, 1999 Yankees and the 2005 White Sox. The feat of losing just one postseason game was especially impressive for the 1999 Yankees and 2005 White Sox since they both had to win divisional series *and* league championship series to reach the World Series.

Morgan took home plenty of hardware following the 1975 and 1976 regular seasons, including a pair of National League Most Valuable Player Awards. Over those two seasons, he averaged 110 runs, 22 homers, 102.5 runs-batted-in, 123 walks and a batting average of .323. Defensively, he committed just 24 errors and was involved in 181 double plays.

Morgan was a runaway winner of the award in 1975, collecting 21-of-23 first-place votes. Teammate Rose, who finished fifth in the voting, received the other two first-place votes. Morgan tallied 321 points, while second-place finisher Greg Luzinski of the Phillies was second with 154. In 1976, it was more of the same, as Morgan tallied 19 first-place votes and 311 points. Teammate Foster was second with five first-place votes and 221 points.

BACK-TO-BACK MVP AWARDS

A list of major league players who have won back-to-back Most Valuable Player Awards through the 2007 season, as selected by the baseball writers:

| NATIONAL LEAGUE | | AMERICAN LEAGUE | |
|---|---|---|---|
| 2001-04 | Barry Bonds, Giants | 1993-94 | Frank Thomas, White Sox |
| 1992-93 | Barry Bonds, Pirates & Giants | 1960-61 | Roger Maris, Yankees |
| 1982-83 | Dale Murphy, Braves | 1956-57 | Mickey Mantle, Yankees |
| 1980-81 | Mike Schmidt, Phillies | 1954-55 | Yogi Berra, Yankees |
| 1975-76 | Joe Morgan, Reds | 1944-45 | Hal Newhouser, Tigers |
| 1958-59 | Ernie Banks, Cubs | 1932-33 | Jimmie Foxx, Athletics |

**Note:** Bonds also won the award in 1990 with the Pirates, giving him a major-league-record seven through 2007. Tied for second with three MVP Awards are Roy Campanella (Dodgers), Joe DiMaggio (Yankees), Stan Musial (Cardinals), Berra, Mantle, Foxx and Schmidt.

Concepcion batted .274 and .281 in 1975 and 1976 during the Reds' World Series title runs, stole 54 total bases, drove in 118 runs and participated in 195 double plays.

Following back-to-back second-place finishes behind the Dodgers in the NL-West in 1977 and 1978, the Reds pulled a stunner by firing Anderson and hiring John McNamara, who produced a division title in 1979, but saw his club get swept by the Stargell-led Pittsburgh Pirates in the NL playoffs. The Pirates took the World Series crown by defeating Baltimore in seven games.

Anderson completed his nine seasons as Reds manager with 863 wins, 586 losses, two World Series titles and four National League pennants. It didn't take long for the colorful skipper to find work as he was hired by the Detroit Tigers midway through the 1979 season.

Morgan was granted free agency by the Reds following the 1979 season and signed with the team he started out with, Houston, which was managed by Virdon. Morgan, then 36, had a sub-par season, but the Astros took the National League West crown before losing to Philadelphia in the NL playoffs.

Morgan spent the 1981-82 seasons in San Francisco; 1983 in Philadelphia, where he played in another Series (a five-game loss to Baltimore), and 1984 in Oakland before retiring with 268 career homers and a batting average of .271. Through 2007, his 1,865 career walks ranked fifth behind Rickey Henderson, Babe Ruth, Ted Williams and Barry Bonds in baseball's history book.

Morgan was also a terror stealing bases, topping the 40 mark nine times. He also led the National League four times in on-base percentage and base-on-balls four times. During one stretch, his on-base percentage exceeded the .400 mark six consecutive seasons (1972-1977). He also ranked among the top five in base-on-balls 16 times.

Morgan was elected to Baseball's Hall of Fame in 1990 on the first ballot with 363 of the necessary 333 votes needed for election. "I take my vote as a salute to the little guy, the one who doesn't hit 500 home runs. I was one of the guys that did all they could to win," Morgan said at his induction ceremony, according to Baseball-Almanac.com. "I'm proud of my stats, but I don't think I ever got on for Joe Morgan. If I stole a base, it was to help us win a game, and I like to think that's what made me special."

For Concepcion, he spent his entire 19 seasons in the majors with the Reds. As the seasons passed and his arm strength grew weak, he took advantage of the Astroturf at Cincinnati's Riverfront Stadium and developed the "one-hop throw" to first base. He was a clutch performer at the plate, hitting above .300 in three of the four World Series he participated in.

Career-wise through 2007, he ranked among the top five in nine offensive categories in the Reds' record book, including hits, doubles, at-bats, sacrifice flies and stolen bases. Ironically, the player whose job was to "turn two" is the Reds' all-time leader in "grounding into double plays" with 266.

Defensively through the 2007 season, he was the Reds' all-time leader in assists (7,024) and double plays (1,390), and fifth in total chances (11,595). He's also the last National League shortstop to be involved in five double plays in one game, that coming on June 25, 1975 in a 2-0 victory at Atlanta.

Following shoulder surgery in 1982, Concepcion had several solid seasons at the plate and in the field. He is credited with grooming another fine Cincinnati shortstop, Barry Larkin, to become his successor. He spent the last seven seasons as the Reds' handyman, playing every infield position. He retired as a player and team captain after the 1988 season.

Concepcion, who attends the Reds' spring training camp in Sarasota, Fla., on a regular basis, is still popular among Cincinnati fans who believe he should be in the Hall of Fame. He's been on the ballot 13 years and on each occasion hasn't come close to election. His career offensive statistics—.267 average and 101 home runs—are comparable or better than several shortstops who are in the Hall of Fame, including the Dodgers' Pee Wee Reese and the Yankees' Phil Rizzuto. Now his biggest obstacle to the Hall are the shortstops of the past 20 years who have hit for average and power. To this day, Aparicio is the only Venezuelan in the Hall of Fame.

"I love Davey, but he's probably borderline for the Hall of Fame," Billingham said. "I'm not going to mention names, but there are players in the Hall who I feel don't belong there."

"If Davey had played for another team, he probably would have been a superstar, but when you played with the Big Red Machine with players like Bench, Perez, Rose, Morgan and Foster, maybe it was tough for Davey to get the full recognition he deserved."

Former Reds teammate and Hall of Fame first baseman Tony Perez didn't agree, once saying: "You can't separate Davey Concepcion from Pete Rose, Johnny Bench, Tony Perez, Joe Morgan or George Foster. Davey was right there with us."

Concepcion, who is a member of the Cincinnati Reds' Hall of Fame, lives in Maracay, Venezuela, where he is treated like royalty. He is referred to as "King David." His homeland has retired his No. 13 jersey, which he selected as a rookie because his mother was born in 1913. Young players wear No. 13 jerseys throughout his country in honor of their hero.

Morgan has stayed in the game as a television analyst and book author. He joined ESPN's "Sunday Night Baseball" in 1990 and has been a popular color commentator ever since. He won Sports Emmys in 1998 and 2005.

## DEFENSE BY THE NUMBERS

A look at the individual fielding statistics of Joe Morgan and Dave Concepcion during the time period they played together at their primary positions, second base and shortstop (PO – putouts; AST – assists; E – errors; DP – double plays; PCT. – fielding percentage):

| | JOE MORGAN, 2B | | | | | DAVE CONCEPCION, SS | | | | |
|--------|-------|-------|-----|------|------|-------|-------|-----|------|------|
| YEAR | PO | AST | E | DP | PCT. | PO | AST | E | DP | PCT. |
| 1972 | 370 | 436 | 8 | 92 | .990 | 194 | 365 | 18 | 75 | .969 |
| 1973 | 417 | 440 | 9 | 106 | .990 | 165 | 292 | 12 | 56 | .974 |
| 1974 | 344 | 385 | 13 | 92 | .982 | 239 | 536 | 30 | 99 | .963 |
| 1975 | 356 | 425 | 11 | 96 | .986 | 238 | 445 | 16 | 102 | .977 |
| 1976 | 342 | 335 | 13 | 85 | .981 | 304 | 506 | 27 | 93 | .968 |
| 1977 | 351 | 359 | 5 | 100 | .993 | 280 | 490 | 11 | 101 | .986 |
| 1978 | 252 | 290 | 11 | 49 | .980 | 255 | 459 | 23 | 72 | .969 |
| 1979 | 259 | 329 | 12 | 74 | .980 | 284 | 495 | 27 | 102 | .967 |
| Totals | 2,691 | 2,999 | 82 | 694 | .985 | 1,959 | 3,588 | 164 | 700 | .972 |

**NOTE:** *Although a large majority of the seasonal and career double plays listed above involved the two keystone partners as a unit playing together at the same time during the noted time period, some were obviously not. The difference is due to many factors, including the number of games played, late-inning substitutions, injuries, a position change, DPs converted independent of each other and, in some cases, games missed due to military service.*

(1) From "Baseball for Dummies," 3rd edition, by Joe Morgan; Copyright 2005 by Wiley Publishing, Inc., Indianapolis, Ind. Reproduced with permission of Wiley Publishing via Copyright Clearance Center, 222 Rosewood Drive, Danvers, Mass., 01923.

Cardinals manager
Whitey Herzog said
Tom Herr "was as steady
as a rock. He never made
mental mistakes and he never
booted a ball in the clutch."

## CHAPTER TWELVE
# 2B TOM HERR &
# SS OZZIE SMITH,
# ST. LOUIS CARDINALS,
# 1982-87

**NAME: Thomas Mitchell Herr**

Nickname: Tom

Born: April 4, 1956, Lancaster, Pa.

Died: Still throwing as of October 1, 2007

Batted/threw: Both/right

Height/weight: 6-feet, 185 pounds

Major league seasons: 13 (St. Louis, 1979-88; Minnesota, 1988; Philadelphia, 1989-90; N.Y. Mets, 1990-91; San Francisco, 1991)

Major league debut: Aug. 13, 1979 (**Cardinals 3,** Cubs 2)

Final major league game: Oct. 4, 1991 (**Giants 4,** Dodgers 1)

Position: Second base

Career games: 1,514

Career double plays: 1,001

DPs with Cardinals at second base (1982-87): 607

Career errors: 80

Career assists: 4,050

Career putouts: 2,951

Career fielding percentage: .989

Gold Gloves: 0

All-Star: 1 time

World Series: 1-2

Career batting average: .271

Turning two: Herr drove in a career-high 110 runs in 1985. He also led the National League in sacrifice flies in 1985 with 13 and in 1987 with 12.

Hall of Fame: No

**NAME: Osborne Earl Smith**
Nickname: The Wizard of Oz
Born: December 26, 1954, Mobile, Ala.
Died: Still throwing as of October 1, 2007
Batted/threw: Both/right
Height/weight: 5-feet-11, 150 pounds
Major league seasons: 19 (San Diego, 1978-81; St. Louis 1982-96)
Major league debut: April 7, 1978 (Padres 3, Giants 2)
Final major league game: Sept. 29, 1996 (Reds 6, Cardinals 3)
Position: Shortstop
Career games: 2,573
Career double plays: 1,590
DPs with Cardinals at shortstop (1982-87): 613
Career errors: 281
Career assists: 8,375
Career putouts: 4,249
Career fielding percentage: .978
Gold Gloves: 13
All-Star: 15 times
World Series: 1-2
Career batting average: .262
Turning two: Smith averaged 31 strikeouts and 30.5 stolen bases per season. He was also named a National League All-Star 12 straight seasons (1981-92).
Hall of Fame: Class of 2002

St. Louis manager Whitey Herzog obviously knew something about Ozzie Smith that no one else did when he traded for the all-field, no-hit shortstop following the 1981 season.

After appearing in just 68 minor league games, Smith was just 18 years old when he made his major league debut in 1978 with perennial cellar-dweller San Diego, where he hit .258, .211, .230 and .222. The only thing "offensive" about Smith was the fact that during his four years in San Diego he was among the leaders in sacrifice hits four times, twice leading the National League with 28 in 1978 and 23 in 1980.

Defensively, he was marvelous, turning 369 total double plays and committing an average of 21 errors per season. He earned his first Gold Glove with the Padres in 1981, the first of 13 straight that he would win.

Herzog, a savvy skipper, enjoyed great success managing the Kansas City Royals to three straight American League West championships (1976-77-78), but each time his clubs lost to the New York Yankees for the AL pennant.

 He spent eight seasons (1956-63) in the major leagues as a first base-man-outfielder with Washington, Kansas City, Baltimore and Detroit, hitting .257 with just 25 home runs.

"Baseball has been good to me since I quit trying to play it," Herzog joked many times.

He worked his way back into the majors as a third base coach for the New York Mets, then became the organization's minor league director. Because of his baseball "smarts," many observers credited Herzog for developing and producing the players who formed the "Miracle Mets," the team that went from ninth place in 1968 to victory over the Baltimore Orioles in the 1969 World Series.

Instead of power, Herzog stressed solid defense, smart base running, speed, line-drive hitting and strong pitching. Fans called it "Whitey Ball."

Ozzie Smith fit that role perfectly.

Herzog, who became the Cardinals' manager in June 1980, always had an eye on Smith. On Dec. 10, 1981, he did something about it. Herzog pulled the trigger, sending disgruntled All-Star shortstop Garry Templeton to San Diego for the light-hitting Smith. It wasn't a popular move among Cardinal fans nor several Padre players, including Hall of Fame pitcher Gaylord Perry, who won 314 games and recorded 3,534 strikeouts during his 22-year major league career (1962-83).

"Ozzie was a great shortstop," Perry once said. "I saw him as a rookie in San Diego (in 1978). I was always hoping they would hit the ball his way because I knew then that my trouble was over."

Templeton came up through the Cardinals' minor-league organization and was groomed to be the big-league club's shortstop for many years to come. He didn't disappoint the Cards during his six-year stay (1976-81), hitting above .300 three times and scoring 80 to 100 runs a season. The switch-hitter was also the first major league player to collect 100 hits from both sides of the plate in one season, that coming in 1979 when he banged out 211 safeties for a .314 average. The only other major leaguer to accomplish that feat is former Kansas City Royal Willie Wilson, who had 230 hits as a switch-hitter the very next year en route to a .326 average.

Despite Templeton's success with the Cardinals, both in the field and at the plate, Herzog wanted Smith.

"Whitey saw me in San Diego and said he wanted me to play for the Cardinals," Smith recalled. "He said the Cardinals could win the pennant with me at shortstop."

"I tried to trade for Ozzie in 1980," Herzog recalled. "But I got him after the '81 season. Ozzie's contract demands made the Padres mad and my relationship with Templeton wasn't the best."

Herzog was never "buddy-buddy" with his players. "If they need a buddy," he always said, "buy 'em a dog."

Herzog knew Smith was a good glove man who couldn't hit that well, "But I figured we could work on that," he said. "Anyway, I estimated he took away two hits from the opposition with his glove every game we played."

"There's no stat kept for saving runs," Smith maintained. "Good defense puts your offense in a position to win."

"The Wizard of Oz," as he became to be known for his acrobatic skills in the field, quickly made the fans forget Templeton in 1982 when he played a key role in leading the Cardinals to the National League pennant and a 4-games-to-3 victory over the Milwaukee Brewers in the World Series.

Speed, strong pitching and defense were the characteristics of Herzog's 1982 Cardinals, who won the National League East title with a record of

92-70. Seven players stole bases in double figures, led by Lonnie Smith's 68, as the Cardinals led the National League with 200 stolen bases.

The pitching staff showcased Joaquin Andujar (15-10), Bob Forsch (15-9), Steve Mura (12-11), John Stuper (9-7) and relief specialist Bruce Sutter (9-8, plus 36 saves). The team's 3.37 ERA ranked third in the league.

That championship club, which hit only 67 home runs during the regular season, included first baseman Keith Hernandez (.299 average, 7 homers, 94 runs-batted-in), Ken Oberkfell (.289) at third, Darrell Porter (.231, 12, 48) behind the plate and the outfield of Lonnie Smith (.307, 8, 69), George Hendrick (.282, 19, 104) and Willie McGee (.296).

At second base was Tom Herr (.266), a solid hitter and a superb fielder who teamed with Ozzie Smith to form the National League's top keystone combination of the 1980s. From 1982 through 1987, they led the league in double plays three times. During their six seasons together, Smith totaled 613 double plays, Herr 607.

"I think that 1982 infield may have been one of the greatest ever," Herzog proclaimed. "Think of it. Hernandez at first, Herr at second, Ozzie at short and Oberkfell at third, plus Porter behind the plate. Talk about some great defensive players."

Between the five Cardinal infielders, they committed just 53 errors. Smith and Herr were involved in 101 and 97 double plays, respectively. Hernandez was second among National League first basemen in DPs with 140 and third in the league with a .994 fielding percentage. Oberkfell committed just 11 errors at the corner, while Porter was charged with eight. Hernandez and Smith both won Gold Gloves.

Herzog's Cardinals outlasted Philadelphia (89-73) for the National League East crown by three games to advance to the NL Championship Series against Atlanta.

The Cardinals, who were in first place for only 48 days, led the Phillies by 5.5 games on Sept. 20, then survived a late-season slump and clinched the NL-East on Sept. 27 when they posted their 91st win and the Phillies lost their 72nd game.

St. Louis made quick work of the Braves in the NL playoff series, winning the first two at home, then wrapping it up in Game 3 in Atlanta.

Porter was the series' Most Valuable Player, posting a .556 batting average, an on-base percentage of .714 and a slugging percentage of .889.

Ozzie also batted .556 in the three-game series against Atlanta, while Hernandez chipped in with a .333 mark. Herr hit only .231, but his sacrifice bunt in the bottom of the ninth inning of Game 2 allowed teammate David Green, who singled, to advance to second base with no outs. Green then scored on Oberkfell's single to give the Cardinals a 4-3 come-from-behind victory.

As a team, the Cardinals pounded out 34 hits, scored 17 runs and batted .330 against the Braves. Forsch, Sutter and Andujar picked up victories as the St. Louis pitching staff held Atlanta to five runs and a team batting average of .169.

The 1982 World Series got off to a rough start for the Cardinals as they dropped the opener to Milwaukee, 10-0. The Brewers eventually built a 3-2 Series lead, but the Cards came back to take Games 6 and 7 by the scores of 13-1 and 6-3.

The big bats in the 1982 Series for the Cards belonged to Dane Iorg, who hit an incredible .529, Hendrick (.321), Lonnie Smith (.321) and Oberkfell (.292). Ozzie hit only .208, while Herr managed a .160 mark, but he did have five runs-batted-in.

Pitching-wise, Andujar started two games and won both of them (1.35 ERA), while Stuper picked up a victory. Future Hall of Famer Bruce Sutter earned a victory and two saves in relief.

Those who doubted Herzog's trade for Smith became believers following the 1982 campaign.

Templeton spent nine-plus seasons (1982-91) with the Padres and never hit higher than .282. His fielding percentage remained in the .960 range, but he still had the necessary skills to "turn two." He appeared in the postseason in 1984 when the Padres won the National League West by 12 games, then outlasted the Chicago Cubs in five games to advance to the World Series against Detroit. Manager Sparky Anderson's Tigers made quick work of the Padres, taking the Series in five games. Templeton, however, did have a solid postseason, hitting .324. He spent the second half of the 1991 season with the Mets before retiring.

Smith was originally drafted in the seventh round by the Detroit Tigers following his junior year at California-Poly in 1976, but he did not sign in favor of completing his senior year. In 1977, San Diego took him in the fourth round and signed him for a whopping $5,000. Seven years later (1983), he became the first shortstop in the major leagues to earn $1 million a season.

Smith set major league shortstop records for assists and total chances.

Through the 2006 season, he was still the major league's all-time leader in double plays by a shortstop with 1,590. That record, however fell in 2007 with the San Francisco Giants' Omar Vizquel reaching 1,665.

Herr, meanwhile, committed just 80 errors at second base during his 13-year career, an average of 6.2 per season. In comparison, Hall of Fame second basemen Joe Morgan (1963-84) and Bill Mazeroski (1956-72) averaged 11 and 12 errors per season, respectively. Herr's career fielding percentage was an impressive .989. Despite those unbelievable figures, he did not win a single Gold Glove Award. Chicago Cubs second baseman Ryne Sandberg won the annual award nine straight years (1983-91). Like Herr, Sanberg averaged less than seven errors (6.6) a season and had the same .989 career fielding percentage.

"I feel my low error total was due to the extensive work that the Cardinal minor league instructors gave me during my minor league career," said Herr, who signed with the Cardinals in 1974 as an amateur free agent. "Once I was identified as a prospect, they spent countless hours with me."

Herr said the key attributes of a major league second baseman are "the adeptness at turning the double play, lateral range, a plus arm and the intelligence to handle the many types of situational defensive plays that you encounter at the position."

"Also, playing good defense is a matter of pride.....always anticipating the ball coming your way and knowing ahead of time what you are going to do with it," Herr said.

"Everything you do should be a sense of pride," Smith said. "It should be in everyday life."

"Any good teammate has to take pride in what he contributes to the product and Tommy was like that."

"The middle of the (baseball) diamond is where you have the people you can rely on," Smith continued. "It's one of the reasons why you put your strongest people up the middle. The team wants to have confidence in its second baseman and shortstop, as well as your center fielder."

Playing on Busch Stadium's Astroturf was a challenge for all infielders, but Smith saw it as an advantage.

"It allowed me to play deeper than normal," said Smith. "By playing deeper, you had more range on the ball. Getting an extra step on grounders was important."

"I prided myself on making not just the great play, but on concentrating on the routine plays," Smith continued. "That's what separated me from the crowd."

Smith spent hours pouring over scouting reports and the habits of opposing hitters. This allowed him to position himself properly and turn potential base hits into outs.

"Having a game plan is part of being prepared," Smith said.

"Ozzie was a great teammate because all he cared about was contributing to winning games," Herr said. "He was very durable and played through many nagging injuries which earned him a great deal of respect from his teammates."

"His work ethic was also exceptional. He was constantly honing his defensive skills, and also turned himself into a productive offensive player through hard work."

"Ozzie and I rarely missed a day of taking ground balls and feeding each other throws," Herr said. "Whitey Herzog required his regular players to take infield every day, and this helped us prepare for game situations. As a result, we were very comfortable with each other in the trust factor of knowing that we were going to give each other good feeds."

"The more you work with a partner, the better you know his capabilities such as arm strength, range, where he likes the ball on feeds and so on," Herr said. "This work develops the trust or chemistry needed to perform at a high level with the game on the line."

Smith said "Each double play takes on its own character. You try to avoid the contact (at second base by a runner) to avoid any serious injuries."

"Tommy and I took pride in frustrating guys who thought they could hurt us," Smith said. "And believe me, those runners are coming at you. It's a matter of pride."

Former Pittsburgh Pirate center fielder Bill Virdon, who managed Houston (1975-82) and Montreal (1983-84), in addition to the Pirates (1972-73) and the Yankees (1974-75), puts Smith at the head of the class when it comes to shortstops. And Virdon played with and saw some great shortstops during his baseball career, including Dick Groat (Pirates and Cardinals) and Gene Alley (Pirates).

"Ozzie Smith was the best I ever saw at shortstop," Virdon said. "Anyone you put with Ozzie was going to be good. Herr was already good, but I think he was always overlooked because Ozzie was so outstanding."

Herzog agreed, saying, "You always hear about (Bill) Mazeroski (Pirates) and (Bobby) Richardson (Yankees), but Tommy Herr was right there. He was as steady as a rock. He never made mental mistakes and he never booted a ball in the clutch."

"And Ozzie, I don't think anyone played shortstop any better than he did," Herzog continued. "And I saw some great ones like (Luis) Aparicio (White Sox) and (Mark) Belanger (Orioles)."

 The pride factor is also in the batter's box, according to Smith, who grew up idolizing the late Roberto Clemente of the Pirates, a career .317 hitter, Hall of Famer and four-time National League batting champion. "It's just hard work and getting the opportunity."

"I believed there was no reason for me not to be a decent offensive player," Smith continued. "You get out what you put into it. That's life."

"Ozzie used every resource available to him," Herzog said.

Once he joined St. Louis, Smith's batting average grew fatter. In 1985, he hit .276, then it made a steady climb to .303 in 1987.

His biggest hit came in the 1985 National League Championship Series against Los Angeles. The Cardinals—who finished the regular season with a 101-61 record, just 87 team homers and an amazing 314 stolen bases—lost the first two games of the best-of-seven series, tied it at two games apiece, then took a 3-2 series lead when the switch-hitting Smith drilled a bottom-of-the-ninth home run into the right-field stands off the Dodgers' Tom Niedenfuer. It was Smith's first home run batting from the left side of the plate. The Cards took the series in six when teammate Jack Clark belted a two-out, top-of-the-ninth three-run homer off Niedenfuer the next day.

"I had learned to pull the ball," Smith said, looking back at his lone postseason homer. "That home run came from the time I put in. For me, 1985 was the moment in time."

"When I got up that day, I didn't know how it was going to end. That was the turning point when people looked at me as more than a defensive player."

Herr and Smith posted impressive offensive numbers in the 1985 National League Championship Series against the Dodgers. Smith batted .435 and had three runs-batted-in, while Herr hit .333 with four doubles and six RBIs. Defensively, they turned nine double plays.

The 1985 World Series against Herzog's old Kansas City team was a bizarre one. The Cardinals won the first two games, 3-1 and 4-2, in Kansas City, but the Royals came back in Game 3 behind pitcher Bret Saberhagen's six-hit, complete-game 6-1 victory.

John Tudor followed with a brilliant five-hitter as the Cardinals took a 3-1 Series lead, 3-0. Tito Landrum and Willie McGee hit homers to back Tudor's second Series win.

The Cards couldn't put Kansas City away in Game 5, as the Royals' Danny Jackson shut down St. Louis, 6-1, sending the Series back to Kansas City for Game 6 and, if necessary, Game 7.

Game 6 was a pitcher's masterpiece, as the Royals' Charlie Leibrandt and the Cards' Danny Cox matched scoreless innings through the seventh. The Cards pushed across a run in the top of the eighth when Brian Harper singled home Terry Pendleton for a 1-0 lead. It stayed that way until the bottom of the ninth.

Herzog brought in Todd Worrell to relieve Key Dayley, who had worked a scoreless eighth. Up to the plate came the Royals' Jorge Orta. He hit a sharp grounder to first baseman Clark, who fielded the ball cleanly and tossed it to Worrell covering the first base bag. Despite television replays that clearly showed Orta was out, umpire Don Denkinger signaled safe. One thing led to another and when it was over, the Royals won, 2-1, on former Cardinal (1982-83) Dane Iorg's two-run single to tie the Series at 3.

Despite a team meeting and pep talk from Herzog prior to Game 7, the stunned Cardinals didn't show up the next night, losing, 11-0, as Series Most Valuable Player Saberhagen again baffled the St. Louis hitters on five hits. George Brett led the Royals' attack with four hits, as the bewildered Cardinals used seven pitchers.

Herzog was ejected in Game 7 by the home plate umpire, who happened to be Denkinger. When asked about the ejection, Herzog simply said, "I had seen enough."

"That was a black day for Cardinal baseball," Herzog said. "But Don (Denkinger) was a good umpire. We run into one another from time to time. It's history."

"The bad call affected the whole ninth inning," Herr said. "Getting the lead-off hitter out when you're protecting a one-run lead is huge. It would have changed the whole inning. It is a sick feeling when a call goes against you in that situation."

Smith batted a disappointing .087 in the Series, Herr .154. As a team, the Cardinals batted .185 against the Royals' pitching staff, which posted an impressive 1.89 earned-run-average.

To this day, Cardinal fans believe had Denkinger called Orta out at first in Game 6, Worrell would have shut down the Royals and St. Louis would have won the Series.

Herr and Smith were back in the playoffs again in 1987, beating the Giants in seven games for the NL pennant, but losing to Minnesota in seven in the World Series. Again, the Cardinals found themselves ahead, 3 games to 2, but they dropped the final two, 11-5 and 4-2. Again, the Cardinals' keystone combo didn't produce big numbers at the plate, with Herr hitting .250, Smith .214.

In 1988, Herr was traded to Minnesota, then played for Philadelphia, the Mets and San Francisco before retiring at the end of the 1991 season with a career batting average of .271 and 1,001 double plays. His best single season came in 1985, when he batted .302 with 110 runs-batted-in, 97 runs, 38 doubles and 31 stolen bases.

A contact hitter, he lacked power with just 28 career homers. As a matter of fact, he did not hit his first major league homer until his 337<sup>th</sup> career game, that coming against San Francisco's Andy McGaffigan at Candlestick Park on May 10, 1983.

Herr had offers in 1992 to remain in baseball as a coach, but he decided against it so he could spend time with his family. In 1999, he penned a book, *"A View From Second Base"* (Double Play Press, 1998).

Today, he is manager of his hometown Lancaster (Pa.) Barnstormers of the Independent Atlantic League. In 2005, the team's first, Herr guided his young club to a record of 64-76. In 2006, Herr's Barnstormers won the league championship by going undefeated (5-0) in two rounds of the playoff. It was Lancaster's first league championship since 1955. Including the playoffs, Herr led the club to an 80-51 record.

As a player, Herr picked up a few of Herzog's managerial trademarks.

"Actually, Whitey did not really run a tight ship," Herr said. "He had only four rules: be on time; run everything out hard until you are out; play smart; have some laughs while you're at it."

"My philosophy is much the same," Herr continued. "I try to emphasize and put the team first, do whatever the situation calls for to help the team win."

Herzog's managing career came to an end halfway through the 1990 season with his Cardinals struggling with a 33-47 record. During his 18 years, he posted a won-loss record of 1,281-1,125, with six division titles, three pennants and the 1982 World Series win. His 822 victories with the Cardinals ranks him third in the team history book behind Red Schoendienst (1,041) and Tony LaRussa (1,055 through 2007).

Now in his mid-70s, Herzog hasn't ruled out making a managerial comeback. He's not sure if "Whitey Ball" could survive today because the game is now "out of balance," he said. "It's a home-run game now. There's no way to build teams anymore. Now, it's how much money you have."

And it's doubtful if anyone could figure out his managerial philosophy which he shared many times with his players and the media: "A slick way to out-figure a person is to get him figuring you figure he's figuring you're figuring he'll figure you aren't really figuring what you want him to figure you figure."

When the 1990s arrived, Smith was still at the top of his game. In 1991, he committed just eight errors, then a National League record for shortstops.

In 1992, he knocked out his 2,000th hit, stole his 500th base and won his 13th straight Gold Glove Award to break the National League record held by Willie Mays and Roberto Clemente. In 1994, he passed Luis Aparicio for career assists for a shortstop.

Smith played parts of the 1994-95-96 seasons before retiring with 2,460 career hits, a .272 average, 580 stolen bases, 1,590 double plays and a .978 fielding percentage.

He played sparingly for manager LaRussa in the National League Division Series in 1996 against San Diego, going 1-for-3. In the Cardinals' seven-game loss to Atlanta in the NL Championship Series, Smith appeared in three games and went 0-for-9. Ironically, Atlanta lost the World Series in six games to the Yankees, who were skippered by first-year manager Joe Torre, the Cardinals' manager from 1990-95.

Smith's relationship with the Cardinals became strained his final season (1996), which was LaRussa's first as the St. Louis manager. Smith was concerned about a lack of playing time (82 games) and has had little to do with the club since. LaRussa has made it perfectly clear that he and Smith will never be golfing buddies.

Not to be forgotten was Smith's on-field acrobatics, which he performed when he took the field. "It was something I did for fan appreciation day.....a way to get the fans excited," he said.

"It became my trademark," Smith said. "In St. Louis, I'd do it on opening day, special days and for playoff and World Series games."

In 2002, the ultimate honor came—induction into the National Baseball Hall of Fame in Cooperstown, N.Y. Needing 354 votes to be elected, Smith collected 433, or 91.74 percent.

"That was a special moment," recalled Smith, who viewed his induction as a vote for the defensive-minded player. "To be inducted into one of the most-elite fraternities in the world was an honor."

Today, Smith is a fixture in the St. Louis community. Most of his charitable endeavors usually benefit children like the Ronald McDonald House and the Boys Club of St. Louis. He also owns two popular restaurants in the St. Louis area and can be found teeing it up at area golf courses.

Smith has also dabbled some in baseball game broadcasts and was also the host of the television show "This Week in Baseball" from 1997-1999.

AIR-TIGHT STARTING INFIELDS

Former St. Louis manager Whitey Herzog's claim that his 1982 Cardinal infield "may have been one of the greatest ever" may be true. The following is a list of some of Major League Baseball's top defensive infields since 1960 listed in chronological order (GG – Gold Glove winner; E – errors; DP – double plays; PCT. – fielding percentage):

| 1963 Baltimore Orioles | E | DP | Pct. |
|---|---|---|---|
| 1B: Jim Gentile | 6 | 122 | .995 |
| 2B: Jerry Adair | 8 | 67 | .985 |
| SS: Luis Aparicio | 12 | 76 | .983 |
| 3B: Brooks Robinson (GG) | 12 | 43 | .976 |
| C: John Orsino | 7 | 8 | .990 |

**Season:** The Orioles posted an 86-76 record, 18.5 games behind the Yankees.

| 1975 Cincinnati Reds | E | DP | Pct. |
|---|---|---|---|
| 1B: Tony Perez | 9 | 113 | .993 |
| 2B: Joe Morgan (GG) | 11 | 96 | .986 |
| SS: Davey Concepcion (GG) | 16 | 102 | .977 |
| 3B: Pete Rose | 13 | 21 | .963 |
| C: Johnny Bench (GG) | 7 | 9 | .989 |

**Season:** The Reds won 108 games and outlasted Boston in seven World Series games.

### 1978 Philadelphia Phillies

| 1978 Philadelphia Phillies | E | DP | Pct. |
|---|---|---|---|
| 1B: Richie Hebner | 6 | 86 | .994 |
| 2B: Ted Sizemore | 12 | 61 | .978 |
| SS: Larry Bowa (GG) | 10 | 87 | .986 |
| 3B: Mike Schmidt (GG) | 16 | 34 | .963 |
| C: Bob Boone (GG) | 6 | 6 | .991 |

**Season:** The Phillies captured the NL-East crown with 90 wins, but lost to Los Angeles, 3-games-to-1, in the playoffs.

| 1982 St. Louis Cardinals | E | DP | Pct. |
|---|---|---|---|
| 1B: Keith Hernandez (GG) | 11 | 140 | .994 |
| 2B: Tommy Herr | 9 | 97 | .987 |
| SS: Ozzie Smith (GG) | 13 | 101 | .984 |
| 3B: Ken Oberkfell | 11 | 23 | .972 |
| C: Darrell Porter | 9 | 8 | .983 |

**Season:** The Cards won 92, then won the World Series over Milwaukee.

| 1998 Baltimore Orioles | E | DP | Pct. |
|---|---|---|---|
| 1B: Rafael Palmeiro (GG) | 9 | 127 | .994 |
| 2B: Roberto Alomar (GG) | 11 | 86 | .985 |
| SS: Mike Bordick | 7 | 91 | .990 |
| 3B: Cal Ripken Jr. | 8 | 22 | .979 |
| C: Lenny Webster | 4 | 5 | .993 |

**Season:** The Orioles finished 79-83, suffering losing streaks of 10, 9 and 8 games.

| 1999 New York Mets | E | DP | Pct. |
|---|---|---|---|
| 1B: John Olerud | 9 | 127 | .994 |
| 2B: Edgardo Alfonzo | 5 | 98 | .993 |
| SS: Rey Ordonez (GG) | 4 | 91 | .994 |
| 3B: Robin Ventura (GG) | 9 | 33 | .980 |
| C: Mike Piazza | 11 | 5 | .989 |

**Season:** New York won 97, but lost to Atlanta in the playoffs.

| 2000 Cleveland Indians | E | DP | Pct. |
|---|---|---|---|
| 1B: Jim Thome | 5 | 101 | .995 |
| 2B: Roberto Alomar (GG) | 15 | 109 | .980 |
| SS: Omar Vizquel (GG) | 3 | 99 | .995 |
| 3B: Travis Fryman (GG) | 8 | 20 | .978 |
| C: Sandy Alomar Jr. | 8 | 6 | .989 |

**Season:** Tribe finished five games behind the Chisox in the AL-Central with 90 wins.

| 2002 St. Louis Cardinals | E | DP | Pct. |
|---|---|---|---|
| 1B: Tino Martinez | 5 | 119 | .996 |
| 2B: Fernando Vina (GG) | 13 | 104 | .981 |
| SS: Edgar Renteria (GG) | 19 | 72 | .970 |
| 3B: Placido Polanco (GG) | 5 | 18 | .974 |
| C: Mike Matheny | 4 | 6 | .994 |

**Season:** The Cardinals won 97, but fell to San Francisco in five in the league championship.

| 2002 Seattle Mariners | E | DP | Pct. |
|---|---|---|---|
| 1B: John Olerud (GG) | 5 | 122 | .996 |
| 2B: Bret Boone (GG) | 7 | 84 | .989 |
| SS: Carlos Guillen | 18 | 68 | .966 |
| 3B: Jeff Cirillo | 9 | 23 | .973 |
| C: Dan Wilson | 2 | 4 | .997 |

**Season:** The Mariners won 93 games, but finished third in the AL-West and failed to make the playoffs.

| 2006 Boston Red Sox | E | DP | Pct. |
|---|---|---|---|
| 1B: Kevin Youkilis | 5 | 110 | .995 |
| 2B: Mark Loretta | 4 | 99 | .994 |
| SS: Alex Gonzalez | 7 | 68 | .985 |
| 3B: Mike Lowell | 6 | 39 | .987 |
| C: Jason Varitek | 4 | 3 | .994 |

**Season:** The Red Sox committed the fewest errors of any team in the majors, but managed only 86 wins and a third-place finish in the AL-East. Despite the low number of errors by the Sox's infield, none of the five starters won a Gold Glove.

DEFENSE BY THE NUMBERS

A look at the fielding statistics of Tom Herr and Ozzie Smith during the time period they played together at their primary positions, second base and shortstop (PO – putouts; AST – assists; E – errors; DP – double plays; PCT. – fielding percentage):

| | TOM HERR, 2B | | | | | OZZIE SMITH, SS | | | | |
|---|---|---|---|---|---|---|---|---|---|---|
| YEAR | PO | AST | E | DP | PCT. | PO | AST | E | DP | PCT. |
| 1982 | 263 | 427 | 9 | 97 | .987 | 279 | 535 | 13 | 101 | .984 |
| 1983 | 178 | 245 | 6 | 60 | .986 | 304 | 519 | 21 | 100 | .975 |
| 1984 | 328 | 452 | 6 | 106 | .992 | 233 | 437 | 12 | 94 | .982 |
| 1985 | 337 | 448 | 12 | 120 | .985 | 264 | 549 | 14 | 111 | .983 |
| 1986 | 352 | 414 | 9 | 121 | .988 | 229 | 453 | 15 | 96 | .978 |
| 1987 | 306 | 350 | 7 | 103 | .989 | 245 | 516 | 10 | 111 | .987 |
| Totals | 1,764 | 2,336 | 49 | 607 | .988 | 1,554 | 3,009 | 85 | 613 | .982 |

**NOTE:** *Although a large majority of the seasonal and career double plays listed above involved the two keystone partners as a unit playing together at the same time during the noted time period, some were obviously not. The difference is due to many factors, including the number of games played, late-inning substitutions, injuries, a position change, DPs converted independent of each other and, in some cases, games missed due to military service.*

Second baseman Bill (left), manager Cal Sr. (middle) and shortstop Cal Jr. (right) on July 11, 1987. This game marked the first time a father managed two sons on the same team during the regular season. Both went hitless in a 2-1 loss to Minnesota.

## CHAPTER THIRTEEN

# 2B BILL RIPKEN & SS CAL RIPKEN JR., BALTIMORE ORIOLES, 1987-92

**NAME: William Oliver Ripken**
**Nickname:** Billy
**Born:** December 16, 1964, Havre De Grace, Md.
**Died:** Still throwing as of October 1, 2007
**Batted/threw:** Right/right
**Height/weight:** 6-feet-1, 186 pounds
**Major league seasons:** 12 (Baltimore, 1987-92, 1996; Texas, 1993-94, 1997; Cleveland, 1995; Detroit, 1998)
**Major league debut:** July 11, 1987 (Twins 2, **Orioles 1**)
**Final major league game:** July 13, 1998 (Royals 6, **Tigers 4**)
**Position:** Second base (also shortstop: 72 games; third base: 62; first base: 13)
**Career games:** 921
**Career double plays:** 577
**DPs with Orioles at second base (1987-92):** 469
**Career errors:** 61
**Career assists:** 2,395
**Career putouts:** 1,670
**Career fielding percentage:** .985
**Gold Gloves:** 0
**All-Star:** 0 times
**World Series:** 0-0
**Career batting average:** .247
**Turning two:** Bill led the American League in sacrifice hits in 1990 with 17. He also played every infield position during his career, except catcher and pitcher.
**Hall of Fame:** No

**NAME: Calvin Edwin Ripken Jr.**

**Nickname:** Iron Man

**Born:** August 24, 1960, Havre De Grace, Md.

**Died:** Still throwing as of October 1, 2007

**Batted/threw:** Right/right

**Height/weight:** 6-feet-4, 225 pounds

**Major league seasons:** 21 (Baltimore, 1981-2001)

**Major league debut:** Aug. 10, 1981 (**Orioles 3,** Royals 2)

**Final major league game:** Oct. 6, 2001 (Red Sox 5, **Orioles 1**)

**Position:** Shortstop (also third base: 675 games)

**Career games:** 3,001

**Career double plays:** 1,682

**DPs with Orioles at shortstop (1987-92):** 668

**Career errors:** 294

**Career assists:** 8,214

**Career putouts:** 4,112

**Career fielding percentage:** .977

**Gold Gloves:** 2

**All-Star:** 19 times

**World Series:** 1-0

**Career batting average:** .276

**Turning two:** In his second full season (1983) in the major leagues, Ripken pounded out 211 hits for a .318 batting average. He was named the American League's MVP.

**Hall of Fame:** Class of 2007

Many years from now when baseball historians talk about the game's greatest shortstops, the name Ripken will be mentioned in the same breath as Honus Wagner, Ernie Banks, Luis Aparicio and Ozzie Smith.

For 21 Major League Baseball seasons, Cal Ripken Jr. was one of the game's greatest ambassadors. He was inspirational and a role model for millions.

New York Yankee manager Joe Torre once said that Ripken was "a bridge, maybe the last bridge, back to the way the game was played."

"I always admired Cal for the way he played and the way he treated the public," said Hall of Fame broadcaster Ernie Harwell, who followed Ripken's career during his 50-plus years in the television and radio booth. "He was a terrific player and a positive influence for the game. He'd stand in the rain for 30 minutes to sign autographs. You don't see that too often these days."

Don Zimmer, who has been in baseball since 1954 as a player, manager and coach, said Ripken was one of the first of a new breed of shortstops.

"My gosh," he said, "look at what he (Ripken) accomplished. He was bigger and stronger. He could play the heck out of shortstop and he could hit and hit with power."

Several dates stand out in Ripken Jr.'s Hall of Fame career:

**June, 1978:** At the age of 17, he's selected by Baltimore in the second round (48th overall) in the amateur entry draft.

**Aug. 10, 1981:** In his first gig with the Orioles after four seasons in the minors, Ripken made his Major League Baseball debut. It was somewhat eventful as he entered the game as a pinch runner for Ken Singleton and scored the winning run in a 3-2 home victory over the Kansas City Royals. The crowd of 19,850 didn't think much of it. After all, here was a 6-feet-4, 225-pound, 20-year-old kid who the Orioles called up from Triple-A Rochester after a two-month strike. He managed five singles in 39 at-bats for a .128 batting average in 23 games that season.

**April 5, 1982:** At the age of 21, Ripken started at third base in the Orioles' opening-day lineup at Memorial Stadium in Baltimore. Batting sixth, he collected a single, double and two-run homer off Kansas City's Dennis Leonard in a 13-5 Baltimore victory.

**May 30, 1982:** In what would eventually become known as "The Streak," Ripken started at third. He would appear in 94 games at third and 71 games at short en route to American League Rookie-of-the-Year honors

**July 11, 1987:** Second baseman and brother Bill, who was selected in the 11th round of the 1982 entry draft, joined the Orioles, marking the first time in baseball history that a father, Cal Ripken Sr., managed two sons on the same major league team during the regular season. Also, Cal's record streak of 8,243 consecutive innings played came to a halt when his father pulled him in the eighth inning of an 18-3 loss to Toronto.

**Sept. 7, 1995:** Cal Ripken broke the record that baseball historians said could never be topped, playing in his 2,131st consecutive game, surpassing the record held by the "Iron Horse," Lou Gehrig of the New York Yankees (1925-39). Play is stopped after the visiting California Angels are retired in the top of the fifth, making the game official. Ripken, who took a 22-minute "victory" lap around jammed-packed Camden Yards, later stroked a two-run homer to power the Orioles to a 4-2 victory.

He then addressed the crowd of 46,272 following the game: "Tonight I stand here, overwhelmed, as my name is linked with the great and courageous Lou Gehrig. I'm truly humbled to have our names spoken in the same breath. This year has been unbelievable. I've been cheered in ballparks all over the country. People not only showed me their kindness, but more importantly, they demonstrated their love of the game of baseball. I give my thanks to baseball fans everywhere. Tonight, I want to make sure you know how I feel. As I grew up here (in the Baltimore area), I not only had dreams of being a big-league player, but also of being a Baltimore Oriole. For all of your support over the years, I want to thank you, the fans of Baltimore, from the bottom of my heart. This is the greatest place to play."

Then-President Bill Clinton paid tribute to baseball's new "Iron Man," saying, "I admire him not only for his talent, but for his constant determination day in and day out. He's been loyal to his team, his fans, the community and professional sports every phase of his career. His determination and talent has been great for baseball and America."

**Sept. 20, 1998:** "The Streak" officially came to an end at 2,632 as Ripken took himself out of the Orioles' starting lineup prior to a game against the Yankees.

**Oct. 6, 2001:** Ripken played in his final game before a crowd of 48,807 at Camden Yards. Playing third base, he went 0-for-3 in a 5-1 loss to the Boston Red Sox.

**Jan. 9, 2007:** Cal is elected to the National Baseball Hall of Fame in his first year of eligibility, being named on 537 of 545 ballots (98.5 percent of the vote). "It was a wonderful moment to get that call and hear, 'Congratulations, you made the Baseball Hall of Fame,'" Ripken said.

Through the 2007 Hall of Fame voting, pitcher Tom Seaver held the record percentage at 98.84, set when he was selected on 425 of 430 ballots in 1992. The right-handed Seaver posted a record of 311-205 during his 20-year career (Mets, 1967-77, 1983; Reds, 1977-82; White Sox, 1984-86; Red Sox, 1986).

Ripken's accomplishments go well beyond "The Streak" and his election to the Hall. For example, he was the first player to win Rookie-of-the-Year honors (1982) and the Most Valuable Player Award (1983) in back-to-back seasons. He won a second MVP Award in 1991 and was selected the All-Star Game's Most Valuable Player in 1991 and 2001.

Defensively, he led the American League in double plays eight times, assists four times and putouts once. He turned 1,565 career double plays at short, 1,682 overall, 12 times exceeding the 100 mark in a season from his shortstop position. He committed just 225 errors at short, an average of 14 per season, an incredible number considering he played the infield's most-demanding position. In 1990, he committed just three errors for a .996 fielding percentage. He booted the ball less than nine times in five seasons.

Hall of Fame shortstop Ozzie Smith, formerly of the St. Louis Cardinals and a 15-time All-Star, has always believed that shortstops "were the best athletes on the field. And what Cal was able to do just reconfirms that," Smith said.

Offensively, Ripken, ironically, holds the major league record for most times grounding into a double play with 350. As a matter of fact, Cal was the last Oriole to step to the plate in the last game played at Baltimore's Memorial Stadium on Oct. 6, 1991. The result? He hit into a game-ending double play.

On the positive side, he led all major league shortstops in home runs, runs batted in, runs scored and slugging percentage each year from 1983 to 1986. And through 2006, he was one of only eight major leaguers to reach 3,000 career hits (3,184) and 400 home runs (431).

Baseball was in Cal and brother Bill Ripken's blood, thanks to their father, Cal Sr., who spent 36 years in the Baltimore organization as a player, scout, coach and manager until after the 1992 season. He died of lung cancer in 1999 at the age of 63, but he lived long enough to see the achievements of his two sons.

Cal Sr. taught his sons how to play baseball, but he was the first to admit that it was Cal Jr. and Bill who did the work. Cal Sr. always said, "Perfect practice makes perfect."

Like the 6-feet-3 Tony Kubek (1957-65) of the New York Yankees before him, Cal, who was originally drafted as a pitcher, was somewhat of a novelty when then-Baltimore manager Earl Weaver moved him from third to short in 1982. Weaver saw him as the successor to another fine shortstop, Mark Belanger, who brilliantly manned the Orioles' shortstop position for 17 of his 18 major league seasons. A weak hitter (.228 career average), Weaver saw the opportunity to replace the veteran Belinger with a big, strong player in Cal, who possessed great defensive skills and power at the plate.

"When I arrived at the park and saw the lineup card and saw I was playing shortstop, I thought Earl had made a mistake," Ripken recalled. "I went to my dad and he told me it was no mistake."

Weaver, a fiery skipper who loved to hassle umpires, managed the Orioles for 17 seasons (1968-82 and 1985-86). He won 1,480 games for a winning percentage of .583 and guided the Birds to four pennants, including the 1970 World Series crown in five games over Cincinnati. The Hall of Famer never played in the major leagues after spending 10 years in the minors as a second baseman. Five of his Baltimore teams won more than 100 games. The record Weaver's probably best remembered for is his 98 career game ejections. Once in 1985, he got tossed from both ends of a double-header.

With Weaver putting Cal at short, Belanger was shipped to the Los Angeles Dodgers for the 1982 season, his last. A heavy smoker, he died at the age of 54 in 1998.

A majority of shortstops in the American League in 1982 ranged in height from 5-feet-10 to 6-feet, except for Boston's Glenn Hoffman, a 6-feet-2, 190-pound stringbean who was a solid performer in the field, but an average hitter at best with no power.

"When you're big and tall like Cal, it's difficult to put a guy like that in the middle of the diamond," said Kubek, who followed Ripken's career as a network television broadcaster. "But Cal had such a strong arm and a quick arm."

"Cal was one of the first big shortstops and he could hit the ball," recalled Harwell, who spent 55 years as a major league baseball television and radio play-by-play personality. "I personally thought he was more suited for third base, but he showed he could play both short and third. His range was limited a little, but boy he knew how to play the hitters."

Midway through the 1996 season, Baltimore manager Davey Johnson moved Ripken to third, snapping a streak of 2,216 consecutive starts at short, so that Manny Alexander could be tried at short. Ripken didn't care for the move, but it lasted just five games as Alexander experienced trouble at the plate and in the field.

"I always enjoyed playing shortstop because I believe it is a position that, when handled properly, can take charge of a game and serve as an anchor for the defense," Cal said.

"Intelligence, positioning and having an understanding of all of the possible scenarios that could happen when the ball is hit is vital to the success of a shortstop."

"Things like great range and a strong arm are vital when playing the position, but I don't think it's the most important thing. The ability to position yourself the right way and understand the little things matter most," Cal said.

"For example, if there is a base hit to the outfield, what should I do as the cutoff man?"

"If there is a fast runner on first base and a fast runner at the plate, you need to be aware of all that can happen when the ball is hit. If it is hit to you, can you turn the double play if you move quickly enough? How important is the double play in that situation or can you just concern yourself with getting one out?"

Kubek said the "great shortstops always try to get as many outs as you can on every play."

"I remember talking about this when I was a player and our (Yankee) coach, Frank Crosetti, told us that you make the double play and you make it as quickly as possible. He didn't believe in the 'Let's-get-at-least-one-out' theory. Double plays prevent rallies and win games."

Crosetti played for the Yankees for 17 seasons and played shortstop for six World Series championship teams. He's the only Yankee to have played with Babe Ruth, Lou Gehrig, Waite Hoyt and Joe DiMaggio. When he retired in 1948, he spent 20 more seasons with the Yankees as their third base coach, appearing in 15 more World Series, so he knew a thing or two about double plays.

Cal Ripken appeared in one World Series, that coming in 1983 when the Orioles took care of the Philadelphia Phillies in five games. That club, managed by Joe Altobelli, finished 98-64, six games ahead of second-place Detroit in the American League East. The Orioles quickly disposed of the Chicago White Sox in four games in the American League Championship Series, then dominated Philadelphia in the World Series. Cal had a rough go of it at the plate, going 3-for-18 with one RBI. He played errorless ball and was involved in three double plays.

Cal has always said that breaking Gehrig's record was his most-special "personal" moment of his career, while catching the last out of the 1983 World Series remains his favorite "baseball" moment.

First baseman Eddie Murray, a Hall of Famer, led the Birds in 1983 with 33 homers, 111 runs-batted-in and a .306 average. Ripken ended all talk of a sophomore jinx by batting .318 with 27 homers and 102 RBIs. The outfield was solid with John Lowenstein (.281), Al Bumbry (.275) and Ken Singleton (.276).

The pitching staff was deep with Mike Flanagan (12-4), Scott McGregor (18-7), Mike Boddicker (16-8) and Storm Davis (13-7).

In the World Series, the Phillies took the opener, then the Orioles swept four straight. Boddicker, Davis, McGregor and Jim Palmer, who had appeared in just 14 games during the regular season, posted victories for Baltimore.

Cal never played in another World Series, although he did appear in two other postseasons in 1996 and 1997, but the Orioles lost to New York and Cleveland, respectively, in the American League Championship Series.

Amazingly, Ripken played with 32 different second basemen during his 2,302 games as a shortstop, including his own brother, Bill (1987-92) , Rich Dauer (1983-85), Harold Reynolds (1993) and Roberto Alomar (1996).

Alomar, who signed as a free agent with the Orioles in 1996 after spending five All-Star seasons in Toronto, and Ripken probably had one of the best "statistical" seasons of any keystone combination, both offensively and defensively.

On the defensive side, they combined for 216 double plays —- 109 for Ripken, 107 for Alomar —- and 912 assists. Offensively, Alomar hit .328 with 22 homers and 94 RBIs.

Ripken chipped in 26 homers and 102 runs-batted-in to go along with his .278 average.

The 1996 Orioles finished second, four games behind the Yankees in the American League East. As the league's wild-card playoff team, the Orioles defeated Cleveland in the divisional series, 3-games-to-1, then were buried by the Yankees in five games in the league championship series. The Yankees went on to beat Atlanta in six games in the World Series.

In 1997, Baltimore manager Johnson moved Ripken to third for good, breaking up a potentially great "keystone combination" with Alomar. Mike Bordick came over from Oakland in 1997 to take over the shortstop position.

Bordick signed with Baltimore after spending seven productive seasons in Oakland. In 562 games over 3.5 seasons (1997-2000), he gave the Orioles a decent bat and strong defense at short (375 double plays and just 36 errors).

The 1997 Orioles posted a 98-64 mark and finally overtook the Yankees in the AL-East by two games. The Yanks didn't go down easy, taking 3-of-4 in Baltimore in mid-September and eventually closing to two games with seven to play. The Orioles held on, though, winning four of their last six, including two crucial one-run decisions at Milwaukee on the last two days of the season.

Ripken's .438 batting average led Baltimore to a 3-games-to-1 victory over Seattle in the divisional series, but then it ran into another roadblock to the World Series, losing to Cleveland in six games. Ripken again turned in a solid performance in the league championship series against

the Tribe with a .348 mark. The Indians came up short in the World Series, losing in seven games to the Florida Marlins, who were managed at
that time by current Detroit Tiger skipper Jim Leyland.

For Ripken, 1997 was the last season he saw postseason play. He left his
mark, though, with a postseason batting average of .336 in 28 games.

Alomar stayed with the Orioles through the 1998 season, then moved to
Cleveland, where he teamed with another outstanding shortstop, Omar
Vizquel.

Playing with 32 different second basemen in 16 seasons was definitely a
challenge for Cal. Some of the second basemen lasted one season, others one game.

WHO'S ON SECOND?

The following is a "Who's Who" of second basemen during the Cal Ripken
shortstop era with games played and double plays turned, as well as Cal's
double-play total for each season. **Not all of the double plays by the second basemen involved Cal. Also, in 1981 and 1982, when he played both
short and third, Cal totaled 52 double plays in 96 games at shortstop:**

**1983:** Rich Dauer (131 games / 72 double plays), Lenn Sakata (60 / 33),
Bobby Bonner (5 / 0), Todd Cruz (2 / 0), John Lowenstein (1 / 0).
**Ripken, 113.**

**1984:** Dauer (123 / 74), Sakata (76 / 30), Vic Rodriguez (7 / 1).
**Ripken, 122.**

**1985:** Alan Wiggins (76 / 54), Dauer (73 / 42), Sakata (50 / 18), Kelly Paris (2 / 0), John Shelby (1 / 0). **Ripken, 123.**

**1986:** Juan Bonilla (70 /34), Wiggins (66 / 38), Jackie Gutierrez (53 / 27), Rex Hudler (13 / 0), Ricky Jones (11 / 5), John Stefero (1 / 0). **Ripken, 105.**

**1987:** Bill Ripken (58 / 53), Rick Burleson (55 / 37), Wiggins (33 / 20), Pete Stanicek (19 / 13), Rene Gonzalez (6 / 1), Ron Washington (3 / 0), Gutierrez (1 / 0). **Ripken, 103.**

**1988:** Bill Ripken (149 / 110), Stanicek (16 / 5), Gonzalez (14 / 5). **Ripken, 119.**

**1989:** Bill Ripken (114 / 81), Gonzalez (54 / 33), Tim Hulett (23 / 12), Juan Bell (2 / 1), Rick Schu (1 / 0). **Ripken, 119.**

**1990:** Bill Ripken (127 / 84), Gonzalez (43 / 16), Hulett (16 / 9), Jeff McKnight (5 / 1), Marty Brown (2 / 0). **Ripken, 94.**

**1991:** Bill Ripken (103 / 75), Bell (77 / 37), Hulett (26 / 5), Shane Turner (1 / 0). **Ripken, 114.**

**1992:** Bill Ripken (108 / 66), Mark McLemore (70 / 44), Hulett (10 / 2), Steve Scarsone (5 / 3). **Ripken, 119.**

**1993:** Harold Reynolds (141 / 102), McLemore (25 / 17), Hulett (4 / 3). **Ripken, 101.**

**1994:** McLemore (96 / 51), Hulett (23 / 21) (strike-shortened season). **Ripken, 72.**

**1995:** Manny Alexander (81 / 44), Bret Barberie (74 / 43), Jeff Huson (21 / 14). **Ripken, 100.**

**1996:** Roberto Alomar (141 / 107), Bill Ripken (30 / 15), Huson (12 / 6), Alexander (7 / 1). **Ripken, 109.**

"Communications was always the key," Cal said of Baltimore's carousel of second basemen. "I made a real effort to get to know my second baseman, whether it was Robbie Alomar, Brett Barberie or Manny Alexander."

"I would try to engage them and have them tell me how they liked to play, where they wanted the ball on a double-play opportunity."

"By sharing information, we were able to understand each other's game more thoroughly and, as a result, play more effectively together," Cal said.

Zimmer shares Cal's views. "I've always gotten a kick out of a shortstop who's been with a team for, say, seven years and a new second baseman comes along," Zimmer said. "A lot of people say they have to play together for a season or two to get used to one another. I've never gone along with that 100 percent."

"If I play short, I have a second baseman next to me," Zimmer said. "If he throws the ball to me chest high, we have a double play. With some communications, I don't think it takes that long to get used to one another. You can work through it. It doesn't take years to develop."

Zimmer spent 12 seasons playing second base, shortstop, third and the outfield (1954-65) for the Dodgers, Cubs, Mets, Reds and Senators. As an infielder (957 games), he was involved in 418 double plays. He then spent 13 seasons managing the Padres, Red Sox, Rangers and Cubs. He's also been a bench coach for the Yankees and Devil Rays. He has a handful of World Series rings earned as a player and as a coach.

"With Cal, if I were a second baseman, I'd do anything Cal said," Kubek joked about the Orioles' 32 second basemen. "Cal could adjust to anyone."

"In all honesty, the best shortstop I ever saw was Belanger," Kubek went on to say. "He made everything look so easy and he never had to dive for a ball. The standard of shortstops in the American League in Belanger's era was Belanger. Cal replaced an exceptional shortstop and did so very well."

Cal's first keystone mate was Rich Dauer, who had teamed with Belanger for four seasons. Dauer and Ripken formed a solid double-play combo, combining for 389 twin-killers in two seasons (1983-84).

Ripken's "longest" keystone partner in terms of games and years was his brother, Bill. They played in 689 games together between 1987-92 and totaled 1,137 double plays ——. 668 by Cal, 469 for Bill. After stops in Texas and Cleveland, Bill rejoined the Orioles for 30 more games alongside his brother in 1996. Their best single-season mark came in 1988 when they totaled 229 double plays.

"It is so important for the second baseman and the shortstop to have a good rapport," said Bill, who committed just 61 errors during his 12-year career (912 games). "You need to know where the shortstop wants the ball on the throw and vice versa. You need to work closely together with the shortstop on cutoffs and relays, and that comes from good communications. The list can go on and on."

"Obviously, Cal and I had a special relationship and we knew each other like the back of our hands. Most times the shortstop isn't your big brother, so you need to take the time to develop that rapport and make sure that you are on the same page," Bill said.

Bill disagrees with Zimmer's philosophy of longevity, saying, "If you look at some of the more-successful keystone combos, it was the ones who played together for an extended period of time like (Lou) Whitaker and (Alan) Trammell (of Detroit, 1977-95), and (Joe) Morgan and (Dave) Concepcion (of Cincinnati, 1972-79)."

The Ripken-to-Ripken keystone combo is the fifth in Major League Baseball history featuring brothers playing second and shortstop in the same game during the regular season.

Prior to the Ripkens, the last brother keystone combination were twins, second baseman Johnny and shortstop Eddie O'Brien of the 1953 Pittsburgh Pirates. Johnny appeared in 77 games and turned 48 double plays, while brother Eddie played in 81 games and was involved in 39 DPs.

There have been more than 350 brothers who have played in the major leagues, but on the same team is a rarity. Two of the most-famous siblings to play together on the same team were Hank and Tommie Aaron. They spent portions of seven seasons together with the Braves. They're the answer to one of baseball's most-amusing trivia questions: Which two brothers have combined for the most career major league home runs? The answer: 768 by Hank (755) and Tommie (13) Aaron.

The first-known brothers-teammates were George and Harry Wright, who both played for the game's first pro team, the 1869 Cincinnati Red

Stockings. George, an infielder, had a career batting average of .302. Brother Harry, a centerfielder and pitcher, hit .272 for his career and posted a 4-4 mark as a hurler. They were also the first set of brothers to be elected to the Baseball Hall of Fame, George in 1937 and Harry in 1953.

The Waner brothers, Paul and Lloyd, were the second set of brothers to play together and earn admission to Baseball's Hall. Both played for the Pittsburgh Pirates from 1927 to 1940. Paul, an outfielder and first baseman, was a .333 career hitter and entered the Hall of Fame in 1952. Lloyd, an outfielder who hit .316, followed his brother into the Hall in 1967.

The third and final brothers-teammates to become Hall of Famers were half-brothers, pitchers Rube and Bill Foster, who played for the Chicago American Giants of the Negro National League from 1923-26. Rube, who founded the NNL in 1920, posted back-to-back 51-0 and 54-1 pitching records. He was voted into the Hall by the Veterans Committee in 1981. Bill is best remembered for pitching and winning both ends of a double-header on the last day of the 1926 NNL season to clinch the pennant for the Giants. He was elected to the Hall by the Veterans Committee in 1996.

Other notable brother-teammate combos include pitchers Dizzy and Paul Dean (1934-37 Cardinals); pitchers Joe and Phil Niekro (1973-74, Braves; 1985 Yankees), who totaled 539 victories between them; pitchers Gaylord and Jim Perry (1974-75 Indians), who combined for 529 victories; and the battery of catcher Rick Ferrell and his brother, pitcher Wes (1934-37, Red Sox; 1937-38, Senators). Dizzy, Phil, Gaylord and Rick are members of the Hall of Fame.

Then there's the Alou brothers of the San Francisco Giants. On Sept. 15, 1963, Felipe, Matty and Jesus played the outfield together against the Pirates at Forbes Field in a 13-5 Giants' victory. Their streak of playing together lasted one inning.

As far as Ripken's "streak" is concerned, Kubek said he used to get upset with writers who questioned Ripken's day-after-day play despite being in the midst of a hitting slump.

"Didn't they (the writers) realize the value of Cal as a defensive player?" Kubek asked. "Didn't they realize the value of Cal as a leader on the field, someone who set a positive example on the field?"

"What Cal did had a positive influence on the game when it really needed it," Kubek said. "Just think of how many people followed his game streak as he got closer to Gehrig's record."

Harwell said Gehrig "probably faced the same criticism."

"For Cal, it brought attention to him and the team," Harwell added. "The fact that he showed up everyday to play overshadowed the criticism."

One of Cal's former managers, Frank Robinson, always said he wished he had more Cal Ripkens because of his "determination and dedication to play."

Robinson managed the Birds for three-plus seasons, posting a mark of 230-285. He replaced Cal Sr., who became manager in 1987 and led the Orioles to a disappointing 67-95 mark. After an 0-6 start in 1988, Cal Sr. was let go and replaced by Robinson. The Orioles proceeded to lose their next 15 games for an 0-21 start en route to a 54-107 season.

When the winless streak hit 0-18, a profile photo of a frustrated Bill with a bat against his forehead appeared on the cover of *Sports Illustrated* on May 2, 1988. The streak finally ended in the 22$^{nd}$ game of the season in Chicago, where the Orioles beat the White Sox, 9-0. Cal collected four hits, including a solo homer.

Although he had them, injuries were never a major problem for Cal, who believed in staying in perfect shape. His most-bizarre injury came prior to the 1996 All-Star Game in Philadelphia. Following a pre-game team photo shoot, pitcher Roberto Hernandez of the Chicago White Sox lost his balance and struck Ripken on the nose with his elbow. The nose was broken, but to no one's surprise, Cal played in the game, won by the NL, 6-0.

Today, Cal and Bill continue to have a positive influence on the game. They own and operate the Ripken Baseball Camps and Clinics. The Ripken Academy is located in Aberdeen, Md., 25 miles north of Baltimore. This facility features youth replicas of Camden Yards, Fenway Park, Wrigley Field and Memorial Stadium.

Their newest venture, The Ripken Experience, opened in June 2006 in Myrtle Beach, S.C. At this overnight camp, players and coaches are treated like major leaguers.

Ripken Baseball also owns the Aberdeen (Md.) Iron Birds of the New York-Penn League, a Class A minor league affiliate of the Orioles, and the Augusta (Ga.) Green Jackets of the Class A South Atlantic League, an affiliate of the San Francisco Giants.

The Cal Ripken Sr. Foundation, founded in 2001 by members of the Ripken family in memory of their patriarch Cal, Sr., works to create baseball and softball programs and facilities that positively impact disadvantaged youth. This program helps thousands of youth annually through a variety of community efforts.

In addition, Cal is a best-selling author. His third book, *"Parenting Young Athletes The Ripken Way,"* was published in April of 2006.

DEFENSE BY THE NUMBERS

A look at the fielding statistics of Bill Ripken and Cal Ripken Jr. during the time period they played together at their primary positions, second base and shortstop (PO – putouts; AST – assists; E – errors; DP – double plays; PCT. – fielding percentage):

| | BILL RIPKEN, 2B | | | | | CAL RIPKEN JR., SS | | | | |
|---|---|---|---|---|---|---|---|---|---|---|
| YEAR | PO | AST | E | DP | PCT. | PO | AST | E | DP | PCT. |
| 1987 | 133 | 162 | 3 | 53 | .990 | 240 | 480 | 20 | 103 | .973 |
| 1988 | 309 | 440 | 12 | 110 | .984 | 284 | 480 | 21 | 119 | .973 |
| 1989 | 255 | 335 | 9 | 81 | .985 | 276 | 531 | 8 | 119 | .990 |
| 1990 | 250 | 366 | 8 | 84 | .987 | 242 | 435 | 3 | 94 | .996 |
| 1991 | 201 | 284 | 7 | 75 | .986 | 267 | 528 | 11 | 114 | .986 |
| 1992 | 217 | 317 | 4 | 66 | .993 | 287 | 445 | 12 | 119 | .984 |
| Totals | 1,365 | 1,904 | 43 | 469 | .988 | 1,596 | 2,899 | 75 | 668 | .984 |

NOTE: *Although a large majority of the seasonal and career double plays listed above involved the two keystone partners as a unit playing together at the same time during the noted time period, some were obviously not. The difference is due to many factors, including the number of games played, late-inning substitutions, injuries, a position change, DPs converted independent of each other and, in some cases, games missed due to military service.*

CHAPTER FOURTEEN

# 2B LOU WHITAKER & SS ALAN TRAMMELL, DETROIT TIGERS, 1977-95

**NAME: Louis Rodman Whitaker Jr.**

**Nickname:** Sweet Lou

**Born:** May 12, 1957, Brooklyn, N.Y.

**Died:** Still throwing as of October 1, 2007

**Batted/threw:** Left/right

**Height/weight:** 5-feet-11, 160 pounds

**Major league seasons:** 19 (Detroit, 1977-95)

**Major league debut:** Sept. 9, 1977 (Red Sox 5, **Tigers** 1)

**Final major league game:** Oct. 1, 1995 (Orioles 4, **Tigers** 0)

**Position:** Second base

**Career games:** 2,390

**Career double plays:** 1,527

**DPs with Tigers at second base (1977-95):** 1,527

**Career errors:** 189

**Career assists:** 6,653

**Career putouts:** 4,771

**Career fielding percentage:** .984

**Gold Gloves:** 3

**All-Star:** 5 times

**World Series:** 1-0

**Career batting average:** .276

**Turning two:** Whitaker was the American League's Rookie of the Year in 1978. Today, his car license plate number reads "AL ROY 78"

**Hall of Fame:** No

**NAME: Alan Stuart Trammell**
Nickname: Tram
Born: February 21, 1958, Garden Grove, Calif.
Died: Still throwing as of October 1, 2007
Batted/threw: Right/right
Height/weight: 6-feet, 175 pounds
Major league seasons: 20 (Detroit, 1977-96)
Major league debut: Sept. 9, 1977 (Red Sox 5, Tigers 1)
Final Major league game: Sept. 29, 1996 (Brewers 7, Tigers 5)
Position: Shortstop
Career games: 2,293
Career double plays: 1,321
DPs with Tigers at shortstop (1977-95): 1,292
Career errors: 235
Career assists: 6,265
Career putouts: 3,448
Career fielding percentage: .976
Gold Gloves: 4
All-Star: 6 times
World Series: 1-0
Career batting average: .285
Turning two: Trammell batted .314 in 1984, then .364 in the American League Championship Series and .450 in the Tigers' five-game World Series win over San Diego.
Hall of Fame: No

It was a match made in baseball heaven.

For 19 seasons (1977-95), second baseman Lou Whitaker and shortstop Alan Trammell of the Detroit Tigers played side-by-side to form Major League Baseball's longest-running keystone combination.

It addition to being baseball's longest, it is generally recognized as the game's finest and most-consistent, both defensively and offensively.

Between the two, they totaled 2,819 double plays—1,527 for Whitaker, 1,292 for Trammell—a major league record for a second baseman and shortstop. Even more impressive is the fact the two committed just 412 errors between them. They also hold the American League record for games played together (1,918).

Whitaker holds the Tigers' team record for most career double plays at 1,527, while Trammell is fourth with 1,321. Second baseman Charlie Gehringer (1924-42) and first baseman Norm Cash (1960-74) are second and third, respectively, with 1,447 and 1,328.

Trammell won four Gold Gloves (1980-81, 1983-84), Whitaker three (1983-85). The two are members of a select group of eight keystone partners who won Gold Glove awards in the same season, doing so twice in 1983 and 1984.

Offensively, Trammell was a career .285 hitter, including a high of .343 in 1987, with 185 homers. Seven times in his 20-year career, he batted above .300. Whitaker hit .276 and 244 homers during his 19 seasons. In 1983, he batted a career-high .320.

"You know, you can talk about (Joe) DiMaggio's 56-hit game hitting streak (1941) and some of these other records that will never be broken, well you'll never see two players spend 19 years together like Lou and Alan did," said Sparky Anderson, who managed the Tigers for 17 seasons (1979-95).

"They were raised by the Tigers, brought up by the Tigers, played their entire careers with the Tigers, and had a love for the city and the uniform," Anderson said. "They would have stayed Tigers forever."

"You'll never see it again, especially now with free agency and players moving from one team to another every two or three years," Anderson said.

"It's a remarkable record," said Ernie Harwell, who broadcasted Tiger games 18 of the 19 years Whitaker and Trammell played together. "There's no question Lou and Alan were extraordinary the way they lasted together."

"I can think of a couple records that might never be broken like (Johnny) Vander Meer's back-to-back no-hitters (for Cincinnati in 1938). Topping that with three in a row would be awfully tough."

Ralph Houk, who managed the New York Yankees to three American League pennants and a pair of World Series crowns in 1961 and 1962, remembers the first time he saw Whitaker and Trammell after becoming the Tigers' skipper in 1974.

"When I took the job at Detroit, general manager Jim Campbell told me he wanted me to take a look at two guys at one of our early spring camps in Lakeland (Fla.)," Houk recalled. "I'll never forget the first time I saw Trammell because he was wearing yellow shoes."

Campbell was a "Tiger lifer" in the front office, first as vice-president and director of minor league operations (1960-62), then vice-president and general manager (1963-78), president and general manager (1979-83), and finally president and CEO (1984-90). He was the architect of two World Series championship teams: 1968, when the Tigers beat St. Louis in seven, and 1984, a five-game Series win over San Diego.

"Jim and I were very impressed with both Alan and Lou, who was playing third base at the time," Houk said. "We talked about moving Lou to second because we already had a good third baseman in Detroit (Aurelio Rodriguez). Jim and I talked about bringing them up together late in 1977."

"They became good friends," Houk said. "They roomed together and really got to know each other. When two guys can spend time together, talk about baseball and the mistakes and good plays they made, it really helps. I had two players similar to that in (Bobby) Richardson and (Tony) Kubek with the Yankees. Those two didn't turn out too bad."

After Whitaker and Trammell led Montgomery, Ala., to the Southern League championship in 1977, the two were promoted to the parent club late in the season. Whitaker, then 20 years old, replaced Tito Fuentes and Trammell, 19, took over for Tom Veryzer.

"The following year (1978), their first full seasons, I knew they were good and I thought they'd play together for a long, long time," Houk said.

"Lou made the switch from third base to second base look natural," Trammell said. "The organization gets the credit for putting us together. Here we were, two young guys in 1977 who obviously had some ability going to the major leagues. Heck, Lou and I both got our first base hits off the same pitcher, Reggie Cleveland of Boston, in September of 1977."

"I look at the 19-year record of our's, and look at Davey Lopes and Bill Russell (of the Dodgers, 1973-81), who played together for nine years. Lou and I more than doubled that," Trammell said. "Will it ever be broken? I don't know. I think it's highly unlikely the way the game is today with free agency, but never say never. I will say those 19 years are something both Lou and I can be proud of."

"Lou and I played at a high level for a long time because of our preparation, passion and dedication," Trammell said.

TEAMMATES FOREVER
To date, no two players in any sport have been teammates continuously on the same team as long as Whitaker and Trammell. A look at Major League Baseball players who were teammates on one team the longest through 2007:

| YRS. | PLAYERS | TEAM | SEASONS |
|---|---|---|---|
| 19 | Lou Whitaker & Alan Trammell | Tigers | 1977-95 |
| 18 | George Brett & Frank White | Royals | 1973-90 |
| 17 | Robin Yount & Jim Gantner | Brewers | 1976-92 |
| 17 | Jim Palmer & Mark Belanger | Orioles | 1965-81 |
| 17 | Roberto Clemente & Bill Mazeroski | Pirates | 1956-1972 |
| 17 | Max Carey & Babe Adams | Pirates | 1910-1926 |

**Note:** *In comparison, the longest-running teammates in the National Basketball Association through 2007 were Karl Malone and John Stockton, who played together for 18 seasons (1986-2003) for the Utah Jazz.*

Whitaker admits he was "disappointed" with the move from third to second.

"All my life I played third," Whitaker said. "I had tears in my eyes when the organization moved me to second, but if I wanted the opportunity to move to the majors quickly, I had to make the change because they already had Rodriguez at third."

Jim Leyland, who was Whitaker's manager at Class A Lakeland (Fla.) of the Florida State League (FSL) in 1976 and is now the manager of the Detroit Tigers, didn't want the organization to make the switch from third to second so quickly.

"They wanted me to switch him over toward the end of the (1976 FSL) season and I begged them," Leyland recalled. "I said, 'Look, I don't think this is a good time. This guy is a top prospect and he's going to be a big leaguer for a long time. I'd hate to take a chance and see him get hurt playing second base when someone slides into him."

As Lakeland's third baseman, Whitaker led Leyland's crew to the 1976 FSL championship. He was also named the league's player of the year with a .376 batting average.

"I convinced Jim Campbell and the Tigers to wait until the instructional league (that 1976 fall) to work with him and work with Eddie Brinkman at second," Leyland said. "The rest is pretty much history. As it turned out, those two (Whitaker and Trammell) turned out to be one of the best (DP combinations) in the game."

Brinkman worked in the Tigers' minor-league organization after spending 15 seasons in the majors as a shortstop, including four with Detroit (1971-74). He was not an offensive threat (.224 career average), but he was an outstanding defensive player, turning more than a thousand DPs during his career. He won a Gold Glove in 1972 during an era when shortstops like Mark Belanger and Luis Aparicio were the perennial winners.

"As a third baseman, Lou was tremendous…absolutely tremendous," Leyland said. "He made the transition easily. He had so much talent. He just played with instinct."

"Those two were etched in stone forever. They were the talk of baseball for a lot of years. When everyone talked about the Tigers, they'd say Trammell and Whitaker were unbelievable, and they were," Leyland said.

"It all worked out," Whitaker said. "I'll tell you this, there will never, ever be two guys like Alan and myself who played as hard day-in-and-day-out as we did."

Trammell credits that to constant infield practice.

"Infield practice never stopped. It was everyday," Trammell said. "Timing is so important. Lou and I wanted to keep that edge. It was second nature where Lou would be (on the double play). That's where the timing comes in. If someone else was playing second base, I had to take that split second to look at second base and that could cost you the double play."

The two didn't disappoint Houk, Campbell or Tiger fans in 1978. Whitaker hit .285 and Trammell .268 as the Tigers improved their record to 86-76 compared to 74-88 the previous season. In the field, they both had 95 double plays.

Houk became the Tigers' skipper in 1974, replacing Joe Schultz who had taken over for Billy Martin during the 1973 season. Detroit suffered four straight losing seasons (1974-77) before things turned around in 1978. The addition of Whitaker and Trammell was attributed to the club's turnaround. Houk retired after the 1978 season, but resurfaced in Boston where he managed the Red Sox from 1981-84. He concluded his 20 years as a manager with a record of 1,619 wins and 1,531 losses.

In 1979, the Tigers went through three managers—Les Moss, Dick Tracewski and Sparky Anderson, who had been fired by Cincinnati following the 1978 season despite a 92-69 record, four National League pennants and two World Series titles.

Anderson had managed another "classic" keystone combination in Cincinnati in second baseman Joe Morgan and shortstop Davey Concepcion from 1972-78. He doesn't dare compare the two double-play combinations.

Former Tiger teammate, pitcher Jack Billingham, saw similarities.

"Lou and Alan were pretty damn close to Morgan and Concepcion," said Billingham, who played for both Cincinnati and Detroit. "I will say that Joe (Morgan) was the best player I ever played with."

"I didn't think Joe and Davey could ever be matched, but I played with Lou and Alan for two seasons (1978-79) and they just got better and better," Billingham said. "They added two years to my career. Being a sinkerball pitcher, and having Lou and Alan backing me up allowed me to win 20-some games (actually 25) my last two seasons. Once those groundballs start sneaking through the infield, you're in trouble. With

Lou and Alan, I didn't have that problem. You're only as good as the people around you."

During his 13 years in the major leagues, the right-handed pitcher won 145 games and posted a respectable 3.83 earned-run-average.

Anderson said there were a few differences between Whitaker and Trammell, "but not in ability."

"Lou never worried about the history or the past," Anderson said. "Alan loved to know the past history. He just loved the history of the game."

"Lou was very quiet, but very durable," Anderson continued. "He never made the game of baseball a life-and-death issue. He believed the game was to enjoy. He was a street player because he learned how to play the game in the street. He never put pressure on himself. He just came to the park everyday to play baseball."

"When I played, I just went to the ballpark to play baseball, not to talk," Whitaker said.

"Lou's always been such a good person," Anderson said. "Every once in a while—and when I say that I mean every three years—we'd sit down and talk. He never bragged about himself. He just loved to play the game."

"Offensively, Lou had fun hitting....and he could hit with power," Anderson said. "He didn't bare down at the plate, whereas a guy like (Pete) Rose bared down every time he batted. And I don't know if I've ever seen a better two-strike hitter. He'd foul away ball after ball until he got on base with a hit or a walk."

Whitaker's relaxed style of play was mistaken by some as nonchalant. Not so, according to Trammell.

"Some people may have thought Lou was nonchalant, but that wasn't true," Trammell said. "They said the same thing about (Hall of Famer) Rod Carew, who was real smooth. Rod just glided. It was just the grace and style Lou and Rod had."

"Lou was as tough mentally as anyone I've played with. And Lou was the best clutch hitter I played with."

"It was just his mold of playing," Harwell said. "It was so easy for Lou. He didn't have the fire that a (Kirk) Gibson had. Lou went about it day-to-day."

Kirk Gibson spent 17 seasons in the majors, 12 with the Tigers (1979-87 and 1993-95). A fierce competitor, he played the outfield and was the Tigers' designated hitter. He is best remembered for his two-run, pinch-hit homer in the bottom of the ninth inning off Oakland relief specialist Dennis Eckersley that propelled the Los Angeles Dodgers to a 5-4 victory over the Athletics in Game 1 of the 1988 World Series. Barely able to walk because of injuries, Gibson's homer is replayed on television constantly, showing him limping around the bases, pumping his right arm up-and-down in celebration. His homer led the way for the Dodgers' five-game World Series victory.

Whitaker avoided the hoopla and focused on playing baseball.

"Lou had everything he needed to be a great second baseman—sure hands, good arm, he was great on the pivot at second base," Harwell said. "He did everything required of a second baseman."

Charlie Gehringer, the Hall of Famer who played second base for the Tigers for, ironically, 19 years (1924-42), once compared himself to Whitaker, saying he considered himself a better offensive player, but not defensively.

"Gehringer always loved Lou," Tiger historian Lew Matlin said. "He said several times, 'Well, I couldn't field with Lou, but I could out-hit him.'"

As a matter of fact, several all-time Tiger teams list both Gehringer and Whitaker at second base.

## GEHRINGER VS. WHITAKER

The following is a quick statistical comparison of Tiger second basemen Charlie Gehringer and Lou Whitaker:

|  | Gehringer | Whitaker |
| --- | --- | --- |
| Seasons | 19 | 19 |
| Years | 1924-42 | 1977-95 |
| Batting average | .320 | .276 |
| Runs scored | 1,774 | 1,386 |
| Base hits | 2,839 | 2,369 |
| Runs batted in | 1,427 | 1,084 |
| Home runs | 184 | 244 |
| Errors | 310 | 189 |
| Double plays | 1,447 | 1,527 |
| Assists | 7,091 | 6,653 |
| Putouts | 5,446 | 4,771 |
| Fielding percentage | .976 | .984 |

Trammell, meanwhile, had a lot of fire in his belly.

"Shortstops can be bias, but I always thought the shortstop was as much the key as anyone," Trammell said. "I loved playing shortstop, playing up the middle (of the infield). I felt like a captain."

Trammell's defensive talents on the diamond was a result of fielding balls off his family home's chimney when he was in elementary and high school.

"I used to mark off a box on the chimney and my goal was to throw the ball inside the box, then field the ball cleanly," Trammell explained. "That was great for my hand-and-eye coordination."

"To be a successful shortstop, you have to have the sixth sense on where all the guys should be," Trammell said. "I was in tune. I loved playing and was always prepared. I always enjoyed the cat-and-mouse game.....where did the batter hit the ball before? We had to read the ball off the bat, pay attention and have to be able to react quickly."

"Whenever there were two outs at the end of a game and there was a groundball hit to Tram, I'd start walking up the (dugout) steps because I knew the game was over," Anderson said. "Alan had such sure, soft hands. There was no one better picking up the baseball. He had such a quick and accurate release. Every time he threw the ball, regardless of where he was on the field, it was thrown overhand."

"I'll never forget one day Trammell was taking some infield practice and (Hall of Famer) Pee Wee Reese happened to be around," Anderson recalled. "I asked Pee Wee who did Trammell remind him of. The answer was Pee Wee Reese. That's just how good Alan was."

"Trammell had great consistency," Harwell said. "In the clutch, you wanted the ball hit to Alan. Fundamentally he was so sound. He concentrated on the game and brought a great passion to it. He had great respect and love for baseball."

As Whitaker and Trammell enjoyed more and more personal success, do did Anderson's Tigers, who posted winning records every season from 1978 through 1983.

Then came 1984, the year Detroit ran away with everything. The Tigers got off to an amazing 35-5 start and coasted to a 104-58 record to easily win the American League East title by 15 games over Toronto.

Trammell led the Tigers with a .314 average while adding 14 homers and 69 runs-batted-in despite missing 43 games due to tendonitis. Whitaker chipped in with a .289 mark, second-highest on the club, plus 13 homers and 56 RBIs. Because the Tigers clinched the AL-East title so early, the keystone mates were rested down the stretch of the regular season in preparation for the playoffs. As a result, they're DP totals were slightly down: Whitaker had 83, Trammell 71.

Dave Bergman was at first, while Howard Johnson patrolled third. The outfield featured Chet Lemon, Larry Herndon and Gibson. The catcher was Lance Parrish. Darrell Evans was a potent designated hitter with 16 homers and 63 RBIs.

Anderson had Barbaro Garbey, Tom Brookens and Ruppert Jones coming off the bench.

Pitching-wiser, the Tigers were loaded, with Jack Morris (19-11), Dan Petry (18-8), Milt Wilcox (17-8), and relief pitchers Willie Hernandez (9-3, 32 saves) and Aurelio Lopez (10-1, 14 saves). Hernandez was named both the American League's Most Valuable Player and Cy Young Award winner that season.

Morris set the tone for the season in the fourth game with a 4-0, no-hit, eight-strikeout victory over the White Sox in Chicago. The Tigers won their first nine games, lost to Kansas City, then rattled off seven straight wins for a 16-1 start. A nine-game win streak in mid-May put them at 35-5. By the end of June, Detroit was 55-21 and, for all practical purposes, the race in the American League East was over. In one-run games, they were 25-11.

In the American League Championship Series, the Tigers, led by Trammell's .364 average, knocked out Kansas City in three games, then took the San Diego Padres in five in the World Series. The Padres were managed by Dick Williams, who won a pair of World Series crowns with the Oakland Athletics in 1972 and 1973. He was also the manager of the 100-to-1 long-shot Boston Red Sox, who went from ninth place in 1966 to the American League pennant in 1967 before losing to the St. Louis Cardinals in seven World Series games.

The Tigers took the 1984 Series opener, 3-2, thanks to Herndon's two-run homer in the fifth inning and Morris's complete-game, eight hitter.

In Game 2, the Padres overcame an early 3-0 deficit to post a 5-3 win, the difference being a three-run homer by the Padres' Kurt Bevacqua.

The Tigers then won the next three games, 5-2, 4-2 and 8-4 behind the pitching of Wilcox, Morris and Petry.

In the fifth and final game, the Padres closed to 5-4 in the eighth, but Gibson put it out of reach with a three-run blast that made the count 8-4.

Trammell was named the World Series' Most Valuable Player based on his 9-for-20 hitting performance (.450). The nine hits tied a record for a five-game World Series. He also had two homers and six runs-batted-in. Whitaker batted .278 with a pair of doubles. His six runs scored tied a record for a five-game Series.

"We had great defensive players, we had great pitching," Whitaker said. "We did it all. We made very few mistakes."

"Lou and Alan were a big, big part of that 35-5 streak and 1984 championship team," Harwell recalled. "Whitaker led off and he'd get on base. Then Trammell would bat second and he'd get on. Before you knew it, the Tigers would have a couple of first-inning runs on the board for their pitchers to work with."

Anderson was named the American League's Manager of the Year. More important, he became the first manager to win World Series titles in both leagues. He won a pair in Cincinnati in 1975 and 1976 in the National League, and the 1984 AL crown with the Tigers. The only other manager to achieve World Series crowns in both leagues is Tony LaRussa, who won in 1989 with Oakland and in 2006 with St. Louis.

Following third-place finishes in the American League East in 1985 and 1986, the Tigers nailed down the division title on the final day of the 1987 season with a major-league best record of 98-64. The Tigers entered the final weekend series at home one game behind Toronto, but swept the three games by scores of 4-3, 3-2 and 1-0 to finish two games ahead.

Doyle Alexander, whom the Tigers picked up midway through the 1987 season from Atlanta after a 5-10 start, pitched seven strong innings in the 4-3 win to run his Detroit record to 9-0. Trammell's homer in the third proved to be the game winner. Rookie relief pitcher Mike Henneman worked the final two innings for Detroit to pick up his seventh save.

In the 3-2 victory that went 12 innings, Morris pitched splendid ball for nine innings, then the Tigers got three scoreless relief innings from the right-handed Henneman, who ran his record to 11-3.

The Tigers nailed down the division title when Frank Tanana hurled a complete-game, 1-0 masterpiece. The lone run came on Herndon's solo homer in the second.

In that final three-game series, Whitaker batted .384, Trammell .375.

Following the last out of the final regular-season game, Whitaker pulled second base out of the infield dirt and signed it: "To Alan Trammell, 1987 AL MVP, - Lou Whitaker."

Trammell had an incredible season, batting .343 with 205 hits, 28 homers, 105 runs-batted-in, 109 runs, 34 doubles and a .551 slugging average from the cleanup position. He was the first Tiger since Al Kaline in 1955 to collect 200 hits and 100 RBIs in the same season. In the final month of the season, he hit .416.

Despite the Tigers' shortstop's heroics, George Bell of Toronto was named the American League's 1987 MVP by a 21-point margin over Trammell. Bell hit .308 with 47 homers and 134 RBIs, but he had a rough final week of the season, going 4-for-27, as the Blue Jays lost their final seven games.

In the 1987 American League Championship Series, the Tigers "got waxed," Trammell said, by the 85-77 Minnesota Twins, 4 games to 1. The Tigers struggled at the plate, including Trammell (.200) and Whitaker (.176), in the surprisingly short series. Pitcher Bert Blyleven picked up a pair of victories for the Twins, while Frank Viola and relief specialist Jeff Reardon each posted wins. In the World Series, Minnesota took down St. Louis in six games.

The Tigers went through a playoff dry spell until 2006, when Jim Leyland led the club to the World Series, only to fall in five games to St. Louis.

From 1988 through 1995, the Tigers experienced some ups and downs. In 1988, the Tigers finished one game behind Boston in the American League East, then lost 103 the following season. From 1990 through 1995, the Tigers suffered four losing seasons.

 Both Whitaker and Trammell continued to play well, though. As a matter of fact, in Whitaker's final three seasons (1993-95), he batted .290, .301 and .293.

For his career, Whitaker averaged less than 10 errors a season. He also played in 2,308 games at second, third on baseball's all-time list for second basemen behind Eddie Collins (1906-28) at 2,650 and Joe Morgan (1963-84) at 2,527.

In 1992, "Sweet Lou," as he was called by Tiger fans, reached two career milestones, recording both his 2,000th hit and his 200th home run.

Meanwhile, an elbow injury that first surfaced in 1983 came back in 1992 to haunt Trammell, limiting him to 28 games. In 1993, however, he rebounded with a .329 batting average, then spent the next three years playing a limited role (216 total games) before retiring in 1996. Trammell is just one of three players to play for the Tigers for at least 20 seasons, the others being Hall of Famers Al Kaline (1953-74) and Ty Cobb (1905-26), both of whom spent 22 years with the club.

Anderson retired at the age of 61 after the 1995 season, which saw the Tigers post a 60-84 mark. He was inducted into the Baseball Hall of

Fame in 2000 by the Veterans Committee with a career managerial record of 2,194 wins and 1,834 losses.

For the time being, the Hall of Fame doesn't appear to be in the picture for Whitaker and Trammell. In 2001, Whitaker's first year on the ballot, he received 2.91 percent of the vote. A player needs at least 5 percent to remain on future ballots, so he'll have to depend on the Veterans Committee.

Trammell has been on the ballot since 2002, but has come up short of the necessary 75 percent of the vote for election by the Baseball Writers Association of America.

"When I look at the Hall of Fame voting for Lou, I think it's shameful," Anderson said. "Lou is one of the finest second basemen in the game. He ranks among the top 10 ever to play the position."

"From those Tiger teams I managed, I think three should be in the Hall of Fame: Jack Morris, Lou Whitaker and Alan Trammell," Anderson said. "They really gave to the game. They said that Frank Robinson (the player) could carry a team for three weeks. Well, Jack, Lou and Alan could carry our Tiger teams for weeks. Those three belong in the Hall of Fame."

Morris, a righty, won 254 and lost 186 games during his 18 seasons (1977-90) in the majors, 14 of which were with Detroit, where he was 198-150. He finished his career with the Twins (1991), Blue Jays (1992-93) and Indians (1994), compiling a 56-36 mark.

In the postseason, Morris won two games for the Tigers in the 1984

World Series and two more for the Twins in the 1991 Fall Classic. In 13 career postseason starts, he posted an impressive 6-1 record.

"The writers who covered the Tigers saw our excellence everyday," Whitaker said of himself and Trammell. "Those writers who maybe saw us play once or twice, they're the (Hall of Fame) voters. Alan and I belong there (in the Hall)."

Tiger fans agree, saying that the offensive and defensive statistics of Whitaker and Trammell are comparable to former Chicago Cub second baseman Ryne Sandberg, who made the Hall in 2005, and former St. Louis shortstop Ozzie Smith, a member of the Class of 2002.

"It's been a mystery to me," Anderson said. "Baseball's greatest double-play combination belongs in the Hall of Fame. There should be no question about it."

Trammell became manager of the Tigers from 2003-2005, compiling a record of 186-300, before he was let go. After losing 119 games in 2003, Trammell's club posted a 72-90 mark the following season, an improvement of 29 wins. In 2005, the Tigers stood 42-44 at the All-Star break, but injuries to key players and inexperienced players caused them to fade the second half of the season to finish 71-91.

His guidance and leadership were instrumental in the Tigers' success in 2006 under Leyland, who acknowledged that Trammell had set the table. Despite his three losing seasons, Trammell re-established professionalism and pride in the Tiger organization.

Prior to the 2006 World Series, Leyland paid tribute to Trammell and his former coaching staff that was let go after 2005. "We're here now with a different staff, but I would be remiss if I didn't mention how hard those guys worked," Leyland said of Trammell and his staff. "They worked their tails off. I'm the fortunate one. I came in and reaped the benefits of a lot of hard work by a lot of people."

When it became apparent he was going to be dismissed as the Tigers' skipper, Trammell said, "Whether I'm there or not, I'll always be a Tiger, and I'll always root for the Tigers."

Tiger fans had the opportunity to thank Trammell for his years of service in Detroit prior to Game 2 of the 2006 World Series when he was introduced and received a long, thunderous standing ovation.

Prior to becoming the Tigers' manager, Trammell was a baseball operations assistant for Detroit, then the club's hitting coach in 1999. He spent the 2000-2002 seasons as a coach with the San Diego Padres.

Today, he's the bench coach for the Chicago Cubs under new manager Lou Piniella.

Whitaker is also enjoying life and his privacy in Lakeland, Fla. He's a regular at the Tigers' spring training camp in Lakeland, helping out wherever he can. Like Whitaker the player, he prefers to remain quiet and stay out of the spotlight.

That was difficult, though, in 1985 when he was named to the American League All-Star Team. En route to Minnesota for the Mid-Summer Classic, Whitaker left his Tiger uniform in his car at the airport in Detroit. Once he arrived in Minnesota, he was forced to purchase a replica

Tiger jersey from a vendor and write his name and "No. 1" on the back with a black magic marker.  He wore a Tigers' mesh hat and borrowed a glove. Obviously, he was in the national spotlight. He then went 0-for-2 in the American League's 6-1 loss.

## DEFENSE BY THE NUMBERS

A look at the fielding statistics of Lou Whitaker and Alan Trammell during the time period they played together at their primary positions, second base and shortstop (PO – putouts; AST – assists; E – errors; DP – double plays; PCT. – fielding percentage):

| | LOU WHITAKER, 2B | | | | | ALAN TRAMMELL, SS | | | | |
|---|---|---|---|---|---|---|---|---|---|---|
| YEAR | PO | AST | E | DP | PCT. | PO | AST | E | DP | PCT. |
| 1977 | 17 | 18 | 0 | 2 | 1.000 | 15 | 34 | 2 | 5 | .961 |
| 1978 | 301 | 458 | 17 | 95 | .978 | 239 | 421 | 14 | 95 | .979 |
| 1979 | 280 | 369 | 9 | 103 | .986 | 245 | 388 | 26 | 99 | .961 |
| 1980 | 340 | 428 | 12 | 93 | .985 | 225 | 412 | 13 | 89 | .980 |
| 1981 | 227 | 354 | 9 | 77 | .985 | 181 | 347 | 9 | 65 | .983 |
| 1982 | 331 | 470 | 10 | 120 | .988 | 259 | 459 | 16 | 97 | .978 |
| 1983 | 299 | 447 | 13 | 92 | .983 | 236 | 367 | 13 | 71 | .979 |
| 1984 | 290 | 405 | 15 | 83 | .979 | 180 | 314 | 10 | 71 | .980 |
| 1985 | 314 | 414 | 11 | 101 | .985 | 225 | 400 | 15 | 89 | .977 |
| 1986 | 276 | 421 | 11 | 98 | .984 | 238 | 445 | 22 | 99 | .969 |
| 1987 | 275 | 416 | 17 | 99 | .976 | 222 | 421 | 19 | 94 | .971 |
| 1988 | 218 | 284 | 8 | 53 | .984 | 195 | 355 | 11 | 67 | .980 |
| 1989 | 327 | 393 | 11 | 99 | .985 | 188 | 396 | 9 | 71 | .985 |
| 1990 | 286 | 372 | 6 | 98 | .991 | 232 | 409 | 14 | 102 | .979 |
| 1991 | 255 | 361 | 4 | 91 | .994 | 131 | 296 | 9 | 60 | .979 |
| 1992 | 256 | 312 | 9 | 72 | .984 | 46 | 80 | 3 | 16 | .977 |
| 1993 | 236 | 322 | 11 | 75 | .981 | 79 | 181 | 3 | 24 | .989 |
| 1994 | 136 | 246 | 12 | 44 | .970 | 117 | 181 | 10 | 44 | .968 |
| 1995 | 107 | 163 | 4 | 32 | .985 | 86 | 158 | 5 | 34 | .980 |
| Totals | 4,771 | 6,653 | 189 | 1,527 | .984 | 3,339 | 6,064 | 223 | 1,292 | .977 |

**Note:** *1981 and 1994 were strike-shortened seasons with the Tigers playing 109 and 115 games, respectively.*

## CHAPTER FIFTEEN

# THE BEST OF THE REST

A QUICK LOOK AT SOME GREAT,
BUT NOT-QUITE-CLASSIC KEYSTONE COMBINATIONS,
LISTED IN CHRONOLOGICAL ORDER:

**2B BUDDY MYER & SS JOE CRONIN (1929-34), Washington Senators:**
Joe Cronin was one of the most-successful and most-beloved sportsmen in the game. His success as a manager and president of the American League (1948-59) overshadows what he accomplished on the field as a player, especially from 1929-34, when he teamed with Buddy Myer to form one of baseball's finest keystone combinations with the Washington Senators. Cronin spent 18 full seasons in the majors, seven with the Senators and 11 with the Red Sox. In the six seasons he played with Myer, the Senators won more than 92 games four times, including 1933, when Cronin, then player-manager, led the Senators to 99 wins and the American League pennant. In the World Series, though, the New York Giants buzzed their way past the Senators in five games. In 1935, the Senators sold Cronin to Boston, where he became player-manager from 1935-44. He retired as a player in 1945 when he broke his leg, but he stayed on and managed the Red Sox to the 1946 American League pennant. The Sox fell to St. Louis in the World Series in seven. During his six seasons with Myer, the two totaled 1,074 double plays—517 for Myer, 557 for Cronin. Myer spent his first two seasons (1925-26) with the Senators, then was traded to the Red Sox in what Washington owner Clark Griffith called "the dumbest move I ever made." He got Myer back in 1929, but had to give

up five players for him. A .303 career hitter, Myer won the AL batting title in 1935 with a .349 mark. He batted .300 or better eight times. He led the American League in fielding in 1931 and 1938, and had a career-high 138 double plays in 1935 with five different shortstops after Cronin left for Boston. Cronin, a member of the Baseball Hall of Fame, batted .300 or better 11 times and drove in 100-plus runs eight times. During his career, he turned 1,165 double plays at short, 1,241 overall. His keystone mate Myer had 963 career DPs at second, 1,134 overall.

**2B JACKIE HAYES & SS LUKE APPLING (1932-39), Chicago White Sox:** Both Hayes and Appling insisted that old Comiskey Park was built on a junkyard. No one knows for sure. Despite the poor playing conditions, Hayes and Appling provided fans with plenty of excitement in the middle of the White Sox's infield. In the eight seasons they formed a keystone combo, they totaled 1,203 double plays. Appling was the leader of the Sox, who failed to win a pennant during the 20 seasons he played (1930-50; he served in the Army in 1944). At the time, he was considered the best lead-off hitter in the game (.310 career average) and he set major league defensive records for shortstops that were eventually broken by another White Sox shortstop, Luis Aparicio. His .388 batting average in 1936 led the league and marked the first time a shortstop won a batting title. A seven-time all-star, he turned 1,424 double plays in his career despite his poor .948 career fielding percentage. He picked up the nickname "Old Aches and Pain" because he constantly complained about his injuries. Appling was named to the Baseball Hall of Fame in 1964. Hayes spent five seasons (1927-31) in Washington before joining the White Sox in 1932. Joe Cronin, who was in baseball from 1926 through 1947, said Hayes was "the best double-play artist in the league." A .265 career hitter, Hayes was involved in 639 double plays at second, 702 overall. His career was cut short in 1940 when he lost sight in one eye. He eventually went completely blind.

**2B TONY LAZZERI & SS FRANK CROSETTI (1932-37), New York Yankees:** Here are two keystoners who both played with Babe Ruth, Lou Gehrig and Joe DiMaggio and won 11 World Series titles between them. Lazzeri started his career with the Yankees in 1926, Crosetti in 1932. For six seasons, they formed the keystone combination of the mighty Yankee teams, totaling 824 double plays from 1932-37. Lazzeri, named to the Hall of Fame in 1991, participated in 808 career DPs at second during his 14-year career. He spent the 1938 season with the Cubs and 1939 with the Dodgers and Giants before retiring. A .292 career hitter, he batted above .300 five times, drove in 100 or more runs seven times and hit 14 or more homers eight times, big offensive numbers for a second baseman in those days. He was a member of five World Series championship teams. Crosetti spent his entire 17-year career (1932-48) with the Yankees and then some. When he retired after the 1948 season, he coached third base for the New Yorkers for 20 years. He participated in 944 double plays at short, 968 overall. His best years, double-play wise, came in 1938 and 1939 when he and new second baseman Joe Gordon totaled 238 DPs. A career .245 batter, Crosetti played on six world championship teams. As the Yanks' third-base coach, he was associated with nine more championship teams.

**2B BILLY HERMAN & SS BILLY JURGES (1932-38), Chicago Cubs:** During the seven seasons Herman and Jurges formed a keystone combination, they totaled 1,269 double plays, which is one of the reasons why the Cubs enjoyed a decade of success in the 1930s. The Cubs posted 10 straight winning seasons and won three National League pennants, but they couldn't win a World Series, losing to the Yankees twice and the Tigers once. Herman, a 1975 inductee into the Hall of Fame and a 10-time All-Star with 1,177 double plays at second (1,202 overall), was a .304 career hitter, topping the .300 mark nine times during his 17 seasons, which also included stops in Brooklyn, Boston and Pittsburgh. When he retired, he managed the Pirates to a 61-92 mark in 1947. Nineteen years later, he managed the Red Sox in 1965 and 1966, posting a two-year record of 128-182. Jurges spent 17 seasons in the big leagues, posting a .258 career batting average and turning 929 double plays at short, 982 overall. He played with the Cubs from 1931-38, the Giants (1939-45) and then back with the Cubs (1946-47). Like his former keystone mate, Jurges managed the Red Sox for portions of two seasons in 1959 and 1960. His record: 59-63.

**2B RED SCHOENDIENST & SS MARTY MARION (1946-50), St. Louis Cardinals:** Here's a keystone combination that didn't set the National League on fire with its bats, but the two did superb jobs manning the middle of the infield for the Cardinals for five seasons, totaling 918 double plays. Schoendienst, voted into the Hall of Fame in 1989 and a 10-time All-Star, was a career .289 hitter, but he lacked power. He did turn 1,368 career double plays at second and posted an impressive .982 fielding percentage. Schoendienst was on the Cardinals' 1946 World Series championship team, which beat Boston in seven games, as well as two Milwaukee Braves' teams that won National League pennants in 1957 and 1958. In the World Series, both against the Yankees, the Braves won in 1957, but lost to the Bronx Bombers in 1958. After retiring in 1963, Schoendienst became the Cardinals' manager from 1965-76, posting a record of 1,041-955 with two National League pennants (1967 and 1968) and a World Series crown (1967 against the Red Sox). Marion spent his entire 13-year career in St. Louis, 11 with the Cardinals and two with the Browns. Marion, who averaged 82 DPs a season, was a .263 career hitter. He had all the necessary tools to be an eight-time All-Star second baseman. He was the surprise winner of the 1944 National League Most Valuable Player Award with his .267 average, six homers and 63 runs-batted-in as the Cardinals won 105 games and defeated the Browns in the World Series. Marion's teammate, Stan Musial, posted much better numbers that season—.347 average, 12 homers and 94 runs-batted-in—yet the outfielder finished fourth in the balloting. Like his keystone partner, Marion became a manager. In 1951, he led the Cardinals to a third-place finish with an 81-73 mark. In 1952 and 1953, he became the player-manager of the St. Louis Browns and experienced little success, posting a two-year record of 96-161. He fared much better with the White Sox in 1955-56 with records of 91-63 and 85-69.

**2B JOHNNY TEMPLE & SS ROY McMILLAN (1954-58), Cincinnati Reds:** Temple and McMillan formed the National League's top keystone combination during the 1950s, totaling 1,008 double plays between them. Temple spent 13 seasons in the majors, eight with the Reds (1952-59), while McMillan had a 16-year career, 10 with Cincinnati (1951-60). The two became keystone partners in 1954 and quickly established themselves as top defensive players, combining for 246 double plays. Temple was a four-time All-Star who was a .284 career hitter. Although he lacked power and the ability to drive in runs, he did score 70 or more runs six times with the Reds, including 1959, when he scored 102. A brilliant bunter, he ranked among the top three in the National League in sacrifice bunts five times. In 1959, he led the NL with 13 sacrifice flies. Temple also spent some time with the Indians, Orioles and Astros before retiring in 1964 with 829 DPs at second. McMillan won three straight Gold Gloves (1957-59) for his play at short and was also a two-time All-Star. During his career with the Reds (1951-60) and then later with the Braves and Mets, he was involved in 1,304 career double plays at short. A .260 hitter, his career average dropped to .243 when he saw less playing time later in his career. McMillan spent a third of a season managing the 1975 New York Mets to a 26-27 mark after replacing the fired Yogi Berra. Although Temple and McMillan never led the Reds to a National League flag, they were involved in one of the most exciting pennant races in 1956 when they finished 91-63, two games behind NL champion Brooklyn and one-game behind second-place Milwaukee.

**2B JULIAN JAVIER & SS DAL MAXVILL, St. Louis Cardinals, 1966-70:** Here's a keystone combination that played a key role in the Cardinals winning National League pennants in 1967 and 1968, yet never received the accolades it deserved. The twosome totaled 784 double plays in the five full seasons they played together—Maxvill with 401 and Javier with 383—but they played in the shadows of two "classic keystone combinations," Pittsburgh's Bill Mazeroski and Gene Alley, and the Chicago Cubs' Glenn Beckert and Don Kessinger. Between the two, they won just one Gold Glove (Maxvill in 1968) and Javier was the lone All-Star selection (1968). Javier, who came from the Dominican Republic, was the Cards' starting second baseman from 1960 through 1970 before a younger Ted Sizemore, acquired from the Dodgers, won the job in 1971. Javier, who hit a career-high .282 in 1969, saw limited action in 1971 before being traded to Cincinnati for pitcher Tony Cloninger. A .257 hitter, Javier was involved in 907 career DPs at second, all with the Cardinals. Maxvill joined the Cards in 1962 and became their regular shortstop in 1966 when Dick Groat was traded to the Phillies. He remained the Cardinals' starting shortstop until midway through the 1972 season when he was shipped to Oakland, then Pittsburgh (1973), then back to Oakland (1974-75). Maxvill was involved in 575 DPs at shortstop during his stay in St. Louis, 649 overall. A .217 career hitter, Maxvill was obviously in the Cardinals' lineup for his defense. In 1967, Maxwill batted only .227 as the Cardinals won the NL pennant and defeated Boston in seven World Series games. The following season, he hit a career-high .253, but the Cardinals lost to Detroit in seven in the Series. With a lineup that included feared hitters like catcher Tim McCarver, first baseman Orlando Cepeda, and outfielders Lou Brock, Curt Flood and Roger Maris, plus a pitching staff that showcased Bob Gibson, Steve Carlton and Nelson Briles, St. Louis didn't need to count on Maxvill for offense. Maxvill won three World Series rings, two with the Cardinals— 1964 vs. the Yankees and 1967 vs. the Red Sox—and one with Oakland in 1974, when the Athletics defeated the Dodgers in five. Javier won two Series rings in 1964 and 1967. He batted .333 in 19 World Series games.

**2B BOBBY GRICH & SS MARK BELANGER (1973-76), Baltimore Orioles:** Grich and Belanger patrolled the middle infield together for four seasons and each won four Gold Gloves during that time. Together, they totaled 877 double plays. Grich spent 17 seasons in the majors, the first seven (1970-76) with the Orioles and the final 10 with the Angels. A career .260 hitter with 224 homers, he was involved in 1,302 double plays as a second baseman. Belanger spent 17 of his 18 seasons (1965-82) with the Orioles and won eight Gold Gloves. A light hitter (.228 career), his forte was defense and great range at short. He totaled 1,054 double plays at short during his career. He won a World Series ring in 1970 when the Orioles beat Cincinnati in five games. He and Grich led the Orioles to American League East titles in 1973 and 1974, but on both occasions they were defeated by eventual world champion Oakland in the American League playoffs. Belanger spent the 1982 season with the Los Angeles Dodgers, as the Orioles were in the process of breaking in a new, young shortstop by the name of Cal Ripken Jr.

**2B DAVEY LOPES & SS BILL RUSSELL (1973-81), Los Angeles Dodgers:** Although they only won one Gold Glove between them— Lopes in 1978—in the nine years they played together, these two anchored baseball's longest-running starting infield with Steve Garvey at first and Ron Cey at third. With this All-Star foursome in the lineup, the Dodgers won 804 games between 1973 and 1981, four National League pennants, a World Series title and had five second-place finishes in the National League West. Lopes and Russell, both originally outfielders, totaled 1,297 double plays. Offensively, they were solid. Lopes was a career .263 hitter with 557 stolen bases. He also played for the Athletics, Cubs and Astros. Russell was a Dodger "lifer," spending 18 seasons (1969-86) with the club and hitting a career .263. While wearing the "Dodger Blue," he played in 2,181 games. Only outfielder Zach Wheat (1909-1926) played more games (2,410) as a Dodger. Russell later managed the Dodgers from 1996-98, taking over for the retired Tom Lasorda, and compiled a record of 173 wins and 149 losses.

**2B RYNE SANBERG & SS SHAWON DUNSTON (1985-91), Chicago Cubs:** Sanberg is generally recognized as the Cubs' greatest second baseman. He came up with the Phillies in 1981, saw limited action, then was traded to Chicago where he spent his first full season (1982) at third base. He moved to second in 1983 when then-second baseman Bump Wills opted for free agency. His double-play partner in 1983 and 1984 was 37-year-old Larry Bowa. In 1985, the Cubs went with the 22-year-old Dunston at short over the aging Bowa. During their six seasons as a keystone combo, Sanberg and Dunston totaled 1,032 double plays. Sanberg was a gem at second as he committed just 109 career errors (less than seven per season), had a career fielding percentage of .989 and was involved in 1,158 double plays at second. He won nine Gold Gloves, was a 10-time All-Star and the National League's 1984 Most Valuable Player. Inducted into the Baseball Hall of Fame in 2005, Sanberg was a solid offensive performer with a career batting average of .285, plus 282 homers and 1,061 runs-batted-in. Dunston was a solid performer both in the field (708 DPs at short) and at the plate, where he averaged .269 for his career. He stayed with the Cubs through the 1995 season, then spent the rest of his 18-year career with the Pirates, Indians, Giants, Cardinals and Mets.

**2B ROBERTO ALOMAR & SS OMAR VIZQUEL (1999-2001), Cleveland Indians:** These two middle infielders each won Gold Gloves all three years they played together in Cleveland and totaled 575 double plays. They probably would have become one of the greatest keystone combinations in the game had the Indians not traded Alomar to the Mets after the 2001 season. He played for the Padres, Blue Jays, Orioles, Mets, White Sox and Diamondbacks in addition to Cleveland, where he batted .323, .310 and .336. Overall, Alomar, now retired, won 10 Gold Gloves at second and turned 1,408 DPs. He did win two World Series rings with the Blue Jays in 1992 and 1993. Vizquel spent 11 seasons in Cleveland (1994-2004) after spending five with the Mariners. During his three years with Alomar, he hit .333, .287 and .255. The keystoners led the Tribe to the postseason in 1999 and 2001, but the club suffered losses to Boston and Seattle, respectively, in the American League Divisional Series. Vizquel also played in two World Series with the Indians, but lost in 1995 to Atlanta and 1997 to Florida. After the 2004 season, he signed with San Francisco as a free agent, where he continues to work his magic in the field, winning an 11th Gold Glove in 2006. With 1,665 career DPs, he is now baseball's all-time leader for shortstops in that category through 2007.

**2B JEFF KENT & SS RICH AURILIA (1998-2002), San Francisco Giants:** The Giants became perennial National League contenders in 1998 with the arrival of the keystone combination of second baseman Jeff Kent and shortstop Rich Aurilia. After several losing seasons, the Giants ripped off 89, 86, 97, 90 and 95 victories between 1998 and 2002 when Kent and Aurilia took command of the Giants' middle infield. And during that time, they totaled 960 double plays. The keystone combo took the Giants within one game of the 2002 World Series title. After placing second in the National League West, the Giants defeated

Atlanta and St. Louis in the playoffs before falling to the Anaheim Angels in seven Series games. Kent was one of the key offensive forces behind the Giants' success that season, with a .313 average, 37 homers and 108 runs-batted-in. Through the 2007 season, Kent, now a Dodger, has 1,209 career DPs at second. Aurilia, who has great range, good hands and a strong arm, was the perfect double-play mate for Kent. In 2000, he recorded a career-high 110 double plays at short. Now back with the Giants after spending the 2005 and 2006 seasons with the Reds, Aurilia started the 2007 season penciled in at all four infield positions. Aurilia handles the bat well, as he proved in 2001 when he crashed 37 homers, drove home 97 runs and batted .324.

**2B ALFONSO SORIANO & SS DEREK JETER (2001-03), New York Yankees:** These two enjoyed three productive seasons together before Soriano was shipped to Texas in the Alex Rodriguez trade following the 2003 season. The two formed a flashy keystone combo that combined for 455 double plays. Offensively, Soriano, an All-Star in 2002 and 2003, batted .268, .300 and .290, belted 95 homers and drove home 266 runs in his three seasons with the New Yorkers. At Texas, he hit a total of 64 homers and drove in 195 runs in 2004 and 2005. In 2006, he played for Washington, where he was moved to left field. Following the 2006 season, he signed with the Chicago Cubs. Jeter, who had 988 DPs through 2007, won Gold Gloves in 2004, 2005 and 2006 as he's maintained his All-Star play at shortstop. The 1996 Rookie of the Year had a .317 career batting average through 2007 and had scored more than 100 runs in 11 of his 13 seasons. An eight-time All-Star, Jeter is a .309 hitter in the postseason. And the Yankees, with Jeter at shortstop, are 4-2 in World Series play. Jeter is now teamed with 25-year-old Robinson Cano, who has had three impressive seasons at second base, batting .314 with 286 career DPs.

## CHAPTER SIXTEEN

# THE FIRST BASEMEN

All successful keystone combinations need a slick-fielding first baseman. Many double plays would not be completed without the first baseman's ability to scoop throws out of the dirt or stretch that extra inch to "turn two." First basemen listed are those who played with "Baseball's Classic Keystone Combinations" and appeared in the most games at that position during each season (DP - double plays; PCT. - fielding percentage):

## JOHNNY EVERS & JOE TINKER
### CHICAGO CUBS

| YEAR | 1ST BASEMEN | DP | PCT. |
|------|-------------|-----|------|
| 1902 | Frank Chance | 21 | .968 |
| 1903 | Frank Chance | 49 | .972 |
| 1904 | Frank Chance | 48 | .990 |
| 1905 | Frank Chance | 54 | .990 |
| 1906 | Frank Chance | 71 | .989 |
| 1907 | Frank Chance | 64 | .992 |
| 1908 | Frank Chance | 56 | .989 |
| 1909 | Frank Chance | 43 | .994 |
| 1910 | Frank Chance | 48 | .996 |
| 1911 | Vic Saier | 44 | .980 |
| 1912 | Vic Saier | 67 | .992 |

Turning Two: Chance, who led the National League in stolen bases with 67 in 1903 and 57 in 1906, is a Hall of Famer, Class of 1946. Saier was the Cubs' starting first baseman from 1911 through 1916 and had 422 career DPs. He had a career batting mark of .263 and average power during his eight-year career.

## CHARLIE GEHRINGER & BILLY ROGELL
### DETROIT TIGERS

| YEAR | 1ST BASEMEN | DP | PCT. |
|------|-------------|-----|------|
| 1932 | Harry Davis | 123 | .989 |
| 1933 | Hank Greenberg | 111 | .988 |
| 1934 | Hank Greenberg | 124 | .990 |
| 1935 | Hank Greenberg | 142 | .992 |
| 1936 | Jackie Burns | 126 | .994 |
| 1937 | Hank Greenberg | 133 | .992 |
| 1938 | Hank Greenberg | 146 | .991 |

**Turning Two: Greenberg,** a five-time All-Star, is a Hall of Famer, Class of 1956. He hit 58 homers in 1938, three short of breaking Babe Ruth's 1927 single-season record of 60. **Davis** spent two seasons with the Tigers (1932-33) and totaled 156 DPs in 185 games. **Burns** spent six successful seasons with the Browns (1930-35), then one with Detroit. He had 776 career DPs at first. He was with the Browns for 6-plus seasons and concluded his career with a .279 average and .992 fielding percentage.

## JOE GORDON & PHIL RIZZUTO
### NEW YORK YANKEES

| YEAR | 1ST BASEMEN | DP | PCT. |
|------|-------------|-----|------|
| 1941 | Johnny Sturm | 117 | .990 |
| 1942 | Buddy Hassett | 130 | .991 |
| 1946 | Nick Etten | 80 | .991 |

Turning Two: **Sturm** played just one season in the majors. **Hassett** spent three seasons with the Dodgers (1936-38), three with the Braves (1939-41) and one with the Yankees. As a first baseman, he had 642 career DPs. **Etten** was a superb first baseman, participating in 148, 144 and 149 DPs from 1943-45. A .277 hitter, he was an All-Star in 1945.

## BOBBY DOERR & JOHNNY PESKY
## BOSTON RED SOX

| YEAR | 1ST BASEMEN | DP | PCT. |
|------|-------------|-----|------|
| 1942 | Tony Lupien | 99 | .992 |
| 1946 | Rudy York | 154 | .994 |
| 1947 | Jake Jones | 110 | .991 |
| 1951 | Walt Dropo | 91 | .987 |

Turning Two: **Lupien** played for the Red Sox for three seasons (1940-42), then the Phillies (1943-44) and the White Sox (1948). He had 532 DPs and an impressive career fielding percentage of .993. **York** spent 12 seasons in the majors (1937-48), but just one-plus with the Red Sox, hitting .276 with 17 homers and 119 RBIs in 1946. **Jones** took the first-base job away from York a third of the way into the 1947 season after being traded from the White Sox (1941-42, 1946, plus part of 1947). His 110 DPs in 1947 with the Red Sox came in 109 games. He lost the job to **Billy Goodman** in 1948. **Dropo** was the Red Sox's first baseman in 1950 and 1951 (238 total DPs), then saw service with the Tigers, White Sox, Reds and Orioles.

## JACKIE ROBINSON & PEE WEE REESE
## BROOKLYN DODGERS

| YEAR | 1ST BASEMEN | DP | PCT. |
|------|-------------|-----|------|
| 1948 | Gil Hodges | 85 | .986 |
| 1949 | Gil Hodges | 142 | .995 |
| 1950 | Gil Hodges | 159 | .994 |
| 1951 | Gil Hodges | 171 | .992 |
| 1952 | Gil Hodges | 152 | .992 |

**Turning Two: Hodges** won Gold Gloves in 1957, 1958 and 1959. He had the perfect build for a first baseman—6-feet-2, 200 pounds and agile. He manned first base for the Dodgers from 1948 to 1961. He totaled 1,584 DPs and committed just 121 errors in 1,851 games in which he played first for the Dodgers. He had an impressive .992 career fielding percentage and 377 homers. He managed the Mets to the 1969 World Series title over Baltimore.

## NELLIE FOX & LUIS APARICIO
## CHICAGO WHITE SOX

| YEAR | 1ST BASEMEN | DP | PCT. |
|------|-------------|-----|------|
| 1956 | Walt Dropo | 95 | .993 |
| 1957 | Earl Torgeson | 72 | .998 |
| 1958 | Earl Torgeson | 54 | .978 |
| 1959 | Earl Torgeson | 58 | .983 |
| 1960 | Roy Sievers | 117 | .993 |
| 1961 | Roy Sievers | 93 | .993 |
| 1962 | Joe Cunningham | 118 | .994 |

Turning Two: **Dropo** was a vacuum cleaner in the three-plus seasons (1955-58) he played first for the White Sox, committing just 19 errors in 342 games. **Torgeson** joined the Sox from Detroit early in 1957 and saw more action at first than Dropo because he had a livelier bat. He lost his job late in the 1959 season when the Sox picked up slugging-first baseman **Ted Kluszewski** from the Reds. "Kluz" was the Sox's starting first baseman in the White Sox's 1959, six-game World Series loss to the Dodgers. **Sievers,** a 17-year veteran with a solid bat, spent two seasons with the Sox and produced back-to-back .295 batting averages. He also played for the Browns, Senators and Phillies. **Cunningham** was another short-lived White Sox first baseman, playing two seasons (1962-63). A career .291 hitter in 12 seasons, he posted a .993 career fielding percentage at first.

### BOBBY RICHARDSON & TONY KUBEK
### NEW YORK YANKEES

| YEAR | 1ST BASEMEN | DP | PCT. |
| --- | --- | --- | --- |
| 1957 | Bill Skowron | 116 | .992 |
| 1958 | Bill Skowron | 112 | .993 |
| 1959 | Bill Skowron | 68 | .991 |
| 1960 | Bill Skowron | 130 | .991 |
| 1961 | Bill Skowron | 146 | .993 |
| 1962 | Bill Skowron | 101 | .991 |
| 1963 | Joe Pepitone | 111 | .995 |
| 1964 | Joe Pepitone | 128 | .988 |
| 1965 | Joe Pepitone | 104 | .997 |

Turning Two: **Skowron,** a six-time All-Star, suited up for the Yankees for nine seasons (1954-62), and provided offensive punch and splendid defense. A career .282 hitter with 211 homers, he exceeded 100 DPs six times for the Yanks. He won five World Series rings, four with New York and one with the Dodgers (1963 against—who else?—the Yankees). **Pepitone** won Gold Gloves in 1965, 1966 and 1969. During those three seasons, he committed just 16 total errors. The Yankees were so impressed with his bat (a disappointing .258) and fielding (.993), they traded Skowron to Los Angeles. Following the 1969 season, Pepitone played sparingly for the Astros, Cubs and Braves.

### BILL MAZEROSKI & GENE ALLEY
### PITTSBURGH PIRATES

| YEAR | 1ST BASEMEN | DP | PCT. |
|------|-------------|-----|------|
| 1965 | Donn Clendenon | 161 | .984 |
| 1966 | Donn Clendenon | 182 | .985 |
| 1967 | Donn Clendenon | 122 | .988 |
| 1968 | Donn Clendenon | 134 | .990 |
| 1969 | Al Oliver | 87 | .991 |
| 1970 | Bob Robertson | 107 | .995 |
| 1971 | Bob Robertson | 107 | .993 |
| 1972 | Willie Stargell | 96 | .984 |

**Turning Two:** The Pirates always seemed to have good-hitting, good-fielding first basemen during the 1960s and the 1970s, starting with **Clendenon,** who owned the job for six seasons (1963-68). He could be counted on for 80-90 RBIs per season. His career ended with the Mets in 1972. In 1969, he was named the Most Valuable Player in the Mets' five-game World Series victory over Baltimore. **Oliver,** an outfielder by trade, took over first in 1969 and did a solid job with a .285 average. He spent nine seasons (1969-77) with the Pirates before being traded to

Texas. He was a career .303 hitter. **Robertson** won the job in 1970 and enjoyed two successful seasons at the plate (53 homers, 154 RBIs). He won a World Series ring in 1971 when the Pirates beat Baltimore in seven. In 1972, Robertson shared playing time at first with **Stargell**, who was then 32 years old. Roberston saw considerable playing time at first in 1973 and 1974, as Stargell returned to the outfield. In 1975, Stargell, then 35, took over first and remained there until he retired in 1982. He played 1,296 games in the outfield and 848 at first. He's a Hall of Famer, Class of 1988. He had 701 DPs at first. "Pops," as he was called by teammates and fans, produced a career batting average of .282 with 475 homers and 1,540 RBIs. He won two World Series rings in 1971 and 1979, both against the Orioles.

### GLENN BECKERT & DON KESSINGER
### CHICAGO CUBS

| YEAR | 1ST BASEMEN | DP | PCT. |
|------|-------------|-----|------|
| 1965 | Ernie Banks | 143 | .992 |
| 1966 | Ernie Banks | 88 | .992 |
| 1967 | Ernie Banks | 111 | .993 |
| 1968 | Ernie Banks | 118 | .996 |
| 1969 | Ernie Banks | 116 | 997 |
| 1970 | Jim Hickman | 46 | .990 |
| 1971 | Joe Pepitone | 75 | .990 |
| 1972 | Jim Hickman | 61 | .992 |
| 1973 | Jim Hickman | 37 | .988 |

**Turning Two: Banks,** who played 1,125 games at short and 1,259 at first, is a Hall of Famer, Class of 1977. He joined the Cubs in 1953 as a shortstop and remained there through the 1961 season. The move to first was an easy one for the two-time (1958-59) National League MVP as he was involved in 1,005 DPs and turned the ball over just 80 times for an eye-popping .994 fielding percentage. He played sparingly in 1970 and 1971. **Hickman** started at first in 1970 and 1972-73. He posted a couple of good seasons, including 1970, when he hit .315 with 32 homers and 115 RBIs. He spent the 1971 season in the outfield so the Cubs could get **Pepitone's** bat in the lineup. Acquired from Houston, Pepitone didn't disappoint as he hit .307 with 16 homers. He spent the 1972-73 seasons as a backup.

## JOE MORGAN & DAVE CONCEPCION
### CINCINNATI REDS

| YEAR | 1ST BASEMEN | DP | PCT. |
|------|-------------|-----|------|
| 1972 | Tony Perez | 111 | .993 |
| 1973 | Tony Perez | 131 | .991 |
| 1974 | Tony Perez | 111 | .996 |
| 1975 | Tony Perez | 113 | .993 |
| 1976 | Tony Perez | 110 | .996 |
| 1977 | Dan Driessen | 116 | .994 |
| 1978 | Dan Driessen | 92 | .996 |
| 1979 | Dan Driessen | 112 | .993 |

**Turning Two: Perez** is a Hall of Famer, Class of 2000. He joined the Reds fulltime in 1965 as a first baseman, then was moved to third for the 1967 through 1971 seasons. In 1972, he moved to first on a permanent basis (1972-76). He also played for the Expos, Red Sox, and Phillies before returning to the Reds for the 1984-85-86 seasons. Career-wise, he was involved in 1,342 DPs as a first baseman, 1,484 overall. He crashed 379 career homers and drove in 1,652 runs. **Driessen** became a Red in 1973 and was bounced between first, third and the outfield until 1977 when he became a regular first baseman for the rest of his 15-year career. He stayed with the Reds until midway through the 1984 season, when he was sent to Montreal, then the Giants, Astros and Cardinals (1987). In 1,375 games at first, he posted an impressive .995 fielding percentage.

## TOM HERR & OZZIE SMITH
### ST. LOUIS CARDINALS

| YEAR | 1ST BASEMEN | DP | PCT. |
|------|-------------|-----|------|
| 1982 | Keith Hernandez | 140 | .994 |
| 1983 | George Hendrick | 72 | .992 |
| 1984 | David Green | 98 | .991 |
| 1985 | Jack Clark | 102 | .988 |
| 1986 | Jack Clark | 66 | .995 |
| 1987 | Jack Clark | 116 | .989 |

**Turning Two: Hernandez** won 11 straight Gold Gloves from 1978 to 1988, five when he was with the Cardinals (1974-82) and six when he was with the Mets (1983-89). He played in 2,014 games, all but seven at first, and participated in 1,654 DPs. He was the National League's co-MVP in 1979 when he hit .344 and drove home 105 runs. He shared the honor with the Pirates' Stargell. **Hendrick** played for six teams during his 18 seasons in the majors, seven in St. Louis (1978-84). An outfielder by trade, he took over first in 1983 after Hernandez was traded to the Mets. Offense was his forte as he hit .278 with 267 homers and 1,111 RBIs. In his one season at first for the Cards, he batted a career-high .318. **Green's** career covered six seasons, five with the Cards (1981-84, 1986) and one with the Giants (1985). He became the Cards' first baseman in 1984 when Hendrick moved back to the outfield. **Clark** gave the

Cards some stability at first, starting for three seasons after being picked up from the Giants (1975-84). He was solid at first, but what the Cards were looking for from him was offense and they got it. Eleven times during his 18-year career he exceeded 20 homers. He surpassed the 80-RBI mark nine times. His finest season with the Cards came in 1987 when he hit 35 homers, drove in 106 runs and batted .286.

## BILL RIPKEN & CAL RIPKEN
### BALTIMORE ORIOLES

| YEAR | 1ST BASEMEN | DP | PCT. |
| --- | --- | --- | --- |
| 1987 | Eddie Murray | 146 | .993 |
| 1988 | Eddie Murray | 101 | .989 |
| 1989 | Randy Milligan | 92 | .995 |
| 1990 | Randy Milligan | 84 | .987 |
| 1991 | Randy Milligan | 92 | .990 |
| 1992 | Randy Milligan | 110 | .994 |

**Turning Two: Murray,** a Hall of Famer (Class of 2003), won Gold Gloves in 1982, 1983 and 1984. He joined the Orioles in 1977 as a designated-hitter, then became the club's starting first baseman from 1978 to 1988. The Orioles pulled a shocker after the 1988 season and traded the talented Murray to Los Angeles, where he continued to excel (1989-91) in the field and at the plate. He also had productive seasons with the Mets (1992-93) and Indians (1994-96). In 2,413 games at first, he totaled 2,033 DPs and had a fielding percentage of .992. Offensively, he's a member the 500-Home Run Club with 504, batted .287 and drove in nearly 2,000 runs. When Murray was traded to the Dodgers, **Milligan,** acquired from Pittsburgh, became the Orioles' starting first baseman for four seasons. During that period, he committed just 31 errors. Offensively, he had average power and a .261 batting average.

## LOU WHITAKER & ALAN TRAMMELL
## DETROIT TIGERS

| YEAR | 1ST BASEMEN | DP | PCT. |
|------|-------------|----|----|
| 1977 | Jason Thompson | 135 | .991 |
| 1978 | Jason Thompson | 153 | .993 |
| 1979 | Jason Thompson | 135 | .994 |
| 1980 | Richie Hebner | 35 | .998 |
| 1981 | Richie Hebner | 36 | .995 |
| 1982 | Enos Cabell | 62 | .992 |
| 1983 | Enos Cabell | 76 | .997 |
| 1984 | Dave Bergman | 63 | .989 |
| 1985 | Darrell Evans | 80 | .984 |
| 1986 | Darrell Evans | 85 | .998 |
| 1987 | Darrell Evans | 86 | .997 |
| 1988 | Darrell Evans | 43 | .993 |
|  | Dave Bergman | 31 | .990 |
|  | Ray Knight | 40 | .991 |
| 1989 | Dave Bergman | 88 | .993 |
| 1990 | Cecil Fielder | 137 | .989 |
| 1991 | Cecil Fielder | 110 | .993 |
| 1992 | Cecil Fielder | 98 | .991 |
| 1993 | Cecil Fielder | 84 | .991 |
| 1994 | Cecil Fielder | 73 | .993 |
| 1995 | Cecil Fielder | 66 | .993 |

**Turning Two:** The Tigers have never had a first baseman who has won a Gold Glove since the award's inception in 1957. During the 19 seasons Whitaker and Trammell played together, they had seven "primary" first basemen. The most-notable one was the 6-feet-3, 250-pound **Fielder,**

who provided strong defense at first and plenty of punch at the plate. In the six-plus seasons he played with the Tigers (958) games, he belted 245 tape-measure homers and had 758 RBIs. He came up with the Blue Jays in 1985, then was sold to the Hanshin Tigers of the Japan Central League where he became a superstar during the 1989 season. Hanshin paid him $1 million, gave him a chauffeur and a full-time interpreter. The Detroit Tigers then signed Fielder as a free agent prior to the 1990 season for $1.25 million, which turned out to be a steal. He gave the Tigers 51 homers and 132 RBIs in 1990. He retired in 1998 after short stints with the Yankees, Angels and Indians. He won a World Series ring in 1996 with the Yankees, who beat the Braves in six games. Fielder, the starting first baseman, batted .391 in the Series. **Thompson** was the Whitaker-Trammell tandem's initial first baseman. He joined the Tigers in 1976, then saw Whitaker and Trammell come aboard in 1977. Thompson was a slick fielder (35 errors in three seasons) and had plenty of power, hitting 31, 26 and 20 homers from 1977-79. He spent the rest of his 11-year career with the Angels, Tigers and Expos. **Evans** was a solid first baseman, defensively. At the plate, he was dangerous. In the four seasons he was the club's "primary" first baseman, he slugged 125 homers and had 352 RBIs. Prior to joining the Tigers, he spent 15 seasons in the National League with the Braves and Giants. **Hebner, Cabell, Bergman** and **Knight** all made positive contributions to the Tigers, but for short periods of time.

## FIRST BASEMEN: MOST DOUBLE PLAYS

The top 25 first basemen in terms of career double plays as first basemen through the **2007 season**:

| | |
|---|---|
| 2,044 | Mickey Vernon (1939-59), Senators, Indians, Red Sox, Braves |
| 2,033 | Eddie Murray (1977-96), Orioles, Dodgers, Mets, Indians |
| 1,782 | Rafael Palmeiro (1986-2005), Cubs, Rangers, Orioles |
| 1,775 | Fred McGriff (1986-2004), Jays, Padres, Braves, Rays, Cubs, Dodgers |
| 1,769 | Joe Kuhel (1930-46), Senators, White Sox |
| 1,733 | Charlie Grimm (1916-36), Athletics, Cardinals, Pirates, Cubs |
| 1,687 | Chris Chambliss (1971-86), Indians, Yankees, Braves |
| 1,654 | Keith Hernandez (1974-90), Cardinals, Mets, Indians |
| 1,646 | Andres Galarraga (1985-2004), Expos, Cards, Rockies, Braves, Giants, Angels |
| 1,619 | Jeff Bagwell (1991-2005), Astros |
| 1,614 | Gil Hodges (1943, 1947-63), Dodgers, Mets |
| 1,611 | Wally Joyner (1986-2001), Angels, Royals, Padres, Braves |
| 1,581 | John Olerud (1989-2005), Jays, Mets, Mariners, Yankees, Red Sox |
| 1,575 | Lou Gehrig (1923-39), Yankees |
| 1,571 | Will Clark (1986-2000), Giants, Rangers, Orioles, Cardinals |
| 1,562 | Jim Bottomley (1922-37), Cardinals, Reds, Browns |
| 1,533 | Mark Grace (1988-2003), Cubs, Diamondbacks |
| 1,528 | Jimmie Foxx (1925-42, 1944-45), Athletics, Red Sox, Cubs, Phillies |
| 1,500 | Don Mattingly (1982-95), Yankees |
| 1,500 | Joe Judge (1915-34), Senators, Dodgers, Red Sox |
| 1,498 | Steve Garvey (1969-87), Dodgers, Padres |
| 1,480 | George Scott (1966-79), Red Sox, Brewers, Royals, Yankees |
| 1,468 | George Sisler (1915-30), Browns, Senators, Braves |
| 1,408 | Mark McGwire (1986-2001), Athletics, Cardinals |
| 1,405 | Willie McCovey (1959-80), Giants, Padres, Athletics |

## CHAPTER SEVENTEEN

# BASEBALL'S TOP KEYSTONERS BY THE NUMBERS

## SECOND BASEMEN

The top players in terms of double plays achieved as second basemen **through the 2007 season,** with years played and teams. Some players achieved DPs playing a different position. Those DPs are not included in the numbers below. (*) **still active:**

| | |
|---|---|
| 1,706 | Bill Mazeroski (1956-72), Pirates |
| 1,619 | Nellie Fox (1947-65), Athletics, White Sox, Astros |
| 1,547 | Willie Randolph (1975-92), Pirates, Yanks, Dodgers, Athletics, Brewers, Mets |
| 1,527 | Lou Whitaker (1977-95), Tigers |
| 1,507 | Bobby Doerr (1937-51), Red Sox |
| 1,505 | Joe Morgan (1963-1984), Astros, Reds, Giants, Phillies, Athletics |
| 1,444 | Charlie Gehringer (1924-42), Tigers |
| 1,408 | Roberto Alomar (1988-2004), Padres, Jays, Orioles, Indians, Mets, White Sox |
| 1,382 | Frank White (1973-90), Royals |
| 1,368 | Red Schoendienst (1945-63), Cardinals, Giants, Braves |
| 1,302 | Bobby Grich (1970-86), Orioles, Angels |
| 1,215 | Eddie Collins (1906-28), Athletics, White Sox |
| 1,209 | Jeff Kent (1992-2007), Mets, Jays, Indians, Giants, Astros, Dodgers (*) |
| 1,177 | Billy Herman (1931-47), Cubs, Dodgers, Braves, Pirates |
| 1,160 | Joe Gordon (1938-43, 1946-50), Yankees, Indians |

## SHORTSTOPS

The top players in terms of double plays achieved as shortstops **through the 2007 season,** with years played and teams. Some players achieved DPs playing a different position. Those DPs are not included in the numbers below. (*) **still active:**

| | |
|---|---|
| 1,665 | Omar Vizquel (1989-2007), Mariners, Indians, Giants (*) |
| 1,590 | Ozzie Smith (1978-96), Padres, Cardinals |
| 1,565 | Cal Ripken Jr. (1981-2001), Orioles |
| 1,553 | Luis Aparicio (1956-73), White Sox, Orioles, Red Sox |
| 1,424 | Luke Appling (1930-50), White Sox |
| 1,307 | Alan Trammell (1977-96), Tigers |
| 1,304 | Roy McMillan (1951-66), Reds, Braves, Mets |
| 1,290 | Dave Concepcion (1970-88), Reds |
| 1,265 | Larry Bowa (1970-85), Phillies, Cubs, Mets |
| 1,246 | Pee Wee Reese (1940-58), Dodgers |
| 1,237 | Dick Groat (1952-67), Pirates, Cardinals, Phillies, Giants |
| 1,217 | Phil Rizzuto (1941-42, 1946-56), Yankees |
| 1,215 | Don Kessinger (1964-79), Cubs, Cardinals, White Sox |
| 1,186 | Bert Campaneris (1964-83), Athletics, Rangers, Angels, Yankees |
| 1,183 | Rabbit Maranville (1912-35), Braves, Pirates, Cardinals, Cubs, Dodgers |

# ALL-TIME DOUBLE-PLAY TEAM

The most double plays achieved by position **through the 2007 season:**

| Pos | Player | DP |
|---|---|---|
| 1B | Mickey Vernon, Senators, Indians, Bosox, Braves (1939-59) | 2,044 |
| 2B | Bill Mazeroski, Pirates (1956-72) | 1,706 |
| SS | Omar Vizquel, Mariners, Indians, Giants (1989-2007) | 1,665 |
| 3B | Brooks Robinson, Orioles (1955-77) | 618 |
| OF | Tris Speaker, Bosox, Indians, Senators, Phillies (1907-28) | 139 |
| OF | Ty Cobb, Tigers, Athletics (1905-28) | 107 |
| OF | Max Carey, Pirates, Dodgers (1910-29) | 86 |
| C | Ray Schalk, White Sox (1912-28) | 226 |
| P | Warren Spahn, Braves, Giants (1942-65) | 82 |

## GROUNDING INTO DOUBLE PLAYS THROUGH 2007

**CAREER**

| | |
|---|---|
| 350 | American League: Cal Ripken Jr., Orioles (1981-2001) |
| 305 | National League: Hank Aaron, Braves, Brewers (1954-76) |

**MOST IN ONE SEASON**

| | |
|---|---|
| 36 | AL: Jim Rice, Red Sox, 1984 |
| 30 | NL: Brad Ausmus, Astros, 2002 |
| | Ernie Lombardi, Reds, 1938 |

**MOST SEASONS LEADING THE LEAGUE**

| | |
|---|---|
| 4 | AL: Jim Rice, Red Sox (1982, 1983, 1984, 1985) |
| 4 | NL: Ernie Lombardi, Reds (1933, 1934, 1938) and Giants (1944) |

**MOST TIMES IN ONE GAME**

| | |
|---|---|
| 4 | AL: Goose Goslin, Tigers, April 28, 1934, vs. Indians (Tigers won, 4-1) |
| 4 | NL: Joe Torre, Mets, July 21, 1975, vs. Astros (Mets lost, 6-2) |

**FEWEST IN ONE SEASON (minimum 150 games)**

| | |
|---|---|
| 0 | AL: Dick McAuliffe, Tigers, 1968 |
| 0 | NL: Craig Biggio, Astros, 1997, and Augie Galan, Cubs, 1935 |

## THE AUTHOR

**John Valerino** was born in Lakewood, Ohio, in 1952, but spent most of his childhood in Windsor, Conn., from where he made frequent trips to Fenway Park in Boston. A 1974 graduate of Florida Southern College in Lakeland, Fla., John spent 30 years at The Ledger in Lakeland, 25 as the newspaper's executive sports editor. He also served as the sports coordinator for The New York Times Regional Newspaper Group from 1989-2003. He covered three Olympic Games, Major League Baseball, as well as college football, basketball and baseball. He won numerous state and national journalism awards. A pitcher in high school with a sizzling fastball and a hanging curve, he was scouted by several clubs until he developed tendonitis his senior year. He and his wife of 25 years, Lorraine, have two daughters, Mackenzie and Quinn, and two grandchildren, Jason and Emma. This book is a product of therapy for an illness John has been fighting to overcome for several years, major clinical depression. He is one of 21 million Americans suffering from the disease.

## THE ASSOCIATE EDITOR

**Michael F. Valerino** was born in Sharpsburg, Pa., in 1919. The first baseball game he attended was Game 1 of the 1927 World Series between the Yankees and his beloved Pirates. Sneaking past security at Forbes Field, he watched his Pirates lose, 5-4, as Babe Ruth collected three singles and Lou Gehrig had two runs-batted-in. The Yanks went on to win the Series in four games. Mike had to wait until 1960 before his Pirates appeared in a Series again, but this time he had a ticket for Game 4 at Yankee Stadium, a 3-2 Pittsburgh win. He graduated from the University of Pittsburgh in 1939 with a bachelor's degree in aeronautical engineering. He earned his Masters from Case Western Reserve in Cleveland to complete the requirements of a nuclear physicist. At Langley Field in Newport News, Va., he helped design the engine cooling systems and radiation shielding panels to protect pilots of World War II-era fighter airplanes. He also spent many years with NASA, where he was involved in the early applications of nuclear medicine and the combustion system for the Space Shuttle. He also worked for Combustion Engineering in Windsor, Conn., as Director of Safety and Licensing for the building of nuclear reactors. He passed away in December 2006 at the age of 87.

## WHAT THEY'RE SAYING

"John's writing is refreshingly vivid and beyond accurate. Drawing on an unparalleled pool of players, managers and historians, John illuminates each player so eloquently that it reads like a statistically rich novel. Not just a home run in our opinion, but rather a ninth-inning, two-out, two-strike, walk off grand slam."

—**Editors,** *Baseball Almanac*

"Baseball is never a static thing, a simple compilation of numbers. It is people doing extraordinary things in an eye-blink and John Valerino's book captures wonderfully this human element. To understand the genius behind the well-turned double play can only be understood by knowing the athletes who were the best at performing it. John does this masterfully, bringing to vivid life the necessary obsession, the required dexterity and the inevitable companionship inherent in the craft. The double play may be the pitcher's best friend, but this book should be a serious baseball fan's best friend. A fan will never look at a double play the same way after reading this book, nor ever dare to under-evaluate it."

—**Bob Padecky,** sports columnist, *Santa Rosa Press Democrat*
    and a member of the Baseball Writers Association
    of America since 1977

"Baseball has needed a book like this for a long time. Pitchers like myself counted on the second baseman and shortstop to make the double plays. Thanks to John, this is a long-overdue tribute to the game's most-important defensive play."

—**Bob Shaw,** former major league pitcher (1957-67)